Refugee Protection in Brazil and Latin America – Selected Essays

Refugee Protection in Brazil and Latin America – Selected Essays

Liliana Lyra Jubilut

POLICY SERIES

TRANSNATIONAL PRESS LONDON

2018

Refugee Protection in Brazil and Latin America – Selected Essays
By Liliana Lyra Jubilut

First Published in 2018 by TRANSNATIONAL PRESS LONDON in the United Kingdom, 12 Ridgeway Gardens, London, N6 5XR, UK.
www.tplondon.com

Transnational Press London® and the logo and its affiliated brands are registered trademarks.

Requests for permission to reproduce material from this work should be sent to: sales@tplondon.com

Paperback
ISBN: 978-1-910781-78-4

Cover Design: Gizem Çakır
Cover Photo: Zaatari refugee camp, Jordan. By Foreign and Commonwealth Office - https://www.flickr.com/photos/foreignoffice/9660903731/in/photostream/, OGL, https://commons.wikimedia.org/w/index.php?curid=28188100

www.tplondon.com

DEDICATION

To Stefania,
who loved Refugees Studies, Academia, her friends and London.

ABOUT THE AUTHOR

Liliana Lyra Jubilut is a Professor of International Law, Human Rights and Refugee Law at the Universidade Católica de Santos, Brazil. She holds a PhD and a Master in International Law (Universidade de São Paulo) and a LLM in International Legal Studies (NYU School of Law). Former Visiting Fellow at the Refugee Law Initiative and Former Visiting Scholar at Columbia Law School.

Coordinator of the Research Group Human Rights and Vulnerabilities ("*Direitos Humanos e Vulnerabilidades*") and a part of the coordination of the UNHCR Sérgio Vieira de Mello Chair at UniSantos since 2013.

Liliana has been working with refugees academically and in practice since 1999. Former Lawyer at the Refugee Center of Caritas Arquidiocesana de São Paulo. Former Consultant of UNHCR-Brazil. Former Coordinator of a nation-wide research project of the Ministry of Justice on Migrants in Brazil. Member of the Migration Research Leaders Syndicate of the International Organization for Migration.

CONTENTS

ACKNOWLEDGMENTS

The author is grateful to the publishers for permissions granted to reprint the following articles in this book:

Chapter 1. The need for international protection in migration by LL Jubilut, SMOS Apolinário, First Published in Portuguese as *"A necessidade de proteção internacional no âmbito da migração"* in: Revista Direito GV 6 (1), 2010, 275-294.

Chapter 2. 1 Refugee Law and Protection in Brazil: a model in South America? by LL Jubilut, First Published in: *Journal of Refugee Studies* 19 (1), 2006, p. 22-44

Chapter 3. Refugee Status Determination in Brazil: A Tripartite Enterprise by LL Jubilut, SMOS Apolinário, First Published in: *Refuge* 25 (2), 2008, p. 29-40.

Chapter 4. Resettlement in Solidarity: a new regional approach towards a more humane durable solution by LL Jubilut, WP Carneiro, First Published in: Refugee Survey Quarterly, 30, 2011, p. 63-86.

Chapter 5. Enhancing refugees' integration - new initiatives in Brazil by LL Jubilut, First Published in: *Forced Migration Review*, 35, 2010, p. 46-47.

Chapter 6. Refugee Population in Brazil: The Quest for Integral Protection by LL Jubilut, SM Apolinário, First Published in Portuguese as *"A população refugiada no Brasil: em busca da proteção integral"* in: Universitas - Relações Internacionais 6 (2), 2008, p. 9-38.

Chapter 7. Humanitarian visas: building on Brazil's experience by LL Jubilut, CSM de Andrade, and AL Madureira, First Published in: *Forced Migration Review*, 53, 2016, p. 76-78.

Chapter 8. Regionalism: A strategy for dealing with Crisis Migration by LL Jubilut, EP Ramos, First Published in: *Forced Migration Review*, 45, 2014, p. 66-67.

Chapter 9. Regional Developments: Americas, F Piovesan, LL Jubilut, First Published in: Andreas Zimmermann. (Org.). Commentary on the 1951 Convention Relating to the Status of Refugees and its 1967 Protocol. 1ed.Oxford: Oxford University Press, 2011, p. 205-224.

Chapter 10. Fora and Programmes for Refugees in Latin America by LL Jubilut, First Published in: Ademola Abass; Francesca Ippolito. (Org.). Regional Approaches to the Protection of Asylum Seekers - An International Legal Perspective. Surrey: Ashgate, 2014, p. 245-266.

Chapter 11. The transformative potential of refuge: the deepening of solidarity and of limits to sovereignty as a legacy of the Cartagena Declaration and its review process by LL Jubilut, SMOS Apolinário, and JCJ Silva, First Published in Portuguese as *"O potencial transformador do refúgio: aprofundamento da solidariedade e da limitação à soberania como legado da Declaraçaõ de Cartagena e de seus processos revisionais"* in: Larissa Ramina; Tatyana Scheila Friedrich. (Org.). Coleção Direito Internacional Multifacetado - Direitos Humanos, Guerra e Paz - Volume III.Curitiba: Juruá, 2014, p. 173-198.

Chapter 12. The Challenges of Protection of Refugees and Forced Migrants in the framework of Cartagena+30 by LL Jubilut, AL Madureira, First Published in Portuguese as *"Os Desafios de Proteção aos Refugiados e Migrantes Forçados no Marco de Cartagena + 30"* in: Revista Interdisciplinar da Mobilidade Humana 22 (43), 2014, p. 11-33

Chapter 13. Latin-America and Refugees: a panoramic view by LL Jubilut, First Published in: Völkerrechtsblog (Blog) 2016.

The author would also like to thank Guita N. Jubilut for her invaluable assistance in the review of the manuscript and Ibrahim Sirkeci for the invitation to publish these selected essays.

The texts reflect the original published works, including the author's bios at the time of publication. Updates on the content, when needed, are presented in footnotes marked with *.

INTRODUCTION

Refugees and their protection have started to be a part of daily conversation in recent years. New flows from Africa to Europe, new crisis in Asia and in the Americas, and record numbers since the Second World War, for instance, have paved the way for news reports in the media, political discourses on the topic and debates on how to actually protect these persons.

In a world scenario of increasingly (i) closed borders, (ii) association of migration to security issues, (iii) lack of political will to ascertain human rights and (iv) disregard for migration as a right *in se*, the challenges on and for refugees' protection have been progressing; as have the need for international protection of persons fleeing well-founded fear of persecution due to their race, religion, nationality, political opinion or membership to a social group, i.e. refugees.

To face said challenges, respect for International Refugee Law and for International Human Rights are key; and the search for (new) strategies to guarantee protection needs to be a constant, including both the development of new international obligations, frameworks and guidelines and the identification and replication of good practices.

Even though international initiatives are in play in this sense (as, for example, the United Nations High Commissioner for Refugees (UNHCR) leading the creation of a Global Compact for Refugees, which was proposed in the New York Declaration of 2016 and is expected to be in place in 2018), advancements in this context have been scarce. Refugees' protection – as well as migration in general – seems to be a topic in which little consensus can be currently found in the global arena, albeit being a global issue.

In light of these, regional approaches and national practices gain relevance, especially if they can be seen as good practices, even if not without flaws; and as initiatives that increase the humanitarian protection space and that can be (perfected) and replicated in other scenarios.

They need, thus, to be identified, described and analysed. This book with a collection of previously published essays is an effort in this regard.

Starting with a general text on the need for international protection in migration, the book focuses on Latin America and Brazil (which compose the 2 main sessions), and presents these examples of regional and national initiatives in refugees' protection.

Both cases count on with practices that have been praised, including by UNHCR, and are examples of Global South approaches to a global issue.

In the case of Brazil, the texts describe the country's practice in "traditional" refugee protection both in terms of refugee status determination and of resettlement. They also highlight the need for integral protection (i.e. the combination of refugees' rights stemming from International Refugee Law and from International Human Rights Law), and challenges in guaranteeing it, through integration or social rights, in the country. Furthermore, they present the practice of humanitarian visas (for entry and for staying in the country) that have been adopted by Brazil.

In the case of Latin America, the texts begin with descriptions of the relevance of regionalism in refugee protection and focus on the expanded definition of refugee status brought along by the Cartagena Declaration and the consequent expansion of the humanitarian space in the region. They also describe the documents adopted in the review process of the Cartagena Declaration, which brought along, for instance, resettlement in solidarity as a regional approach to a traditional durable solution for refugees. Lastly, the texts present current challenges in refugee protection in the region, either by positing topics that need to be tackled or by describing the region's current landscape in relation to refugees.

With texts written from 2006 to 2016, the book allows for a perception of Latin America and Brazil's practices in recent years, describing a decade-worth of developments, key issues and scenarios in the time of the writings, and presenting the contextualization of the initiatives in historical and political terms whenever possible. As they were written as individual texts and for different audiences, some of the same information and arguments may appear in different texts throughout the book as the aim was to have complete and thorough pieces in themselves; but one hopes that the final result will be a volume that presents a comprehensive outlook of refugees' protection in Brazil and in Latin America, with each text bringing valuable information and contributing different aspects to form this panoramic description and analysis.

The texts stem from Human Rights, International Refugee Law and International Law foundations and perspectives, but also draw on other areas, such as International Relations. This is due both to the multidisciplinary approach that is needed for proposals on refugees' protection and to the backgrounds, interests and perspectives of the different co-authors that collaborated in the texts.

The texts aims to both provide sources and information on the little known practices on protecting refugees in Latin America and in Brazil, as well as to aid in the search of actions that allow for actual, durable and integral refugees' protection in the region and beyond.

Liliana Lyra Jubilut
November 2017

THE NEED FOR INTERNATIONAL PROTECTION IN MIGRATION (2010)[*]

Liliana Lyra Jubilut[**] and Silvia Menicucci. O. S. Apolinário[***]

Introduction

The legal analysis of the complex theme of migration made by the international doctrine has been recently demonstrating an effort to systematize international protection rules enforced for different migration situations under an International Migration Law (Cholewinski; Perruchoud; Macdonald, 2007)[1]. This proposal, in fact, consists of rules usually considered as part of International Human Rights Law, International Refugee Law, International Humanitarian Law, International Labor Law, Economic International Law and International Criminal Law.

It is, therefore, necessary to question the autonomy of this suggested new area in International Law, and the risk of considering the situation of forced migrants — such as the case of refugees and forcefully displaced persons classically distinguished from (economic) migrants due to their private needs and demands resulting from persecution or other serious violations, which arise from strong legal liabilities from the States to protect them — as subject to a generic International Migration Law. More than that, it must be questioned if the establishment of an International Migration Law would not shadow the particularities of each type of migrant, instead of improving the protection of human rights for persons on the move (McAdam, 2007).

In view of that, the purpose of this paper is to define, with the support of the doctrine and International Law itself, when possible, the main situations of

---

[*] The translation of this paper was done by Revista Direito GV and revised by the autores.

[**] Master and juris doctor in international law by the Universidade de São Paulo, LL.M. in International Legal Studies by New York University School of Law (USA). Professor of International Law at Faculdade de Direito do Sul de Minas. Consultant for the Creation of the Brazilian Refugee Council and was a lawyer at the Refugee Center of *Caritas Arquidiocesana de São Paulo* in partnership with UNHCR and the Brazilian government.

[***] Master and juris doctor in international law by the Universidade de São Paulo, Professor of International Law at UNICEUB; former lawyer at *the Centro de Acolhida para Refugiados da Caritas Arquidiocesana do Rio de Janeiro* in partnership with UNHCR and the Brazilian government

[1] The authors defend the idea of a unitary regulatory regime for the legal analysis of human movement, understanding that the multiple answers to immigration, although different, may be gathered. This book has a different perspective from the 2003 publication Migração e Normas Jurídicas Internacionais, which defended the idea that a regime which is coherent with international rules regarding migration had not yet appeared. That publication also reflects the denomination from the Migration International Law and Legal Affairs Department within the scope of the International Organization for Migration (IOM).

migrants, in order to verify the relevant protection instruments and the need to increase international protection, observing the particularities of each group.

Thus, the purpose is not to exacerbate the technical aspect of the distinctions between migrants. Instead, from such distinctions, this study checks the means to improve international protection and, consequently, the protection of persons on the move.

1 The Context of the Proposal of an International Law of Migration

Migration is part of the history of humankind and constitute an ever-growing phenomenon. It is estimated that there are more than 200 million international migrants in the world nowadays,[2] i.e. 3% of the world's population, and 26 million of internally displaced persons.[3] Migration is a theme which covers legal, political, social and cultural aspects; being inherently multidisciplinary and causing deep reactions in several societies. According to the International Organization for Migration:

> *Migration is one of the defining issues of the twenty-first century. It is now an essential, inevitable and potentially beneficial component of the economic and social life of every country and region. The question is no longer whether to have migration, but rather how to manage migration effectively so as to enhance its positive and reduce its negative impacts.*[4]

Despite being a fact in the international scenario, it is currently verified that there is no broad international provision which regulates the conduct of States regarding all the variables existing in migration. What exists are international rules which, by regulating issues such as safety, nationality, statelessness, freedom of movement of people, family unification, human rights, health, trafficking of people, refuge, asylum, deal with the theme of migration; or, also, rules for general protection of human beings which also apply to persons on the move.

On the other hand, some situations of migrants, especially refugees and, more recently, of internally displaced persons, can count on developed or under-development international protection systems and, more than that, due to their special condition compared to that of other migrants, these individuals count on international solidarity, and even with empathy.

The result is often the absence or insufficiency of rules to solve any incoherence between the rules in several fields, with a view for the precedence of human rights within the context of migration. Furthermore, this normative absence or insufficiency reflects upon the gap of specific domestic protection mechanisms, or domestic mechanisms which simply enable the attainment of a situation of regularity for immigrants.

---

[2] The United Nations Organization has recently announced that, due to the new global economic crisis, 10 million people may become migrants. Information obtained in: O Estado de São Paulo newspaper, December 27, 2008, Economy Pages. Available at: <http://www.estadao.com.br/ economia/ not_eco299536,0.htm>.

[3] Information available at: <http://www.iom.int/jahia/Jahia/about-migration/facts-and-figures/global-estimates-and-trends>. Access in January 2009.

[4] Information available at: <http:/ / www.iom.int/jahia/Jahia/lang/en/pid/241>. Access in January 2009.

In view of that, there is a tendency to try to frame all the situations of migrants in the few existing specific international legal rules, which, on the one hand, causes the lack of criteria in using the distinctions between migrants, and, on the other hand, prevents the development of new forms of protection, minimizing, at the same time, the effectiveness of the few existing rules.

An example of this is the fact that several migrants who have left their country of origin or their country of residence due to reasons other than the well-founded fear of persecution, that is, those who are not deemed as refugees according to international legal criteria, are seeking for the protection of refuge, as this institute is one of the most precise ones amidst the complex theme of immigration.

Along with this indiscriminate resource to the protection of refuge is the fact that, since the attacks on September 11, 2001, a growing tension between antiterrorist rules and migration policies have been experienced, reflecting on internal rules, with serious infringements to the protection of human rights. This situation becomes more serious with the economic crisis, xenophobia, fights against transnational crimes, which end up undermining the protection to vulnerable groups of migrants, such as migrant workers, women and children victims of trafficking, stateless persons, internally displaced persons and refugees.

Considering the aforementioned aspects, there is a natural tendency of seeking increased protection by trying to establish a new branch of International Law specifically designed for migration and strongly grounded on the advances obtained in favor of the protection to refugees. However, this paper intends to demonstrate that the protection provided by refuge, even if improved as a result of instruments such as the Convention of the former African Unit (1969)[5] and the Cartagena Declaration (1984),[6] should not be used for several migration situations, otherwise the institute of protection may be weakened and protection to refugees and to migrants in general may be minimized.

2 Brief Historical Considerations Regarding the Appearance of International Rules for the Protection of Persons on the Move

Until the 19th century, many countries had not adopted any type of difference regarding the rights of nationals and foreigners, and free movement between countries was allowed. Nevertheless, there are examples of persecutions, exile penalties, famines which forced people to move, as well as encouraged migration to colonize conquered lands, within the context of colonialism and imperialism.

The First World War brought changes regarding that, with restrictions to freedom of residence and differences between the rights of nationals and foreigners. Furthermore, this context triggered the establishment of international laws for refugees, with developments taking place in the League of Nations (FISCHEL DE ANDRADE, 1996). The Second World War, in turn, brought an enormous flow of displaced and stateless persons, who had no means to return to their place of origin, having been recognized as refugees.

---

[5]   Available   at: <www.acnur.org/t3/portugues/documentos/?tx_danpdocumentdirs   _pi2%5 Bpointer%>. Access in January 2009.

[6] Available at: <http://www.unhcr.org/basics/BASICS/45dc19084.pdf>. Access in January 2009.

In view of this challenge, the international society started an institutionalization process, in order to offer protection to those people — refugees and stateless persons — by means of the establishment of the United Nations High Commissioner for Refugees (UNHCR) and the adoption of treaties, such as the 1951 Convention and the 1967 Protocol regarding the status of refugees,[7] and the 1954 and 1961 conventions about statelessness.[8]

Article 14 of the Universal Declaration of Human Rights (1948),[9] a matrix document of the universal international system for the protection of human beings, provided the right to all victims of persecution to seek and being granted asylum in other countries. Article 13 established, in a more general manner, that everyone has the right to freedom of movement and residence within the borders of each State, as well as the right to leave any country, including their own, and to return to their country.

At the same time, it developed the internationalization of human rights, with the establishment of a UN's human rights system and regional systems, such as the inter-American, African and European systems. Regarding migration within the Inter-American scope, Article 8 of the American Declaration of the Rights and Duties of Man (1948)[10] provides that every person has the right to settle within the territory of the State of which he/she is a national, to move about freely within such territory, and not to leave it except on his/her own will.

Article 12 of the International Covenant on Civil and Political Rights (1966)[11] provided that: 1) everyone lawfully within the territory of a State shall, within that territory, have the right to liberty of movement and freedom to choose their residence; 2) everyone shall be free to leave any country, including their own; 3) the above-mentioned rights shall not be subject to any restrictions except those provided by Law and necessary to protect national security, public order, public health or morals or the rights and freedoms of others, consistently with the other rights recognized in this Covenant; 4) no one shall be arbitrarily deprived of the right to enter his own country.

Therefore, the international instruments ensure, regarding migration, the freedom of movement, which may only be restricted in view of the due process of law, and the right of asylum.

In a general manner, human rights rules also establish the idea of universality of human rights, grounded on the principle of non-discrimination. Thus, national and foreigners must have the same rights.

However, being in irregular situations may put many migrants in a situation which does not allow them to carry out their civil, political, social, economic and cultural rights, for fear of being found by authorities and for being subject to the

---

[7] See: <http://www.unhcr.org/protect/PROTECTION/3b66c2aa10.pdf>. Access in January 2009.
[8] See: <http://www.unhcr.org/protect/PROTECTION/3bbb25729.pdf>; <http://www.uncr.org/protect/PROTECTION/3bbb286d8.pdf>. Access in January 2009.
[9] Available at: <http://www.unhchr.ch/udhr/lang/eng.htm>. Access in January 2009.
[10] Available at: <https://www.cidh.oas.org/Basicos/Portugues/b.Declaracao_Americana.htm>. Access in January 2009.
[11] Available at: <http://www2.ohchr.org/english/law/ccpr.htm>. Access in January 2009.

consequent enforcement of measures to make them return to their country of origin.

Notwithstanding the restriction measures imposed by States to migration, these eventually generate a situation of irregular migrants with no documentation.[12] Therefore, as the labor rights derive from a labor relation, the International Labor Organization (ILO) drafted treaties to provide for the situation of migrant workers, and, in 1990, a milestone in the UN's human rights system was the International Convention on the Protection of the Rights of All Migrant Workers and Members of their Families.[13]

The Convention, in force since 2003, is very comprehensive and ensures rights to migrant workers who are either in regular situations or not in the host country. However, international acceptance of such treaty is very much reduced, with only forty member-States.[14,15]

Nationally, States may adopt internal rules regarding the rights of migrants (foreigners); however, they must comply with the obligations undertaken internationally and the minimum international standards. As the protection to refugees has been, for a long time, an international concern and obligation[16], most States create rules to protect this category of migrants, which does not occur in relation to the others. Furthermore, it is observed that due to the context of an economic crisis and concerns with national safety, States have been adopting restrictions to migration. As mentioned before, the combination of these factors leads some persons considered as economic migrants to seek refuge as a manner to obtain regularization of their entrance and stay in the country of destination. Besides that, due to the lack of procedures within the national arena to grant protection to other people who need it, but who do not qualify as refugees, said persons also end up seeking protection in refuge.

This incorrect use of the rules of refuge also occur within the international scenario, in which discussions are taking place on the use of protection granted by refuge in cases, for instance, of international displacement resulting from environmental disasters, indicating that International Law did not create specific protection forms for new cases of migration which require international protection.

It is noted that there is no structured international protection to persons on the

---

[12] It must be pointed out that more recent doctrine does not use the expression *illegal migrants,* in order not to (1) criminalize a conduct which is generally an administrative infringement, and (2) stigmatize migrants by attributing to them a malfeasance.

[13] Available at: <http://www2.ohchr.org/english/law/cmw.htm>. Access in January 2009. There was also the adoption, in 2000, of a Protocol against the Smuggling of Migrants by Land, Sea and Air, supplementing the United Nations Convention against Transnational Organized Crime; This document is not still in force, but can be seen at: <http://www2.ohchr.org/english/law/organizedcrime.htm>. Access in January 2009.

[14] There is a campaign by the Brazilian civil society and of human rights protection agencies in order to have Brazil ratify that convention. IOM estimates that there are 1.5 million foreigners living in Brazil and 3 million Brazilians living abroad. Information obtained at: <http://www.iom.int/jahia/ Jahia/pid/444>. Access in January 2009.

[15] Information obtained at: <http://www2.ohchr.org/english/bodies/ratification/ 13.htm>. Access in January 2009.

[16] Currently, 147 States are part of the 1951 Convention or the 1967 Protocol. Information obtained at: <http://www.unhcr.org/protect/PROTECTION/3b73b0d63.pdf>. Access in January 2009.

move, which leads to improper use of the few existing mechanisms and, in practical terms, to the vulnerability of these persons. In view of that, and in order to contribute to filling this gap, it is relevant to present the differences between the situations of migrants, so that it is also possible to assess which are the most appropriate manners to ensure at least the most essential rights to these persons. This will be done hereinafter.

3 The Classical Difference Between Voluntary and Forced Migration

Studies regarding population, demography and movement of persons usually include the movement of economic migrants, refugees and displaced persons within the wide concept of migration, which is analyzed as a process. However, said inclusion has not been applied, in practical terms, to the expression *migrant*, which is not understood as a generic term, comprising several categories, such as refugees, displaced persons and economic migrants. A migrant is generally considered an economic migrant or a migrant worker and is understood to be different from a refugee or other persons who have been forced to be displaced due to an external factor against their will.

The Constitution of the International Organization for Migration[17], for instance, refers to separate movements for 1) migrants and 2) refugees, displaced persons and other individuals who need to make use of international migration services[18], as follows:

Article 1

The purposes and functions of the Organization shall be:

to make arrangements for the organized transfer of migrants, for whom existing facilities are inadequate or who would not otherwise be able to move without special assistance, to countries offering opportunities for orderly migration;

to concern itself with the organized transfer of refugees, displaced persons and other individuals in need of international migration services for whom arrangements may be made between the Organization and the States concerned, including those States undertaking to receive them [...]

On the one hand, this distinction is relevant, as it helps to understand that the nature and the scope of the protection to be ensured to a refugee, for instance, are different from those granted to a working migrant, which may be kept under the protection of the State from which he/she is a national, in view of the complementary nature of international protection[****]. However, on the other hand, it should start from the point of view of migration in general, and not of categories of migrants, as, in fact 1) both forced migrants and volunteer migrants are migrants and 2) the difference from the point of view of migrants may lead to discrimination processes or categorization of persons who, in fact, share the same inherent quality

---

[17] Available at: <http://www.iom.int/jahia/Jahia/about-iom/constitution/chapter-I-purposes-and-functions>. Access in January 2009.

[18] See: PERRUCHOUD, Richard, Persons falling under the Mandate of the International Organization for Migration (IOM) and to Whom the Organization may Provide Migration Services.

[****] The notion of complementary is used here in the sense that the main (or primary) responsibility for the protection of human beings rests with the States.

of dignity.

Therefore, since the distinction between forced migration and voluntary migration is relevant for the current system of protection of persons on the move, as the protection to be granted to the persons in each of these situations is different, the main peculiarities of each situation are revealed bellow.[19]

Hence, migration may be divided into forced migration and voluntary migration.[20] Voluntary migration comprises all the cases in which the decision of migrating is freely taken by the individual, due to personal convenience, with no intervention of external factors. These are applicable, therefore, to persons and members of their families who move to another country to pursue better social and financial conditions to themselves and to their family members. These persons may have a regular or irregular migratory status, due to their entrance or stay in the country of residence, having or not observed the legal requirements provided for in the country.

Forced migration, in turn, occur when the volitional element of displacement is nonexistent or minimized and comprise a wide range of situations.

The classical forced migration situation is the refuge that protects people who had or have to leave their country of origin or of habitual residence due to a well founded fear of persecution because of their race, religion, nationality, political opinion or membership in a social group, as provided for in the 1951 Convention and the 1967 Protocol; or, in the case of Latin America, also because of gross and generalized violation of human rights.

The 1951 Convention and the 1967 Protocol provide for the rights of refugees and asylum seekers and the duties of States towards them, as well as regulate the protection of other persons who are under the protection of UNHCR, such as stateless, repatriated and resettled persons.[21]

Besides refugees, internally displaced persons, either due to armed conflicts, environmental disasters or serious infringement of human rights are also ranked in that situation. These persons continue under the protection of their State, what makes the international protection peculiar.

A third group of persons on the move subject to forced migration is that of those environmentally displaced, often referred to as *environmental refugees*. Environmental changes, especially those related to the weather, have been causing the displacement of millions of persons, a phenomenon which tends to become more serious. At times, these persons may become internal displaced persons; at other times, they may even cross international borders. In the latter case, it has been debated whether they could fall into the protection system for refugees, which does not seem appropriate, as they lack the basic feature of this system, namely, persecution.

---

[19] It must also be observed that, although the terms *forced migrants* or *volunteer migrants* are used in the text, this will be done based on the idea previously exposed, that is, in order to distinguish the migratory phenomena experienced by these persons on the move, and not as a manner to classify human beings.

[20] About migration classifications, see: JUBILUT, Liliana Lyra, Migrações e Desenvolvimento, em AMARAL JR., Alberto do (org.), *Direito Internacional e Desenvolvimento* (São Paulo: Manole, 2005, p. 123—54).

[21] See: <http://www.unhcr.org/protect/PROTECTION/3b66c39e1.pdf>. Access in January 2009.

Forced migration also include persons who had to move due to situations regarding their economic, social or cultural rights. In these cases, there may be a serious lack of enforcement of said rights or the realization of works and activities designed to speed up the development in the short term, but which cause immediate displacements.

Besides that, some individuals need migration services, such as those facing violations of their human rights in their own country and are still in that country (political prisoners, for instance), generally in situations of internal political tension or non-international armed conflict, or any other atypical kind of migration in which the individual is not featured as a migrant, refugee or displaced person.

It can be concluded, therefore, that within this wide group, it is necessary to differentiate those who can count on the protection of their own country of origin or residence and those who cannot claim this protection, in order to consider manners to improve the international protection to all.

4 International Protection in the Area of Migration

4.1 Economic Migrants and Their International Protection

There is no legal definition for the word *migrant*. In general, in States' local legislation, the reference is only to *foreigners* and to their rights to enter, stay and work. In the international scenario, there are several definitions for *migrant workers*, the one adopted by the 1990 Convention on the Protection of the Rights of All Migrant Workers and Members of their Families, comprises part of the UN's human rights system, is worth mentioning.

According to that, a migrant worker is a person who performs a paid activity in a State from where they are not a national. The definition includes migrants bearing no documents or migrants in an irregular situation (due to their entrance, stay or work), workers who perform their activities on the borders, seasonal workers, offshore workers, travelling workers and self-employed workers; and excludes refugees and stateless persons, students and trainees.[22]

Therefore, it can be said that the specific international protection in relation to migrants is poor, so it should be revised. In view of the current international scenario, adopting and enforcing new protection mechanisms will not be feasible. Thus, it is essential that, on the one hand, the States of origin of these people act by means of diplomatic protection, in order to protect them while they are abroad, and that, on the other hand, general human rights instruments be enforced, as they are universal (i.e. applied to all people) and must be observed in all situations.

Thus, minimum protection would be ensured, while trying to adjust the States' interests with the migrants' needs and preparing more specific protection documents.

4.2 Refugees, Persons Under Analogous Conditions as Refugees and Their International Protection

As aforementioned, refugees are forced migrants who can count on the most

---

[22] See articles 2 and 3 in the International Convention on the Protection of the Rights of All Migrant Workers and Members of their Families.

complete protection system. That system offers a clear definition of refugee status and the rights and duties resulting from that situation.

Besides counting on the universal system provided for in the 1951 Convention and in the 1967 Protocol, refugees count on the protection within the regional scenarios, which also provide extended protection to other situations, as in the African and American cases.

The Convention of the former African Unity Organization, currently African Union, which governs the specific aspects of refugees' problems in Africa, was adopted in 1969 to be a binding regional instrument. It is the only legally binding regional treaty regarding refugees. It has been adopted amidst conflicts that took place at the end of the colonial time in Africa and that led to a succession of movement of persons at a large scale. It considers to be a refugee any person who is compelled to leave his/her country owing to external aggression, occupation, foreign domination or events seriously disturbing public order in either part or the whole of his/her country of origin or nationality. Therefore, these people are not required to prove the well-founded fear of persecution.

In 1984, a group of government officials and jurists adopted the Cartagena Declaration, a non-binding regional instrument. The Declaration recommended that the definition of refugee used in Latin America should also include, besides the universal provisions, any person who had fled from their country because their lives, safety or freedom had been threatened by generalized violence, foreign aggression, internal conflicts, massive infringement to human rights, or other circumstances which have seriously disturbed the public order.

Within the domestic arena, each State is free to legislate internally, expanding the protection granted by refuge to other cases not provided for in International Law. However, International Law currently grants protection in compliance with the provisions set out in the 1951 Convention and in the 1967 Protocol.

The 1951 Convention and its Protocol provide States-parties with the legal basis of protection through the principle of *non-refoulement*, that is, the impossibility to return the asylum seeker (while the request for refuge is pending) and the refugee to a country where there is a threat of persecution. UNHCR in turn has the mandate, provided for in its Statute, adopted by the UN' General Assembly in 1950, of ensuring international protection to refugees and to seeking lasting solutions for their problems. UNHCR's mandate has been extended, since then, by means of resolutions of the UN's General Assembly, which assigned to it the responsibility for categories of persons not comprised by the 1951 Convention and its Protocol: persons who fled from a conflict or events which seriously disturb public order (refugees protected by the African Convention and the Cartagena Declaration); refugees under the UNHCR mandate; repatriates; stateless persons; and, in some situations, internally displaced persons. [*****]

However, the provision of protection by UNHCR does not make those persons refugees. Besides, it must be pointed out that the Statute and the resolution of the

---

[*****] UNHCR mandate had also been extended temporarily through several UN resolutions, but nowadays it has a continuous mandate.

UN's General Assembly regarding UNHCR's mandate define its responsibilities and duties, being, therefore, different from a treaty which binds the signatory States, specifying the rights and obligations of the persons recognized as refugees.

It is worth pointing out that the Palestinians are deemed a special case in International Law. In 1948, the United Nations Relief and Works Agency for Palestine Refugees in the Near East (UNRWA)[23] was established to assist Palestinians who have been displaced when the State of Israel was created. The UNRWA defines as Palestinian refugees all persons and their descendants who resided in Palestine two years before the hostilities in 1948 and who lost their homes and means of subsistence as a result of the conflict. The UNRWA was not assigned a mandate to protect the Palestinian refugees. This responsibility was left to the countries where they claimed refuge.

Stateless persons, in turn, are those who are not considered by any State as a national, as provided for in their legal systems. A stateless person may be a refugee and, in this case, he/she would be under the protection of International Law and national legislations regarding refuge, but he/she does not necessarily falls in the criteria for the recognition of refugee status.

Statelessness is closely related with displacement, which explains the involvement of UNHCR with this theme. Displacement may be the cause of statelessness (displacement followed by the redefinition of territorial borders); may be a consequence of statelessness (when the stateless person is forced to leave the place of residence); may be an obstacle to a lasting solution for refugees (when a State refuses to allow the entrance of repatriates, when the previous nationality cannot be proven due to the lack of documents or even birth records).

In the international scenario, the 1954 Convention relating to the Status of Stateless Persons contributed to standardizing and improving the status of stateless individuals and to ensuring that they enjoy, without discrimination, their human rights, that is, the Convention is intended to ensure human rights to stateless persons. In turn, the 1961 Convention on the Reduction of Statelessness defines forms upon which stateless people may acquire or preserve a nationality by means of bonds to a State through birth or ascendency, and aims at solving situations which cause statelessness. However, none of the two conventions establishes a process of claiming for a status of permanent legal residency due to statelessness.

It is also interesting to mention the asylees. This is because, especially in Latin America, refuge and asylum coexist, both being types of the internationally recognized right of asylum. Asylum has its origins in the Classic Age. Nowadays, it is a discretionary act from the State intending to protect persons who suffer persecution, usually political-related. It may be granted in the State's territory (territorial asylum) or in embassies, consulates or legations (diplomatic asylum).

It is noted, therefore, that asylum is different from refuge, because the latter is not discretionary. Instead, it is based on the well-founded fear of persecution and may be based on other reasons than political opinion. Table 1 presents asylum and

---

[23] Available at: <http://www.un.org/unrwa/>. Access in January 2009.

refuge in a scheme format.[24]

Table 1. Similarities and differences between asylum and refuge

		ASYLUM	REFUGE
Similarities		Objectives: both aim at the protection of individuals by a state other than that of their origin and/or habitual residence.	
		Grounds: both are grounded on international cooperation and solidarity.	
		Legal grounds: both are grounded on the respect to human rights and, consequently, both can be understood as comprised by international human rights law.	
		Nature: both have humanitarian nature.	
		Ensured protection: mandatory exits of these persons are limited.	
Differences		Dated as of ancient age.	It was only codified in positive law in the 20th century.
		It is currently practiced especially in Latin America.	It has universal scope.
		Theme of regional treaties since the 19th century.	It has as a basis universal treaties; it only became a theme of regional treaties as of the 1960s.
		Discretionary cases of granting.	Clear hypotheses of recognition of refugee status.
		Limited to political issues.	Five reasons: political opinion, race Religion, nationality and membership in a social group.
		Based on persecution itself	Its essential element is the well-founded fear of persecution, that is, the persecution does not have to taken place
		There is no international body in charge of inspecting the practice of asylum.	There is an international body in charge of supervising the practice of refuge.
		It does not require that the individual be out of his state of origin and/or nationality (in the modality of diplomatic asylum).	It requires that the individual be out of his state of origin and/or nationality.
		There are no exclusion clauses.	It has limitations regarding persons who may enjoy it (exclusion clauses),so that it is consistent with the UN's principles and purposes as it is an organ of this organization that supervises its enforcement.
		There are no cessation clauses.	The protection granted by the refuge can be ceased (cessation clauses).
		Decision of granting asylum is constitutive.	Recognition of the refugee status is declaratory.
		No international obligations to the host state result from the granting.	International obligations to the host state arise from the recognition of refugee status.
		Local integration policies do not result from the granting	Local integration policies must result from the recognition of refugee status

It is noted that, within the international scenario, refugees and persons in analogous conditions to that of refugees (exception made to persons under asylum)

---

[24] Graph scheme presented by Liliana Lyra Jubilut at: JUBILUT, Liliana Lyra, Migrações e Desenvolvimento, em AMARAL JR., Alberto do (org.), *Direito Internacional e Desenvolvimento* (São Paulo: Manole, 2005, p. 123—54).

have protection, with documents and specific international agencies in charge of ensuring the respect to human rights for these persons on the move. As protection is carried out in the territories of the States, there is a possibility of improving specific situations, but the international protection ensured is reasonably developed.

4.3 Internally Displaced Persons and Their International Protection

For internally displaced persons, the UN's Guiding Principles on Internal Displacement[25] define as *internally displaced persons* those persons or groups of population who have been forced to flee and abandon their homes or their usual places of residence, due to armed conflicts, situations of generalized violence, infringements to human rights and natural calamities or those caused by man, or in order to avoid its effects, and which do not cross any internationally recognized border of a State.

Internally displaced persons, as they remain in their own country of origin, may not be considered refugees — nor were initially under the provisions of the UNHCR's mandate. There is no international treaty or agency specifically assigned to protect these persons. Currently, protection is done by the cluster approach of agencies operating in several areas (such as UNICEF and the World Health Organization), and by UNHCR, which was assigned the responsibility of protecting internally displaced persons.

As the internally displaced persons remain in their States, international protection only occurs upon the observation of some criteria: 1) request or authorization by the General Assembly or another UN's higher and competent agency; 2) consent from the State concerned and, where applicable, of other entities involved in the conflict; 3) access to the affected population; 4) appropriate safety conditions for UNHCR's personnel and relevant partners; 5) clear obligations and responsibilities; 6) appropriate capacity and resources.

Agencies and international organs operate according to the aforementioned UN's Guiding Principles, a non-binding instrument inspired by International Human Rights Law, International Humanitarian law and International Refugee Law. The Guiding Principles consolidated the most important principles of international protection for internally displaced persons and are intended to guide States, non-governmental actors, intergovernmental and non-governmental organizations regarding internal displacement. Furthermore, it is worth pointing out that, in cases where the internal displacement results from a situation of internal conflict, the International Committee of the Red Cross (ICRC) understands that its action is required, in view of its mandate.

It is observed that the protection system for internally displaced persons has been developing from practice. Currently, it is supported by governing principles which take into consideration the specificity of the situation of displaced persons and try to respond to the basic needs of this population, and may be appointed as the starting point of an international protection to these migrants.

---

[25] Available at: <http://www.unhcr.org/protect/PROTECTION/43ce1cff2.pdf>. Access in 2009.

4.4 Individuals Displaced Due To Environmental Issues and Their International Protection

The protection to be granted to persons displaced due to environmental reasons has been subject to international debate (LOPEZ, 2007). Environment International law has been developed with preventive and punitive regulations regarding environmental degradation, and International Human Rights Law and International Humanitarian Law deal with the adverse effects of environmental degradation for human beings.

The migration resulting from a temporarily or permanently degraded environment is an unquestionable fact; however, International Law does not have provisions regarding the correlation between environmental degradation and human migration. The few studies about this theme usually focus on how the arrival of a number of migrants may affect the environment, as in the case of the construction of refugee camps, and not on how environmental degradation may cause displacements.

The milestone event in the development of studies regarding migration caused by environmental reasons was a report from the 1985 United Nations Environment Programme (UNEP) (EL-HINNAWI, 1985). From the point of view of International Law, the expression *environmental refugees* is not correct, as the definition provided by International Law to the word *refugee* comprises specific criteria which enable a person to receive the protection of refuge. The 1951 Convention was not drafted to include persons displaced due to environmental reasons, and this is not possible, even if the instrument is construed to update it to the current context. The main issue highlighted by the doctrine (KOZOLL, 2004) is that in most situations, persecution or a concerted action by an identifiable entity or by the State is not in place.

As opposed to the victims of persecution, persons who move due to an environmental disaster may, in general, use the aid and the support of their government, even if said support is limited. This cannot be mistaken with the situation in which the pursuing agent uses the environmental degradation as a means of persecution. In this case, the reason for persecution may be one of those provided for in the 1951 Convention, and the form of persecution is the environmental damage; hence, that individual is a refugee. Accordingly, there must be a well-founded fear of persecution.

However, there is a possibility of, at a regional and national level, granting protection by means of refuge, as international organizations or States extended the protection granted by the institute of refuge to persons fleeing from events which seriously disturb public order. This provision could be enforced to persons who leave their countries due to environmental disasters (MCCUE, 1993).

There is a need to develop a specific system for environmentally displaced individuals, as they do not fall in the definition of refugees, and the remodeling thereof seems to be unlikely and undesirable, as, in a restrictive scenario of migration, this remodeling may jeopardize the existing protections, thus minimizing the guarantees to refugees.

4.5 Individuals Displaced Due To Economic, Social and Cultural Rights and Development and Their International Protection

Nowadays, the difference between the status of refugee and the situation of economic migrants is not easy when the infringement to economic, social and cultural rights is at stake.[26] Historically, it must be remembered that, due to ideological conflicts which marked the period of the Cold War and reflected on the doctrine and on the international rules of human rights, economic, social and cultural rights have been considered, for a long time, by some authors and States, as aspirations and not as human rights. However, it is worth seeking for elements defining the status of refugees and to check if persons displaced due to economic, social and cultural rights may resort to refuge, or if another type of protection must be granted.

Considering the need of a well-founded fear of persecution to characterize refugee status, the motivation resulting from infringement to economic, social and cultural rights gets more complicated, as infringement to those rights occurs more due to negligence than by means of a formal act or actions arranged by a pursuing agent. Besides, it is usually difficult to separate the situation of an individual from the general condition in his country of origin or habitual residence. However, there are cases in which there is an intersection between the fact of membership in a social group and the access to education and health. However, in these cases, the persecution may be characterized being based on membership in a social group.

Likewise, there is a myriad of situations of individuals and human rights treaties which define certain groups, such as the Committee on the Elimination of Discrimination against Women, the Convention on the Rights of the Child, the aforementioned Convention on the Protection of the Rights of All Migrant Workers and Members of their Families, and the Convention on the Rights of Persons with Disabilities. Besides those, there are other groups defined by common features which lead to discrimination, such as people infected by the virus of AIDS, or with other diseases.

There are reasons to consider the deprivation of economic and social rights in certain cases; for instance, the deprivation of the rights to work, education and health, as grounds to recognize refugee status.

The dilemma of economic, social and cultural rights lies in the fact that, if a State fails to provide said rights for the whole population by means of policies and programs, it is difficult to argue individual cases, claiming that said rights are not fulfilled. What can be argued is that, due to their political opinions, ethnic group or membership in a social group, these individuals are deprived by an agent — the State or another entity with sufficient power — of working, receiving education or health care. The essential point is that the State, or another agent acts against the individual, and this constitutes persecution.

Less clear is when there is no action by this agent, but, instead, negligence. The States may argue that the resources are not enough to enable the protection of

---

[26] For further details about the theme, see: FOSTER, Michelle, *International Refugee Law and Socio-Economic Rights:* Refuge from Deprivation (Cambridge: Cambridge University Press, 2007).

certain rights, such as, for instance, treatment to people infected with HIV.

Therefore, a request for refuge in which there are economic, social and cultural rights being infringed may be met in case of discrimination to a given group; otherwise, it will be difficult to demonstrate the well-founded fear necessary to characterize the refuge.

If the infringement to economic and social rights becomes a ground by itself, only for the recognition of refugee status, there may be significant increase in the international movement of persons seeking appropriate standards of living.

An analysis that could be done is the following: if the State of origin tried and has been trying to improve the implementation of economic, social and cultural rights of its population, without discrimination, there would not be grounds to claim persecution. However, if the State fails to carry out this task, discriminating a part of the population in providing the services required to ensure these rights, there is an argument grounded on discrimination to a certain social group, which was a basis for refuge originally provided in the 1951 Convention, and which was applied, for instance, to the gypsies persecuted during the Nazi regime.

However, some individuals who have been denied the right to development, in compliance with the Declaration on the Right to Development (1986)[27], are still deprived of international protection.

The right to development is object of several debates within the international arena; in the UN, the right to development is considered to summarize all human rights, based on the interdependence and non-severability of human rights (OLIVEIRA, 2004). Therefore, when serious and regular infringements to human rights are observed, it should be asked whether the deprivation of the right to development would not configure a situation which requires international protection.

The situation of those States lacking democratic rules, combined with high poverty levels affecting the population at large may result in something unsustainable for the individuals, namely high indexes of child and mother mortality, undernourishment and illiteracy. It can be simply said: "Unfortunate are those who were born in this country!"; by means of international cooperation, it is possible to repair the State's condition of development – however, this is a long-term task —; or one may even try to establish a difference between those situations of lack of development, those who result in persons requiring international protection, since the future with hunger and diseases is an external factor which compels the individuals to migration, even when no persecution is characterized.

In these cases, there are elements to argue for the enforcement of extended protection as provided for in the 1969 African Convention and the 1984 Cartagena Declaration, which do not demand the existence of persecution to grant the protection of refuge, but only the characterization of objective situations, among which life threatened by massive infringement of human rights, or even issues concerning the public order, in view of a weak State incapable of providing the

---

[27] Available at: <http://www2.ohchr.org/english/law/rtd.htm>. Access in January 2009.

minimum conditions necessary to live.

Finally, regarding economic, social and cultural rights and the effectiveness of the right to development, it must be pointed out the displacement of persons due to construction works aiming at improving the country's infrastructure, such as the construction of hydroelectric plants or river diversion works. In those situations, displacement occurs due to the existence of economic, social and cultural rights, and not due to the lack thereof. Nonetheless, with different grounds, the same practical result would be produced: the need for persons to leave their places of residence.

That situation requires a different protection system from the ones referred to herein, as the persons displaced due to these conditions remain under the responsibility of their States, being, thus, closer to the condition of internally displaced individuals and, consequently, submitted to the protection system thereto, which is under construction.

It can be noted that both the lack of effectiveness and the performance of works intending to ensure these rights may cause migration due to economic, social and cultural rights, which poses a number of challenges in the seeking of international protection in migration.

Conclusion

The political, social, economic and environmental realities are causing movements of persons involved in increasingly complex situations, with no international provision of protection, demanding the enforcement of International Human Rights Law and humanitarian principles, and the creation, by States, of complementary protection systems (McAdam, 2005).

The international society must be concerned with the fact that the defining criteria of refugee status and the responsibilities of the States bound to this status lose their accuracy by the use of the institute of refuge to protect persons who are not listed by International Law as entitled to receive this specific protection (Feller, 2006). This concern must not, however, prevent or adversely affect the protection from other persons on the move, either as a result of forced migration or voluntary migration.

Since migration is a given in the international scenario, International Law must attempt to ensure regulations which comply with the interests of the States and the need to protect human beings and all the aspects and dimensions of their dignity.

This protection does not seem to come from International Migration Law , as the situations of migrants are apparently very different in their causes and motivations, and the existing protection levels are very different, what could lead to injustices if they referred to uneven situations in a similar manner.

The protection basis already exists in International Human Rights Law. Instead of advocating for the theoretical creation of an autonomous branch of International Law, the focus must be on the practical protection of migrants, in order to, from the reality and the factual development of protection, start thinking about theoretical constructions. Accordingly, the use of conventional and unconventional mechanisms of the international system and regional human rights systems in cases in which the States infringe the obligations undertaken in human rights treaties, within the context of migration, may contribute to the dignity of migrants being respected.

References:

CHOLEWINSKI, Ryszard; PERRUCHOUD, Richard; MACDONALD, Euan (Eds.). *International migration law: developing paradigms and key challenges.* Hage: T.M.C. Asser Press, 2007.

EL-HINNAWI, Esam. *Environmental refugees*, 4. ed. Nairobi: UNEP, 1985.

FELLER, Erika. Asylum, migration and refugee protection: realities, myths and the promise of things to come. *International Journal of Refugee Law*, v. 18, n. 3–4, p. 509–36, 2006.

FISCHEL DE ANDRADE, J. H. *Direito internacional dos refugiados: evolução histórica (1921-1952).* Rio de Janeiro: Renovar, 1996.

FOSTER, Michelle. *International refugee law and socio-economic rights: refuge from deprivation.* Cambridge: Cambridge University Press, 2007.

JUBILUT, Liliana Lyra. Migrações e desenvolvimento. In: AMARAL JR., Alberto do (Org.). *Direito internacional e desenvolvimento.* São Paulo: Manole, 2005. p. 123–54.

_____. *O direito internacional dos refugiados e sua aplicação no ordenamento jurídico brasileiro.* São Paulo: Método, 2007.

LOPEZ, Aurelie. *The protection of environmentally-displaced persons in International Law*, v. 37, p. 365–409, 2007.

Disponível em: <http://www.lclark.edu/org/envtl/objects/37-4_Volume_ Index.pdf>. Acesso em janeiro de 2009.

MCADAM, Jane. Book reviews, international migration law: developing paradigms and key challenges. *International Journal of Refugee Law*, v. 19, n. 4, p. 776–9, 2007.

_____. Complementary protection and Beyond: how States deal with human rights protection. United Nations High Commissioner for Refugees. *Working Paper n. 118*, 2005.

MCCUE, Gregory S. Environmental Refugees: applying International Environmental Law to involuntary migration. *Georgetown International Environmental Law Review*, v. 6, p. 151–2, 1993.

KOZOLL, Christopher. Poisoning the well: persecution, the environment, and refugee status. *Colorado Journal of International Environmental Law and Policy*, v. 15, p. 271–2, 2004.

OLIVEIRA, Silvia Menicucci de. *O direito ao desenvolvimento: teorias e estratégias de implementação.* 2006. Tese (Doutor em Direito Internacional) – Faculdade de Direito, Universidade de São Paulo, São Paulo, 2006.

PART I: REFUGEE PROTECTION IN BRAZIL

JUBILUT

REFUGEE LAW AND PROTECTION IN BRAZIL: A MODEL IN SOUTH AMERICA? (2006)[*]

Liliana Lyra Jubilut[**, 1]

Introduction

Brazil's commitment to the protection of refugees dates from the beginning of the universalization of the rules on this institution in the early 1950s. However, for some two decades, there were no effective policies for the reception of refugees in Brazil. Such policies only emerged at the end of the 1970s. Since then, and especially with the re-democratization of Brazil in the 1980s and the country's subsequent commitment to human rights at home and abroad, Brazil's activities on refugee protection have evolved considerably.

In 1997, the Refugee Act was passed (Law 9.474/97 of 22 July) and more recently Brazil has both become a country of resettlement and allowed the re-opening of an office of the United Nations High Commissioner for Refugees (UNHCR) on its territory. As a consequence of these changes, Brazil has started to be regarded as a model for the protection of refugees in South America, as stated by UNHCR itself:

> *Nowadays, the countries in the region are at different stages of the process of internal consolidation of their international commitments.* **Brazil became the regional leader with the approval of a refugee act in 1997** *(ACNUR 2003: 8;*

---

[*] Acknowledgements: This article is extensively based on Chapter IV of my dissertation for the Master in Laws (International Refugee Law and its Implementation in Brazil) presented to the Law School of the University of São Paulo (2003). The relative lack of citations in the paper reflects both the small amount of literature on the issue of refugee law and protection in Brazil, and the fact that most data was gathered by virtue of personal testimonies. Furthermore, most of the analysis derives from practical work in the field rather than from a theoretical approach to the issue. The English version of this paper would not have been possible without the valuable aid of Mrs. Dina L. Nicolaewsky and Mrs. Taroub Y. R. Nahuz, to whom I must express my gratitude. I would also like to express my gratitude to Mrs. Cezira Furtim for sharing her experience in working with refugees in São Paulo since the first centre for refugees was established in this city. Most of the historical data in this paper is based on her testimony. Lastly, I would like to thank everyone at the Refugee Centre of Caritas Arquidiocesana de São Paulo and Professor Alberto do Amaral Junior for his supervision of my dissertation for the Master in Laws.

[**] Refugee Center, *Caritas Arquidiocesana de São Paulo.*

[1] Since this paper was accepted for publication the author has left the Refugee Centre to pursue an LL.M. at New York University. Her current address is 10 Hanover Square, apt. 6M, New York, NY 10005, USA.

author's translation, emphasis added).

This leadership role has been attributed to Brazil for two main reasons: the fact that the Brazilian Refugee Act was the first national law on the matter in the region,[2] and Brazil's political and economic importance in South America. In view of this, the present paper aims: 1) to describe the development of refugee law and protection in Brazil and 2) to analyse whether or not Brazil is fulfilling its role as a model in South America regarding the protection of refugees. These two aims have a relevance which goes beyond the country and region themselves. The first goal is relevant in so far as an assessment of the development of refugee protection in Brazil has been missing from the broader international literature on Refugee Law and an analysis of the robustness of Brazil's system could contribute to international perceptions of refugee protection. The second aim, of assessing Brazil's role as a regional model, is important for more than the refugee protection aspects, since other countries in the region tend to look to Brazil when it comes to international relations in general and to the protection of refugees in particular. For example, they use the Brazilian law on refugees as a model when adopting internal regulations on the theme and some have been inspired by the practice of refugee protection in Brazil.

This status is due to the fact that Brazil views itself, and is often held by outsiders to be, a country with 1) continental dimensions; 2) peaceful relations with several neighbours; 3) a history of peace-building diplomacy; 4) linguistic unity in a multi-ethnic environment and 5) better results in the face of the challenge of development than the majority of countries in South America (Lafer 2004). Thus it is important to analyse the extent to which Brazil is playing a refugee protection role which is commensurate with its international and regional standing. To achieve this twofold aim, this article is divided into three parts. The first part describes the historical process of the incorporation of International Refugee Law into Brazil's national legislation and political thinking. This historical overview covers the period from the early 1950s to 1988 when Brazil approved its current Constitution. This overview also explains the origins of UNHCR's initially difficult presence in Brazil, and shows that from the beginning, and in spite of the domestic politics of the time, Brazil played a leading role in the development of refugee protection in the South American region. The second part explores three major issues for any analysis of whether Brazil in fact constitutes a legal model that can be followed in the protection of refugees across South America. The first issue is the current status of refugee law and protection in Brazil. The two key pieces of domestic legislation that regulate refugee law in Brazil (the 1988 Federal Constitution and the 1997 Refugee Act) are examined. The second major issue is the distinctions in understanding and practice in Brazil between 'domestic asylum' and 'refuge'. The final issue is the process of refugee status determination in Brazil. The third part describes the most recent developments in refugee policy in Brazil, especially the previously mentioned re-opening of the office of UNHCR and the beginning of a resettlement

---

[2] Both Argentina and Bolivia passed internal regulations on the creation of an organ vested with the responsibility of granting refugee status prior to Brazil. However, these are not laws and do not tackle the defining aspects of refugee status (in the case of Argentina) nor the rights and duties of refugees (in both cases); therefore, Brazil was the first country in the region to have a comprehensive internal law on refuge.

programme. The conclusion analyses the seemingly positive and negative aspects of the path followed by Brazil regarding refugee law and protection, specifically in the light of the question of its role as a model in South America.

The Beginning of Refugee Protection in Brazil

Brazil has been a country of immigrants since it was first colonized by the Portuguese in the sixteenth century. In spite of this, the treatment of foreigners has varied through the years, especially during the First and Second World Wars and the 24-year dictatorship (1964-1988). Brazil ratified and incorporated the 1951 United Nations Convention on the Status of Refugees into its legal system in 1961 and the United Nations 1967 Protocol on the Status of Refugees in 1972; being therefore, the second country in South America to ratify the Convention and the fifth in the region to ratify the Protocol. Furthermore, it was, along with Venezuela, the first South American country to be part of the Executive Committee of UNHCR; both have been members of ExCom since 1958. Despite this international commitment, Brazil's practice did not respect the international standards on refugee protection. An example of this was its maintenance of the 1951 Convention's geographic restriction (to apply to refugees from Europe only), despite having signed the 1967 Protocol which eliminates it (Fischel and Marcolini 2002a: 37). This was due to the fact that Brazil adopted international refugee law during the early years of the dictatorship when the government often signed treaties committing itself internationally but did not implement them or respect their provisions in its internal practice.

Initial conditions for implementation were, thus, far from ideal, especially because this period also saw significant displacements across South America, due to the persecution of populations following the establishment of nondemocratic regimes, which led in turn to refugees. In this scenario a UNHCR office was needed and in 1977, UNHCR entered into an agreement with the Brazilian government for the establishment of an ad hoc office in Rio de Janeiro (ACNUR 1997). Between 1977 and 1982 this office's activities within Brazil were virtually clandestine, with its main work involving the resettlement of South American refugees in other countries, often beyond the region. This was a result of the fact that the geographic restriction suited the military dictatorship of Brazil at the time, since it was unwilling to shelter people who were fleeing similar regimes in the region. Thus, Brazil only allowed these people to pass through its territory before being resettled in other States. About 20,000 Argentines, Bolivians, Chileans and Uruguayans were resettled from Brazil to Australia, Canada, Europe, New Zealand and the US (Fischel and Marcolini 2002a).

These high numbers were no inducement for Brazil to withdraw the geographic restriction in practice. Similarly, Brazil continued to refuse to recognize UNHCR as an official international organization (in fact a subsidiary organ of the UN), highlighting the dictatorship's unwillingness to commit itself internally to international law.

During this period of almost clandestine activity, UNHCR was able to operate largely as a result of the support of domestic non-governmental organizations involved in human rights activities (Fischel and Marcolini 2002a: 37). These partners were three Catholic non-profit organizations: *Comissão Justiça e Paz* (Justice and Peace Commission), composed primarily of scholars and lawyers who worked on the legal aspects of the Catholic Church's humanitarian work with victims of human rights violations, including refugees; *Caritas Arquidiocesana do Rio de Janeiro* (Archdiocesan Caritas of Rio de Janeiro, or CARJ) and *Caritas Arquidiocesana de São Paulo* (Archdiocesan Caritas of São Paulo, or CASP)-two local branches of Caritas International, a confederation of 154 national Caritas organizations operating in 184 countries. These three organizations conducted refugee protection activities in two cities: São Paulo, where CASP and the Justice and Peace Commission were active[3] and Rio de Janeiro, where CARJ was active.

These partnerships were of vital importance for UNHCR's work, as the Brazilian NGOs provided both legal and social assistance to refugees, making up for the previously mentioned limitations on the competence of UNHCR in the country at the time. An important result of these partnerships was the opportunity to make the practice of the geographic limitation more flexible, as 150 Vietnamese, some Cubans and 50 Baha'i families were received by Brazil as foreign residents. They were not recognized as refugees but were granted rights and protection. The Vietnamese, after some years, began to participate in a micro-credit project for the establishment of sewing workshops, which still operates today. This marked, in fact, the first local integration of refugees into Brazilian society.

The protection of refugees started to change slightly when the Brazilian government recognized UNHCR's status as an international organization in 1982 and when, in 1984, with the re-democratization of some Latin American countries, the repatriation of refugees began. After this date, non-European refugees were allowed to stay in Brazil for a period not limited by resettlement opportunities and were granted documentation issued by UNHCR and endorsed by the Federal Police. The national authorities indicated their understanding that the refugees were UNHCR's responsibility, not Brazil's (Fischel and Marcolini 2002a: 37-38).

The Protection of Refugees after Re-democratization

The 1988 Federal Constitution

Following re-democratization, many changes in refugee protection activities were introduced in quick succession. In 1989, the office of UNHCR was transferred to Brasilia and Brazil withdrew, not only formally but now practically, its geographic limitation to the application of the Convention. In 1990, the reservations to articles 15 and 17 of the 1951 UN Convention, which together with the geographic restriction had been adopted by Brazil, were withdrawn. In 1991, the 394 Inter-Ministry Rule was elaborated, increasing the rights of refugees and establishing a specific administrative process for the granting of refugee status, involving both UNHCR, which analysed the individual cases, and the Brazilian Government, which gave the final decision on the matter. This was a result of three factors: the re-democratization of Brazil; the 1988 Federal Constitution; and the growing

---

[3] The involvement of the São Paulo Catholic Church with refugees was based on the ideals of the former Cardinal-Archbishop of São Paulo, Dom Paulo Evaristo Arns, who was decorated with the Nansen medal for his work with refugees in 1985.

interest in human rights.

In general the procedure for determining refugee status was as follows: UNHCR interviewed the person seeking refugee status and elaborated a legal opinion recommending, or not, the granting of that status. This legal opinion was then sent to the Ministry of Foreign Affairs, which presented its view on the matter and sent it to the Ministry of Justice, which made the final decision. The decision was then published in the official gazette of the Brazilian government *(Diário Oficial da União)* and an official document was sent from UNHCR to CASP and CARJ, based on which, if the decision was positive, the Federal Police issued an identity document for the newly recognized refugee. The caseload at this time was small, around 200 (Fischel and Marcolini 2002a: 38).

In 1992, with the arrival of nearly 1,200 Angolans fleeing the civil war in their country, Brazil adopted a more flexible approach towards refugees. Brazil decided not to limit itself to the definition of the 1951 UN Convention and its 1967 Protocol, but to broaden the definition criteria to encompass the new refugees and allow for their protection. This marked the beginning of Brazil's use of a more comprehensive definition of refugee status, following the example of the Cartagena Declaration of 1984, which, in addition to the universal definition of refugees, stipulates that people fleeing their countries due to gross violations of human rights, foreign aggression, internal conflicts or other circumstances which threaten their lives, security or liberty are refugees.

The next step in Brazil's history of refugee protection was the elaboration of a Bill to create a specific Act on refugee status determination, which is the landmark of the present phase of International Refugee Law in Brazil. This law shows that Brazil has, after a precarious start, decided to commit itself to the cause of refugees, and is the main reason why Brazil is considered a model in the protection of refugees in South America. The creation of a specific and comprehensive Act on refugee status determination would not have been possible without the existence of the 1988 Federal Constitution, which is the beacon of Brazilian re-democratization and, as a result, is extremely protective of human rights. Two analytical tracks need to be taken in order to discern the impact of the 1988 Federal Constitution on refugee protection: 1) the domestic provisions of the Constitution and 2) the Constitution's provisions for Brazil's external approach.

The 1988 Federal Constitution establishes the fundamental principles and core objectives by which Brazil must be guided in its national and international actions. They constitute the foundations and goals of all subsequent Brazilian legislation. Among these principles and objectives are the 'dignity of the human being' (Article 1) and the obligation to promote the welfare of all without discrimination (Article 3), as well as the prevalence of human rights and the concession of political asylum (Article 4, II and Article 4, X, respectively). In addition to this, Article 5 of the 1988 Federal Constitution establishes that all persons are equal before the law, without discrimination of any kind and assures the inviolability of the rights to life, to freedom, to equality, to safety and to property of Brazilians and resident foreigners alike. The 1988 Federal Constitution thus lays down the equality of rights of Brazilians and foreigners, including applicants for refugee status and refugees.

On this basis, foreigners who seek refuge in Brazil find the Brazilian national juridical system with all its guarantees and obligations at their disposal.[4] These principles and rules form, albeit indirectly, the legal foundations of the institution of refuge in the Brazilian juridical system. Refuge is thus understood to be a protection of human dignity based upon non-discrimination, as a branch of human rights and as a form of asylum. Among the external provisions of the 1988 Federal Constitution, the most important for the present discussion are the provisions related to treaties, as such international agreements and conventions provide the basis of international refugee protection. In order for international treaties to take effect in Brazil-with all their impacts on national laws-legislative approval is required. This requirement is described as 'practical' as it is not directly expressed in the 1988 Federal Constitution but derives from jurisprudential interpretation-including decisions of the Supreme Court (*Supremo Tribunal Federal*)[5] -of three different articles of the Constitution (namely articles 21, 49 and 84).

On becoming part of the Brazilian legal system, a treaty acquires one of two distinct hierarchical positions: 1) an ordinary law or 2) a constitutional status, if both Houses of the Brazilian Congress have approved it with a quorum of three fifths of the votes. This second possibility is more recent as it was only incorporated into the 1988 Federal Constitution in December 2004 by the 45th Constitutional Amendment. Prior to this date all treaties were regarded as having the same force as an ordinary law. Some scholars had argued that where human rights are concerned international regulations should be given constitutional status-basing their position on Article 4, II (principle of prevalence of human rights) and Article 5, § 2 (which stipulates international treaties as a source of human rights) of the 1988 Federal Constitution (Piovesan 1996: 87-88)-or even, and as a matter of general application, should be higher in position than any internal legislation (Comparato 2001: 59; Hathaway 1991: 132).

This point is important to the study of International Refugee Law in Brazil in so far as all treaties already incorporated into the Brazilian legal system prior to the 45th Constitutional Amendment, including the 1951 UN Convention and its 1967 Protocol, have the status of an ordinary law and are thus liable to change as a result of further domestic legislation. This situation can lead to tension between Brazilian law and practice and the international rules, making the implementation of the latter difficult and tending to widen the gap between the theoretical commitment to international law, and its actual practice in Brazil. As regards refugee protection, however, this problem has been minimized due to the establishment of a specific act on refugee status, incorporating international law directly into the Brazilian internal legal system.

---

[4] This is the commonly accepted extensive interpretation of the wording of Article 5 vis-iA-vis the establishment of the principle of human dignity in Article 1, by which it is understood that equality before the law and, therefore, equality of rights, includes all foreigners and not only those who reside in Brazil, as every human being has an inherent dignity. There are, however, limitations on some rights of foreigners in Brazil, especially political rights, allowed for by the Federal Constitution and therefore regarded as legal. Any limitation of the rights of foreigners that is not based on the provisions of the Constitution is illegal in Brazil.

[5] Mainly the *Recurso Extraordinario* 80.004 (extraordinary appeal 80.004); the *Carta Rogatória* 8.279 (rogatory letter 8.279) and the decision on the *Ação Direta de Inconstitucionalidade* 1.490-3 (direct actions of unconstitutionality 1.490-3).

The Refugee Act: Law 9.474/97

The Difference between Domestic Asylum and Refuge

Although there are certain international standards to be upheld, the implementation of refugee protection is a domestic affair in the hands of the individual states, which means that each state can create specific rules to improve their protection of refugees, adapting the international standards to local conditions (Article 5 of the 1951 UN Convention). It is in this context that Brazil passed a specific and exclusive act for refugees: Law 9.474 of 22 July 1997, hereafter referred to as the Refugee Act or the Act. Having a specific act on refuge is positive, as it allows for a better correspondence between legal provisions, local conditions and the needs of refugees.

The exclusive character of this law is also significant since, analysing the list of countries which have signed the 1951 UN Convention and/or its 1967 Protocol, one finds that although the majority of states have national legislation on the subject, either by way of constitutional rules or by infraconstitutional legislation (Lauterpacht and Bethlehem 2001), most of these laws have one of two flaws. On the one hand many laws deal with the subject of refugees within the context of immigration legislation. Alternatively, some laws, as, for instance, to mention only South American states,[6] Chile's (Decree 1094, altered by Law 19.479 of 1996) and Venezuela's (Lei Organica sobre refugiados o refugiadas, asilados o asiladas of 3 October 2001), focus on asylum specifically which is important as, to the present day, in Brazil as in most Latin-American countries, domestic asylum and refuge remain two different legal institutions (Barreto n.d.; San Juan 2004; Fischel de Andrade 1998: 398, 400, Fischel de Andrade 2000: 82-84).

'Domestic asylum' and 'refuge' as understood and practised in South America are similar in that they share the same purpose: granting protection to individuals who fear persecution in their country of origin or habitual residence. Further similarities include their basis in respect for human rights and international solidarity and their humanitarian character. Besides this, both are currently founded on the same provision of International Law: article 14 of the Universal Declaration of Human Rights. Perhaps because of all these similarities domestic asylum and refuge as understood in Latin America are commonly confused. The key differences between the two concepts are that:

Domestic asylum:

- dates back to ancient times;

- is a discretionary act of the state;

- does not have legal limitations regarding its concession;

- is limited to political persecution which has to exist in fact;

- can be granted inside the state of origin or residency of the person fleeing

---

[6] As one of the aims of this paper is to show the relevance of Brazil as a regional model in refugee protection, all comparisons among laws will be made with the states of South America. The national legislations on refuge analysed followed the official list of national legislation on the UNHCR web page for Latin America (www.acnur.org).

persecution;

- only allows for the possibility of living legally in a state and

- is based on a constitutive decision by the granting state (i.e. it is the decision by the state which makes the person being granted asylum an asylee).

Refuge, however:

- began in the early decades of the twentieth century;

- is regulated by international norms;

- has an international organization that supervises it (UNHCR);

- has limitations regarding its concession (exclusion clauses);

- is based on a well-founded fear of persecution for reasons of race, religion, nationality, social group or political opinion;

- can only be granted to people outside their state of origin (i.e. requires alienage)

- generates responsibilities regarding the protection of the refugee by the granting state and

- is granted by a declaratory decision (i.e. it is the situation in the country of origin or residence and not the decision of the state which makes a person a refugee).

The co-existence of these two institutions in Latin America can be explained by the fact that the states of this region, while desiring closer integration with the international community by incorporating international regulations on refuge, wanted and needed to maintain their tradition of granting protection to persecuted people who either lay outside the definition of a refugee according to the 1951 Convention or to whom granting refuge was not a wise political move.

This need derived from the historical political atmosphere of Latin America, which has only begun to change recently, and in which instability was a constant as dictatorships, coups and persecution were the norm throughout the region. These processes often victimized important political figures (e.g. presidents or prime ministers) whose continued presence in the country in question could mean either death to the individual or instability to the country.

Their protection as 'Convention Refugees' was, most often, impossible (some fell under the exclusion clauses, for example) but they needed to be able to leave their countries as an essential prerequisite to peace. Their human rights to life, security and fair trial when required also had to be respected. So, as these people could not be refugees according to the Convention (i.e. granted refuge) they needed an alternative form of protection (asylum) so that they themselves would be protected and security in the region could be established and maintained.

The granting of this form of asylum in the region was so important that regional conventions on the theme were established[7] even before the universal norms on

---

[7] As, for instance, the Convention on Asylum (Habana, 1928); the Convention on Political Asylum

refuge were created and the existence of an American International Law on it was advocated (see Haya de La Torre, 1950, International Court of Justice). This particular historical context means that two differently defined institutions of refuge and asylum still co-exist today as two distinct ways to protect human beings from persecution.

This co-existence has, however, both positive and negative aspects. On the one hand, a discretionary (and predominantly political) institution such as domestic asylum can preserve the humanitarian character of the institution of refuge, thereby shielding its application from politically motivated criticism. On the other hand, as there is some confusion about the roles of the two institutions (as for example always referring to refugees as political refugees, as the only cause of granting asylum is political persecution which is not the case for granting refuge) the adequate application of both can be put in jeopardy.

The process of asking for asylum in Brazil is completely different from that of refugee status determination and has a political rather than a juridical nature, which can be noted from the facts that there are no exclusion clauses for the concession of asylum and that the granting of asylum is in the competence of the President of Brazil. Consequently, the 1997 law refers only to 'refuge': the protection of refugees and their status determination, as there is a completely different set of rules and practice for asylum (which predate the regulations on refuge by approximately 150 years).

The Provisions of the Refugee Act

The Refugee Act is the result of the 1996 Human Rights National Programme. Its drafting process involved both the Brazilian government and representatives of UNHCR, demonstrating a political desire to create a national law in accordance with international standards. The Act deals with seven key issues:

- Title I stipulates the definition of refugees,

- Title II deals with entry into Brazilian territory and application for refugee status,

- Title III establishes the competence of the National Committee for Refugees (*Comitê Nacional para Refugiados*, hereafter referred to as CONARE), which is the organization responsible for deciding whether to grant refuge,

- Title IV specifies the rules for refugee status determination,

- Title V deals with the possibilities of expulsion and extradition,

- Title VI establishes the hypotheses of loss and cessation of refugee status,

- Title VII is related to durable solutions, and

- Title VIII stipulates the final provisions.

(Montevideo, 1933); the Declaration of Rights and Duties of Men on Territorial Asylum (IX Pan-American Conference, 1948); the Convention on Political Asylum (Montevideo, 1939) and the Convention on Diplomatic Asylum (Caracas, 1954).

Definition of a Refugee -In defining a refugee, the Refugee Act adopts, in general, the same criteria as the 1951 UN Convention, in particular the classic definition of a refugee (Article 1, I and II) and the cessation clauses (Article 38). However, there are important differences between the universal Convention and the Brazilian law with regards to the exclusion clauses and the extension of the benefits of refuge. With regard to the exclusion clauses, the Act adds to the 1951 UN Convention the possibility of denying refuge to people who have committed terrorism or are involved in drug trafficking (Article 3, III). This could be seen as an unlawful limitation of refugee status as it is not provided for in the Convention and Brazil did not make a reservation on the subject when ratifying it. However, it could also be regarded as updating and specifying the text of the 1951 UN Convention in so far as both terrorism and drug trafficking could fall under the category of serious non-political crimes or acts contrary to the purposes and principles of the UN, which are exclusion clauses provided for in the treaty, thus the Brazilian addition would not be going against International Refugee Law.

Furthermore, the Refugee Act has a provision which, it could be argued, is more in keeping with the concept of the rule of law than the 1951 UN Convention: under the Brazilian law, an exclusion clause can only be applied when the person asking for refugee status has actually committed an act which falls within the exclusion clauses and not when 'there are serious reasons for considering that' the person has done so, as stated in the Convention.

The Act is innovative in the extension of the benefit of refuge as it allows the family of the refugee in Brazil to receive refugee status (Article 2) and also broadens the classic definition of a refugee to include gross violations of human rights as a legitimate reason for granting refuge.[8] In this way, the 'spirit of Cartagena' is adopted, in a reference to the aforementioned more comprehensive definition of refugee status adopted in the Cartagena Declaration of 1984 (Article 1, III).

Regarding the 'spirit of Cartagena', Brazil was the second country in the region to include gross violations of human rights as a reason for granting refugee status in its internal legislation (Bolivia being the first, according to Article 2 of Supreme Decree 19.640 of 4 July 1983) and the first one to do so in a domestic law. This inclusion demonstrates human solidarity, a consciousness of Brazil's international responsibility and a comprehension of the bonds of International Refugee Law and International Human Rights Law. These trends are reinforced by the provision of Article 48 of the Refugee Act which stipulates that this law has to be interpreted in keeping with the Universal Declaration of Human Rights, the 1951 UN Convention and its 1967 Protocol, as well as any international Human Rights document to which Brazil is committed.

---

[8] While the majority of Brazilian scholars understand that this posture resulted merely in an extension of the definition of refugee status, a new theory proposes that, in fact, the adoption of more comprehensive criteria for granting refuge means a completely new approach to the definition of refugee status. This new theory is based on the idea that there has been a change of focus in the definition criteria of refugee status, as the traditional definition relies on the causes of persecution and the definition proposed by the Cartagena Declaration focuses on the objective situation of the country of origin.

Entry and Application for Status - Regarding the entry of refugees into the country, the Refugee Act assures the possibility of making a request for refuge to any immigration authority (Article 7, preface) and the impossibility of deporting someone who has asked for refuge until the end of the refugee status determination procedure (Article 7, I). This is the domestic realization of the principle of *non-refoulement.*

The Act does not stipulate a maximum period for requesting refuge after entering Brazilian territory, as do other countries such as Peru (art. 13, Law 27.891, 2002) and Colombia (art. 6, Decree 2.450, 2002). The Act also establishes that an irregular entry does not prejudice the possibility of asking for refugee status (Article 8). This means that any criminal and administrative procedures arising from an illegal or irregular entry into Brazil, which could result in the deportation or expulsion of the alien due to the Foreigners Statute (*Estatuto do Estrangeiro*-Law 6.881/80)***, are halted until the end of the determination of refugee status (Article 10, preface and Titles I and II) and terminated in the event of a positive answer to the request for refugee status.

The Act also forbids the extradition of refugees and applicants for refugee status pending a decision on their cases, with the exception of cases where national security or a threat to public order are involved, in which case the refugee or applicant will not be sent to his/her country of origin or residence or to a place where his/her life, liberty or welfare may be in jeopardy.

CONARE - The Refugee Act establishes CONARE as the organ responsible for refugee status determination. In addition to its responsibility for first instance decisions on refugee status, CONARE is charged with guiding public policies to make protection, assistance and legal aid to refugees effective. This body is also responsible for the elaboration of normative instructions to clarify any aspect of the Act. CONARE is presided over by a representative of the Ministry of Justice, while the vice-president is a representative of the Ministry of Foreign Affairs. Other members of CONARE represent the Ministries of Health, Work and Labour and Education and Sports. There are also representatives of the Federal Police and of civil society (now represented by CASP) and UNHCR has voice-no-vote status. This makes CONARE the body with the broadest composition of any similar bodies in South America. In Ecuador, for example, the committee vested with responsibility for protecting refugees has only three members (art. 4, decree 3.301, 1992).

Still regarding composition, it is interesting to note that in most South American states, the organ responsible for the granting of refuge includes a representative from the national immigration authorities, which is not the case in Brazil. In this way, Brazil avoids possible prejudice against economic migrants, particularly in time of economic downturn, being also directed against refugees, and Brazilian society at large gets a greater understanding of the particular status of refugees, leading to a stronger spirit of solidarity with their plight.

*** In 2017 Brazil adopted a new law on migration: Law 13.445, which replaces the *Estatuto do Estrangeiro.*

Another distinguishing characteristic of CONARE compared to similar organs in the region is that civil society, represented by an NGO that works with refugees, is not only present but is also entitled to vote. In other countries, these three trends (a representative of a non-governmental organization which works with refugees and is entitled to vote) are not present simultaneously. For example, in Argentina and Uruguay civil society is not represented; in Paraguay the representative of the NGO cannot vote and in Bolivia civil society is represented by the church and by Universidad Mayor de San Andres but there is no mention of the fact that these organs work or have to work with refugees.

The presence of civil society is extremely relevant as an international commitment by a country binds not only the government but also the society at large: involvement in the decision-making process is important as a means of sharing the responsibility for the actual protection of refugees between the government and civil society. An additional facet of this role is that civil society can exercise pressure on the government on behalf of refugees. This broad composition has been both praised and criticized: praised for expanding the theme of refuge to all governmental organs, which would reflect on the lives of refugees, and criticized for the fact that, with rare exceptions, the majority of the representatives of these ministries are not qualified on the subject. CONARE decided to study a change in its composition to 1) invite representatives of other Ministries (e.g. the Ministry of Cities and the Ministry of Social Development) and 2) make the current members participate more actively.

The establishment of CONARE and its success in providing first decisions on refugee status determination (in addition to budgetary matters) were the reasons for the withdrawal of the office of UNHCR from Brazil, in 1998. This success, however, has not been repeated in its other two functions as to date there are no public policies regarding refugees in Brazil and the normative instructions approved by it are often more restrictive of the rights of refugees than the Refugee Act.

Cessation and Loss - The cessation clauses and the reasons for losing refugee status are stated in articles 38 and 39 of the Refugee Act. Cessation is legally possible because the granting of refuge is dependent on the objective situation in the state of origin or residence of the refugee. This situation can change and improve so that the need for protection disappears. Furthermore, misconduct on the part of the refugee could lead to loss of refugee status. 'Misconduct' is understood as gross violation of international law. Committing ordinary criminal offences is not listed in the Act as an exclusion clause, as is the case in most national legislations in the South American states. If refugee status ceases or is lost, the individual is placed under the general system of rules for foreigners in Brazil, the aforementioned Foreigners Statute (Article 39).

In all the decisions on the non-application of refugee status, i.e. denial, cessation and loss, an appeal is possible (Article 40). This appeal is addressed to the Minister of Justice and has to be presented within 15 days of the date of the notification of the decision of CONARE to the applicant.

Initial Criticism of the Refugee Act - The Act stipulates that refugee status determination is free of charge and is a matter of urgency, but does not stipulate timeframes for government decisions on refuge as do other national legislations, for example in Paraguay. This is the first point in which it is found wanting in comparison with legislation in other South American countries. A second criticism of the Act is that it does not list the economic, cultural and social rights of refugees. This is especially relevant as, although the 1988 Federal Constitution establishes the equal rights of Brazilians and foreigners, in practice refugees find many constraints in accessing the labour market and higher education. A third point found wanting is that although the Act establishes the process of refugee status determination, there is no provision for refugee status determination in the event of a massive influx of refugees.

The Process of Refugee Status Determination in Brazil

As noted above, CONARE is responsible for determining refugee status in Brazil. The procedure leading to the granting of such status is as follows.[****] The first step is a deposition from the applicant to the Federal Police, which is entered into the Declaration Term (*Termo de Declarações*). This deposition contains:

- the personal identification data of the applicant,
- his/her civil status,
- the circumstances of entry into Brazil and
- a brief description of the reasons for which refuge is being asked.

Usually, when the plea for refuge involves a family only one deposition is required. The Declaration Term serves as the proof of the legal status of the person seeking refuge in Brazil and is their first documentation in the country. Following this, the applicant is directed to a Refugee Centre operated by either CASP or CARJ. At the Refugee Centre a more detailed questionnaire must be completed. This questionnaire is used by CASP and CARJ in asking the Brazilian Government to grant the applicant another document: the Provisional Protocol (*Protocolo Provisório*). According to Article 21 of the Refugee Act the Provisional Protocol is provided by the Federal Police after CONARE gives its authorization, is valid for 90 days, and is renewed for as long as the refugee status determination process continues, as it is the applicant's identity card in Brazil. The Act stipulates that every member of the family group asking for refuge is entitled to a Provisional Protocol, although in practice this seldom happens.

The Provisional Protocol is the basis for the provision of two further documents: a Labour and Social Welfare Card (*Carteira de Trabalho e Previdência Social*)-needed to find registered jobs and a Natural Person Registry (*Cadastro de Pessoas Físicas*)-an important document for financial purposes.

This is unusual compared with other countries in the region which only provide

---

[****] CONARE's normative resolution 18, of 2014, regulates the current procedure for RSD in Brazil.

people seeking refuge with identity cards, thus constraining their ability to integrate into society.

Two interviews follow the completion of the questionnaire. The first interview is with a lawyer who is trained and paid for by UNHCR. The lawyer elaborates a Legal Opinion on Eligibility (*Parecer de Elegibilidade*). This document will be the basis for decisions on any financial assistance. Although financial aid is limited, all applicants for refugee status are eligible to use the public health system, as well as public housing facilities (shelters), and to benefit from food price discounts with CASP's and CARJ's partners or from government food programmes. In line with the exclusive competence of the Brazilian Government to grant refuge in its territory, the second interview is with a representative from CONARE.

Significantly, the Refugee Act regards all the information provided by the applicant at any stage of the process of refugee status determination as confidential. This provision is not found in the majority of national legislations of the South American states but is extremely important in ensuring both the security of the individual and the confidence each applicant has in providing full details on his/her story.

After this interview the representative of CONARE reports his/her findings to the Preliminary Analysis Group (*Grupo de Estudos Prévios*), a sub-grouping of representatives of CONARE, consisting of the Ministry of Foreign Relations, UNHCR and, after 2004, an NGO representing Brazilian society. The NGO in the Preliminary Analysis Group is the Migration and Human Rights Institute (*Instituto de Migrações e Direitos Humanos*, hereafter referred to as IMDH), which as a result of an agreement with CASP[9] has established an orientation centre for the refugee population in Brasilia.[10] The establishment of this centre shows an increase in public interest in the refugee issue and helps to spread the work with refugees to other cities in Brazil.

The representatives of IMDH and UNHCR on the Preliminary Analysis Group receive the Legal Opinion on Eligibility from the lawyers at the Refugee Centres as a basis for their position in each case. UNHCR participates actively in the Preliminary Analysis Group, although it has a voice-no-vote status in CONARE. This might be seen as 'compensatory', and is also a peculiarity of Brazilian refugee law and protection in comparison to other states in the region.

The Preliminary Analysis Group elaborates an opinion recommending that refugee status be granted or refused. This opinion is then sent to the CONARE

---

[9] This agreement was made possible due to a new partnership between CASP and the *Secretaria Especial dos Direitos Humanos da Presidência da República* (Special Office of Human Rights of the Presidency, hereafter referred to as SEDH/PR) which began in January 2004 and increased the budget of CASP with personnel, allowing, therefore, the transfer of funds to IMDH.

[10] The intention of entering into a similar agreement has been signed between CASP and *Caritas Diocesana de Santos* (Diocesan Caritas of Santos). The establishment of this centre is, at the time of writing, waiting for an answer to funding requests to SEDH/PR. The need to have centres in Brasilia and in Santos derives from the fact that the former is the capital of Brazil and the city where CONARE functions (as well as all State Ministries) and the latter is the biggest port of Brazil and, therefore, the gateway for many applicants for refugee status. It is important to note, though, that the centres do not tackle refugee status determination processes (which rest with CASP and CARJ) and are only in charge of orientation and guidance to improve aid to refugees and applicants in their cities.

plenary, where it is discussed and the official decision on the case is taken. In the case of a positive decision by CONARE the refugee must register with the Federal Police, sign a Responsibility Term (*Termo de Responsabilidade*) and will receive official documentation as a refugee in Brazil. This official document is called the National Register of Foreigners (*Registro Nacional de Estrangeiros*, RNE) and it proves that the refugee may lawfully reside permanently in Brazil due to his/her status as a refugee. The possession of an RNE based on refugee status for over six years enables the refugee to change his/her legal status in Brazil by requesting to become a permanent foreign resident.[11]

If CONARE's decision is negative, the applicant has 15 days after the official notification to either leave Brazil or present an appeal to the Minister of Justice, as mentioned above (articles 29, 31 and 41). The appeal process has suspensive effect on the requirement to leave (article 30). If the decision on the appeal is negative the refugee status determination is over. In this case the applicant is not entitled to any documents provided by the Brazilian government and falls under the general system of rules for foreigners, being, therefore, subject to any compulsory measure of departure deportation, expulsion or extradition (article 32). The compulsory measure of departure, however, cannot be to a place where the life or integrity of the applicant is still in jeopardy, which would violate the principle of *non-refoulement* (article 32). This may give rise to a contradictory situation as the government will neither deport the person to his/her country of origin or residence because of lack of security, nor does it recognize the person as a refugee and, hence, will not allow this person to stay legally in Brazil. This problem in addition to the three points found wanting earlier are the main weaknesses of the Act.

Another important point for reflection is that the procedure for determining refugee status in Brazil is entirely administrative and that the Refugee Act does not provide any possibility of recourse to the judicial system. It is said that a specific provision for access to the judicial system need not be mentioned in the law as it is implicit, on the basis that the 1988 Federal Constitution stipulates that laws cannot exclude from the appreciation of the judiciary any violation or possibility of violation of rights (Article 5, XXXV). However, as refugees are foreigners and are not familiar with the Brazilian legal system, the assurance of being able to take their cases to the judiciary seems relevant and a major aspect of the right to an effective remedy for violations of human rights. Besides this, if, in practice, the process is limited to CONARE it is limited to the Executive Branch, which is the most political branch of the state, and the very apolitical nature of the granting of refuge could be in jeopardy.

In spite of these flaws, and in comparison to the individual legislations of the other South American states, the Brazilian legislation still offers the best combination for the protection of refugees. What is more, the majority of national

---

[11] Permanent foreign residents have, in theory, a stable permanence in Brazil whereas, due to the cessation clauses, refugees could have their status withdrawn in the event that the objective situation of the country of origin or residence changes substantially. However, in practice, the Brazilian government has never withdrawn its protection based on the cessation of refugee status. It is possible to combine both statuses (permanent foreign resident and refugee) in which case the individual can benefit from a more comprehensive protection.

laws on refugees in the region are more recent than the Brazilian Refugee Act, and are broadly inspired by it. All this leads to the conclusion that regarding its legal foundations, Brazil can be considered a model for refugee protection in South America. Whether the same model standard is maintained through innovative policies is analysed in the following section.

Recent Developments in International Refugee Law in Brazil

There have been two important recent developments on refugee law, policy and practice in Brazil. One is the establishment of a resettlement programme. The other is the re-establishment of UNHCR's presence in the country.

Resettlement

As UNHCR sought new or emerging countries of resettlement in the late 1990s (Fischel de Andrade and Marcolini 2002b), three factors made Brazil a potentially interesting place for a new resettlement programme. Firstly, Brazil had shown an interest in deepening its commitment to the protection of refugees. Secondly, it has, as described above, a well-thought-out and well-structured administrative process of refugee status determination. Thirdly, Brazil is a country of migrants with a vast territory and a history of tolerance, providing the basis for good opportunities for the integration of newcomers.

In light of this, and based on the UNHCR competence to sign special agreements (Zieck 1998), a Framework Agreement for the Resettlement of Refugees in Brazil (based on article 46 of the Refugee Act) was negotiated and signed in 1999. This agreement defined the criteria and the ways by which this lasting solution would be implemented within Brazil. An initial commitment to the resettlement of 30 families outside the Rio- Sao Paulo axis (already in charge of the protection of refugees generally as described above) was established by the Brazilian government. In September 2001 a closed seminar was held in Rio de Janeiro to make official the willingness of the cities of Mogi das Cruzes (in the State of São Paulo), Natal (Rio Grande do Norte), Porto Alegre (Rio Grande do Sul) and Santa Maria Madelena (Rio de Janeiro) to begin the resettlement policy in Brazil.

A group of Afghan refugees was the first to be resettled. However, due to the terrorist attacks of September 11, 2001 on the United States and the political instability which followed in the region from which the refugees would come, their resettlement in Brazil was suspended. As a result only the city of Porto Alegre remained in the resettlement project and, on 12 April 2002, received 10 Afghans who had received initial protection in Iran before being resettled to Brazil. On 26 April of the same year, 13 other Afghans, who had initially sought protection in India, were also resettled. The resettled refugees were assisted initially by a non-governmental organization- *Central de Orientação e Encaminhamento* (Orientation and Guidance Centre)-but the assistance programme was soon transferred to a Catholic organization called Sociedade Padre Antonio Vieira (the Father Antonio Vieira Society of the Company of Jesus) which is a current partner of UNHCR. All the resettled refugees had been selected, registered and accepted by CONARE prior to their arrival in Brazil.

Of the 23 refugees who were part of the first resettlement group in Brazil, 18 voluntarily requested repatriation, and returned to Afghanistan following the changes in the circumstances in that country. In spite of this, new groups of resettled refugees were received in 2004. Also in 2004, the twentieth anniversary of the Cartagena Declaration was celebrated with meetings involving UNHCR, civil society and governments of Latin America. One goal of these meetings was to put forward proposals for new actions on refugee protection in the region. Brazil used this occasion to propose the concept of 'resettlement in solidarity' through which countries in the region (especially in South America) could offer their help to other countries in the region facing more difficult situations regarding refugees (Carneiro 2005). Ecuador and Costa Rica are two of the countries in need of particular assistance in this area as they have large numbers of refugees and forced migrants from Colombia. As a result of this proposal the main group of resettled refugees received by Brazil in 2004 was made up of Colombian refugees from Ecuador (although resettlement arrivals in 2004 also included individuals who had been refugees in Cuba). The Brazilian government approved the resettlement of 97 people, but only 75 people arrived and were resettled in 12 cities across the country.[12]

In the first half of 2005, 14 other people out of the 97 already approved arrived; two other cases were discussed and resettled immediately due to security reasons and 30 people have been approved to be resettled and are expected to arrive in Brazil shortly at the time of writing. All of them are Colombian refugees. There has also been an increase in the number of cities receiving resettled refugees and the total number is now 15 with the prospect of three more cities joining the programme in 2006.[13] UNHCR has been supported in this expansion of the resettlement programme in Brazil by *Caritas Brasileira* in the State of São Paulo, the *Núcleo de Estudos Brasileiros* (Brazilian Studies Centre) in the State of Rio Grande do Norte, and the aforementioned IMDH and the Father Antonio Vieira Society of the Company of Jesus. This brief description shows that resettlement is becoming an established practice of refugee protection in Brazil. In light of this it can be said that, once again, Brazil has played a leading role in the region, not only in establishing a resettlement programme but also introducing new concepts and approaches to improve refugee protection in South America, which are already being followed by other countries (especially Chile).

Re-opening of the Office of UNHCR in Brazil

As previously mentioned, UNHCR established an office in Brazil in the late 1970s and remained in the country till 1998. Before its departure from Brazil, the UNHCR office was subordinate to a UNHCR regional office located in Buenos Aires (Argentina): the Regional Office for the Southern part of South America. After the closure of its office in Brazil, the implementing partners (i.e. CARJ and

---

[12] The cities are: Bento Gonçalves, Caxias do Sul, Porto Alegre, Santa Maria, all in Rio Grande do Sul; Campinas, Guararema, Jundiaí, São José dos Campos, Taubaté, all in São Paulo; Lajes, Natal, and Poço Branco, all in Rio Grande do Norte.

[13] The other cities already in the programme are: Passo Fundo, Rio Grande do Sul; São Leopoldo, Rio Grande do Sul; and Tremembé, São Paulo. The probable new cities of resettlement will be Vitória, Espírito Santo; Vila Velha, Espírito Santo; and Gravataí, Rio Grande do Sul.

CASP) started to report directly to the regional office. A UNHCR representative remained in Brazil, though with more limited power.

With Brazil becoming a resettlement country and in recognition of its good practice regarding refugee law, UNHCR decided to re-establish itself in the country. The UNHCR office was reopened in March 2004 and has already proved valuable. Geographical proximity has brought the work of UNHCR closer to the work of the implementing partners and has improved the position of UNHCR in CONARE. It also has brought UNHCR closer to the Brazilian government as a whole, allowing greater UNHCR involvement in the politics regarding refugees.

The presence of UNHCR in Brazil has also created greater opportunities for information campaigns among the general public. In this area two important initiatives should be mentioned: the first is the establishment of Sergio Vieira de Mello Chairs in universities. UNHCR aims to use these Chairs to expand education in International Humanitarian Law and International Refugee Law as well as stimulate the access of refugees to higher education, while honouring a Brazilian international servant, killed in Baghdad, who started his work in UNHCR. The second activity is the organization of workshops for the Federal Police and general public in cities on Brazil's borders, to help ensure the upholding of the right to request refuge. The re-opening of the UNHCR office in Brazil has also facilitated negotiations on current projects, among which resettlement, and projects for the near future (especially a project of access to credit for refugees, which could, in the long run, benefit the local community as well). For all these reasons it can be said that, as in the legal aspects, Brazil has evolved into a model for refugee protection in South America in regard to policy as well.

Conclusion

The practice of International Refugee Law in Brazil has evolved considerably since the establishment of the Refugee Act. From a country which only accepted refugees from Europe, which did not recognize UNHCR as an international organization, which forced refugees from the region to be resettled elsewhere in the world and its own nationals to plead for refugee status abroad, Brazil has become, over a period of 30 years, a receiver of refugees (with approximately 3,500 refugees of over 65 nationalities) and is proposing new approaches for the protection of refugees in South America. As things currently stand, the protection of refugees in Brazil has some positive and some negative aspects. The negative aspects are mainly:

- the lack of a deadline for the government to decide the requests for refuge;

- the lack of stipulation of economic, social and cultural rights in its specific law for refugees;

- the lack of provisions for refugee status determination in the event of massive influx of refugees;

- the fact that the organ vested with the responsibility of first decisions on refuge-CONARE-is within the Executive Branch of the State, which can lead to political bias;

- the fact that access to the judicial system is not stated explicitly in the specific law for refugees, and

- the lack of public policies for refugees.

On the other hand the positive aspects are:

- the existence of a specific and exclusive law for refugees;

- respect for the minimum international standards of International Refugee Law (e.g. the principle of non-refoulement);

- a broad definition of the concept of refugee;

- the absence of a time limit for requesting refugee status once inside Brazil;

- a comprehensive process of refugee status determination regulated by law;

- the broad composition of CONARE encompassing representatives of all organs related to the integration of refugees, as well as a representative of civil society and of UNHCR as a voice-no-vote member, and the fact that CONARE specifically does not include a representative of the organ responsible for immigration to Brazil;

- the granting of documents to applicants for refugee status;

- permission for applicants for refugee status to work;

- the idea and practice of resettlement in solidarity;

- the constant public information effort and

- the important role played by civil society in all phases of the protection of refugees (decision-making/protection, assistance and local integration).

Analysing the positive and negative aspects, one sees that the positive outweigh the negative, and that the negative aspects have not, thus far, jeopardized refugee protection in Brazil. Furthermore, many positive aspects are innovations by Brazil in comparison to the countries of the region. On this basis Brazil can be seen as a model in South America regarding refugee protection. This role can be justified by Brazil's demonstration of a humane position with regard to refugee protection in comparison to the logic that has been operating in the contemporary world. This can be seen both in its inclusion of traditional and new actors in the decision-making process concerning refugee status determination, as well as in the local integration of refugees and in the newly established resettlement programme.

One could explain this position in a realistic light: as Brazil receives a small number of refugees, the issue is not yet regarded as a 'refugee problem'. However, whatever the reasons for doing so, Brazil is adopting a post-Westphalian logic in the only way to ensure real protection to refugees and to fulfil its international legal commitment. This is the most conspicuous and relevant aspect.

After its re-democratization, the openness and political will to continually improve its policies and laws regarding the protection of refugees not only have been a constant in Brazil but seem to be spreading to the general public, which may lead to more progress in the area. Brazil, therefore, is proving that it is possible to combine governmental needs and the offer of protection and integration to those in need-relying especially on tolerance-and is also showing a consciousness of the need to comply with the international obligation of solidarity and protection of human beings. This, in spite of the existing flaws in its refugee protection system, makes Brazil a model in South America, and, as a consequence, a contributor to the evolution of International Refugee Law and protection at large.

References

BARRETO, L. P. T. (n.d.) *'Das diferenças entre os institutos jurídicos do asilo e do refúgio'* (On the differences between the legal institutions of asylum and refugee). (available at http://www.mj.gov. br/snj/artigorefugio.htm)

CARNEIRO, W. P. (2005) 'A Declaração de Cartagena de 1984 e os desafios da proteção internacional dos refugiados, 20 anos depois' (The 1984 Cartagena Declaration and the challenges of the international protection of refugees, 20 years later) in da Silva, C. A. S. and Rodrigues, V. M. *Refugiados* (Refugees), Vila Velha: 55-78.

COMPARATO, F. K. (2001) *A afirrnação hist6rica dos Direitos Humanos* (The historical affirmation of human rights) Sao Paulo: Saraiva.

FISCHEL DE ANDRADE, J. H. (1998) 'Regional Policy Approaches and Harmonization: a Latin American Perspective', *International Journal of Refugee Law* 10(3): 389-409.

_____ (2000) 'Regionalização e Harmonização da Definição e dos Procedimentos para a Determinação da Condição de refugiados no âmbito do Mercosul' (Regionalization and Harmonization of the Definiton and Process for Refugee Status Determination in the MERCOSUR) in Casella, P. B. *Mercosul: Integração, Regionalização e Globalização* (MERCOSUR: Integration, Regionalization and Globalization), Rio de Janeiro: Renovar: 63-98.

FISCHEL DE ANDRADE, J. H. and MARCOLINI, A. (2002a) 'Brazil's Refugee Act: Model Refugee Law for Latin America', *Forced Migration Review* 12: 37-38.

_____ (2002b) 'A política brasileira de proteção e reassentamento de refugiados: breves comentários sobre suas principais características' (The Brazilian policy of protection and resetlement of refugees: brief notes on its main characteristics), *Revista Brasileira de Política Internacional (Brazilian Review of International Politics)*, 45(1): 168-176.

HATHAWAY, J. (1991) *The Law of Refugee Status,* Canada: Butterworths.

JUBILUT, L. L. (2003) *'O Direito International dos Refugiados e sua implementação no ordenamento jurídico brasileiro'* (International Refugee Law and its implementation in Brazil) Dissertação de Mestrado apresentada à Universidade de São Paulo (Masters in Law dissertation presented at Universidade de São Paulo).

LAFER, C. (2004) *A identidade internacional do Brasil e a política externa brasileira: Passado, Presente, e Futuro* (The international identity of Brazil and the Brazilian foreign policy: Past, Present and Future), São Paulo: Perspectiva.

LAUTERPACHT, E. and BETHLEHEM, D. (2001) 'The Scope and the Content of the Principle of Non-refoulement', Annex I, UNHCR Global Consultation Briefing Paper.

PIOVESAN, F. (1996) *Direitos Humanos e o Direito Constitucional Internacional* (Human Rights and International Constitutional Law), São Paulo: Max Limonad.

SAN JUAN, C. (2004) 'Análisis de legislación comparada' (Analysis of Comparative Legislation) in ACNUR, *El asilo y la protección internacional de los refugiados en América Latina* (Asylum and the International Protection of Refugees in Latin America): 215-241, available at http:llwww. acnur.org/biblioteca/pdf/3193.pdf (consulted 07/07/2005).

ZIECK, M. (1998) 'UNHCR's "Special Agreements"', *Essays on the Law of Treaties: a Collection of Essays in Honour of Bert Vierdag,* Martinus Nijhoff Publishers: 171-187.

REFUGEE PROTECTION IN BRAZIL AND LATIN AMERICA

Printed Brochures and Web pages

www.caritas.org

www.unhcr.ch

www.acnur.org

ACNUR (1997) 20 anos de trabalho humanitário no Brasil (1977-1997): 0 mandato do ACNUR (20 years of humanitarian work in Brazil (1977-1997): UNHCR'S mandate)

ACNUR (2003) Refugiados no Sul da América do Sul: Argentina, Bolívia, Brasil, Chile, Paraguai e Uruguai (Refugees in the South of South America: Argentine, Bolivia, Brazil, Chile, Paraguay and Uruguay)

Caritas Arquidiocesana do Rio de Janeiro. Folder sobre as atividades (Brochure on the activities of CARJ)

Caritas Arquidiocesana de São Paulo. Folder sobre as atividades (Brochure on the activities of CASP)

Central de Orientação e Encaminhamento. Folder sobre as atividades (Brochure on the activities of the Orientation and Guidance Center)

REFUGEE STATUS DETERMINATION IN BRAZIL: A TRIPARTITE ENTERPRISE (2008)

Liliana Lyra Jubilut* and **Silvia Menicucci de Oliveira Selmi Apolinário****

Introduction

International refugee law, especially the 1951 Convention relating to the Status of Refugees (Refugee Convention) and its 1967 Protocol, defines who is a refugee. To enable States Parties to these treaties to implement their provisions, refugees have to be identified. The determination of refugee status, although mentioned in article 9 of the Refugee Convention, is not specifically regulated and each State Party can establish the procedure that it deems most appropriate, considering its particular constitutional structure.

With regard to refugee law and protection, Brazil can be seen as both an "old" and a "new" country.[1] It is an "old" country insofar as Brazil was involved in the first international initiatives of refugee protection,[2] has been a member of the Executive Committee (ExCom) of the United Nations High Commissioner for Refugees (UNHCR) since 1958, and ratified the 1951 Refugee Convention and its 1967 Protocol in 1961 and 1972, respectively.[3] And it is a "new" country given that

---

* Liliana Lyra Jubilut holds a Ph.D. in International Law from Universidade de São Paulo, and an LL.M. in international legal studies from NYU School of Law, and is Professor of International Law and Human Rights at Faculdade de Direito do Sul de Minas.

** Silvia Menicucci de Oliveira Selmi Apolinário holds a Ph.D. in international law from Universidade de S. Paulo, and is Professor of International Law and Human Rights at PUC-Rio (Rio de Janeiro) and International Humanitarian Law at UniCEUB (Brasília).

Both authors were lawyers at the refugee centres in S. Paulo and Rio de Janeiro and were directly involved in RSD in Brazil.

[1] Liliana L. Jubilut, *O Direito Internacional dos Refugiados e sua aplicação no ordenamento jurídico brasileiro* [International refugee law and its application in the Brazilian legal order] (São Paulo: UNHCR; Método, 2007).

[2] José Henrique Fischel de Andrade, "O Brasil e a Organização Internacional para Refugiados (1946–1952)" [Brazil and the international organization for refugees] (2005) 48 *Revista Brasileira de Política Internacional* [Brazilian Journal of International Politics] 60; José Henrique Fischel de Andrade, *Direito Internacional dos Refugiados: evolução histórica (1921–1952)* [International refugee law: Historical evolution 1921–1952] (Rio de Janeiro: Renovar, 1996).

[3] The Refugee Convention was signed by Brazil on 28 July 1951, approved by the Legislature through Decree 11, 7 July 1960, and promulgated by the Executive through Decree 50.215, 28 January 1961. The 1967 Protocol was signed on 31 January 1967, approved by the Legislature through Decree 93, 30 November 1971, and promulgated by the Executive through Decree 70.946, 7 August 1972. The geographic limitation and reserves were only suspended by Decree 98.602, 20 December 1989, and Decree 99.757, 4 December

the National Refugee Act, Law 9.474,[4] was passed in 1997 and that in the beginning of the twenty-first century it became an emerging resettlement country.[5]

As the most important developments have occurred in the last decade or so, one can see that refugee law and protection in Brazil has evolved significantly in a short period of time. However, there is always room for improvement. Refugee status determination (RSD) in Brazil is nowadays a tripartite enterprise, involving UNHCR, the Brazilian government, and civil society. The involvement of civil society is a heritage from the early beginnings of refugee protection in Brazil, when there was no government procedure in place and UNHCR had to rely heavily on civil society in order to guarantee any form of protection whatsoever. This tripartite character, and especially the participation of civil society, seems to be an impressive feature of RSD in Brazil as it guarantees a more democratic procedure and involves all actors needed to ascertain integral protection to refugees. It thus seems to aid in the establishment of a better RSD protection and is a practice that should be analyzed to see if indeed it can be regarded as a "best practice."

In light of the above, this paper aims to describe the practice of RSD in Brazil, assess its main qualities and flaws, and verify whether or not there are lessons to be learned from RSD in Brazil with a view to improve best practices of RSD in general.

To achieve these aims, this article is divided into three parts. The first part will provide an overview of RSD in Brazil, both before and after the National Refugee Act of 1997. The second will analyze RSD procedures in Brazil, through three lenses: the internal context in which they occur; the general norms of international refugee law in relation to RSD; and the most protective standards that should apply to the protection of human beings in light of an holistic approach to international law and international human rights law. And finally, the paper will assess if and how the experience of RSD in Brazil can assist in the development of a better-structured RSD system in the world.

RSD in Brazil before the 1997 National Refugee Act

The 1997 National Refugee Act was a turning point in the history of refugee law and protection in Brazil. It established a national law that not only translates the main universal protection clauses to the Brazilian legal system but also enlarges the traditional protection by establishing the possibility of recognizing a person as a refugee due to gross violations of human rights, following the regional formula created in 1984 by the Cartagena Declaration,[6] which concluded:

> *3. To reiterate that, in view of the experience gained from the massive flows of refugees in the Central American area, it is necessary to consider enlarging the concept of a*

1990, both issued by the Executive.

[4] Law 9.474, 22 July 1997, defines mechanisms to implement the Refugee Convention of 1951 and establishes other provisions.

[5] José Henrique Fischel de Andrade and Adriana Marcolini, "A Política Brasileira de Proteção e de Reassentamento de Refugiados—breves comentários sobre suas principais características" [The Brazilian policy of refugee protection and resettlement—Brief comentaries on their main characteristics] (2002) 45 *Revista Brasileira de Política Internacional* [Brazilian Journal of International Politics] 168.

[6] Cartagena Declaration on Refugees, 22 November 1984, Annual Report of the Inter-American Commission on Human Rights, OAS Doc. OEA/Ser.L/V/II.66/doc.10, rev. 1, at 190–93 (1984–85).

refugee, bearing in mind, as far as appropriate and in the light of the situation prevailing in the region, the precedent of the OAU Convention (article 1, paragraph 2) and the doctrine employed in the reports of the Inter-American Commission on Human Rights. Hence the definition or concept of a refugee to be recommended for use in the region is one which, in addition to containing the elements of the 1951 Convention and the 1967 Protocol, includes among refugees persons who have fled their country because their lives, safety or freedom have been threatened by generalized violence, foreign aggression, internal conflicts, massive violation of human rights or other circumstances which have seriously disturbed public order.

Furthermore, it established an administrative RSD procedure in Brazil and a body—the National Committee for Refugees (in Portuguese, Comitê Nacional para Refugiados, or CONARE)—vested with the responsibility of analyzing each individual case. Both of these features were newly introduced by the National Refugee Act. Prior to 1997 RSD in Brazil was regulated by an interministerial rule, Inter-Ministry Rule 394 (and not by a specific bill), and was conducted mainly by UNHCR. This mechanism was designed in the context of the changing regimen in Brazil. During this period, the state looked for ways to strengthen the application of treaties directed towards the protection of human beings, since this was a factor in acquiring legitimacy within international society. In particular, Brazil suspended some of the reservations it had made to the Refugee Convention and stopped adopting the geographical limitation allowed for in this document.[7] Recalling the dictatorship regime that existed prior to the mid-1980s in Brazil is key to understanding how RSD in Brazil was built and designed. During this period, despite repression by the military authorities, some NGOs (specifically those linked to the Catholic Church in Rio de Janeiro and São Paulo), with the support of UNHCR, assisted nationals from Argentina, Chile, Uruguay, and Paraguay to get protection in a third country. This action was developed with no support from the state. In fact, the people involved in these assistance actions were risking their lives and liberty, given that some of the people being protected were under military investigation due to their political opinions. This resulted in a very strong bond between Brazilian civil society and UNHCR and in the development of an expertise in refugee protection encompassing both the international community and the internal civil society.

After promulgation in 1988 of the Federal Constitution, which established a regime based on the rule of law, human rights, and democracy, refugee protection started its transformation into a tripartite structure. In the early 1990s, the development of RSD in Brazil faced the challenge of receiving a large number of asylum seekers from Angola, who left their country due to armed conflict. Most of them were recognized as refugees by the procedure created by the above-mentioned interministerial rule. This interministerial rule established that UNHCR

---

[7] As stated by Guy S. Goodwin-Gill and Jane McAdam while explaining the definition of a refugee: "Originally, the definition, […] limited the application of the Convention to the refugee who acquired such status 'as a result of event occurring before 1 January 1951'. An optional geographic limitation also permitted states, on ratification, to limit their obligations to refugees resulting from 'events occurring in Europe' prior to the critical date"; Guy S. Goodwin- Gill and Jane McAdam, The Refugee in International Law, 3rd ed. (Oxford: Oxford University Press, 2007), 36.

was to conduct the analysis of individual cases and recommend them (or not) to the Brazilian government for its final approval:

> *In general the procedure for determining refugee status was as follows:* UNHCR *interviewed the person seeking refugee status and elaborated a legal opinion recommending, or not, the granting of that status. This legal opinion was then sent to the Ministry of Foreign Affairs, which presented its view on the matter and sent it to the Ministry of Justice, which made the final decision. The decision was then published in the official gazette of the Brazilian government (Diário Oficial da União).*[8]

Following this notification, the Federal Police issued an identification document to the refugee. It is interesting to note that during this period the Brazilian government always followed the legal opinion that was proposed by UNHCR. Furthermore, NGOs linked to the Catholic Church, especially Caritas Arquidiocesana do Rio de Janeiro and Caritas Arquidiocesana de São Paulo, continued to be the historical partners of UNHCR, being responsible for the actual assistance to and orientation of asylum seekers and refugees.

RSD in Brazil after the 1997 National Refugee Act

With the approval of the National Refugee Act, there was a substantial change in RSD in Brazil: the transfer of RSD responsibility to the Brazilian government with UNHCR maintaining a supervisory role. Caritas Arquidiocesana do Rio de Janeiro and Caritas Arquidiocesana de São Paulo continued to be part of the new structure, keeping the role of providing reception, assistance, and orientation to asylum seekers and refugees. With the beginning of the resettlement program in Brazil, there was an increase in the number of NGOs working with refugees in Brazil.[9] The National Refugee Act is the zenith of a process of improving refugee law and protection in Brazil, which had as other landmarks the recognition of UNHCR as an international body in 1982; the approval of the Federal Constitution in 1988; and the lifting of the geographic and temporal restrictions in 1989. It also translates into an increased concern with human rights in the country after the dictatorship, which led to Brazil being more willing to commit to and respect international obligations regarding human rights.

As mentioned, the National Refugee Act defines who is recognized as a refugee in Brazil[10] and the RSD procedure to be applied. It also establishes the rights and

---

[8] Liliana Lyra Jubilut, "Refugee Law and Protection in Brazil: A Model in South America?" (2006) 19 *Journal of Refugee Studies* at 26.

[9] Brazil received mainly refugees from: Afghanistan who were living in refugee camps in Iran and India; from Colombia, who were under the protection of Ecuador and Costa Rica; and from Palestine, who were living in refugee camps in Jordan. The resettlement initiative has also extended the protection net of civil society in Brazil. Nowadays there are three NGOs that are UNHCR resettlement partners in Brazil: *Associação Antonio Vieira* (in Porto Alegre, Rio Grande do Sul), *Caritas Brasileira Regional São Paulo* (in the state of São Paulo), and *Centro de Direitos Humanos e Memória Popular* (in Natal, Rio Grande do Norte). UNHCR has a sixth partner in Brazil, which is *Instituto de Migrações e Direitos Humanos* (in Brasília, Distrito Federal).

[10] "Art. 1—An individual shall be recognized as a refugee if: I—due to well founded fears of persecution for reasons of race, religion, nationality, social group or political opinions, he or she is out of his or her country of nationality and cannot or does not wish to rely on the protection of such country; II—having no nationality and being out of the country where he or she had previously retained permanent residence, cannot or does not wish to return to such country based on circumstances mentioned in item I above; III—due to severe and generalized violation of human rights, he or she is compelled to leave his or her country of

duties of a refugee and the special regimen that applies to people awaiting the decision on RSD—i.e., the asylum seekers (these rights include the impossibility of forced return, deportation, expulsion, or extradition, and the suspension of all administrative and criminal procedures due to irregular entries). In its fourth title, the National Refugee Act establishes the procedure for RSD in Brazil, stating that:

> *Art. 17—A foreigner shall appear before a competent authority and state his or her desire to request recognition of the condition of refugee.*
>
> *Art. 18—The competent authority shall notify the requester to give information and such notification shall set the date for commencement of procedures.*
>
> *Paragraph One—The competent authority shall inform the United Nations High Commissioner for Refugees- UNHCR- on the existence of a proceeding for request for refuge and shall enable UNHCR to offer suggestions to facilitate the development of the proceeding.*
>
> *Art. 19—In addition to the information, given if necessary with the assistance of an interpreter, a foreigner shall complete a request for recognition as a refugee, including a complete identification, professional qualification, schooling of the requester and members of his or her family group, as well as report on the circumstances and facts that form the basis of the request for refuge, indicating the appropriate evidences*
>
> *Art. 20—The record of the information and supervision of the request form completion shall be effected by qualified officials and in condition to guarantee information confidentiality.[11]*

In light of the above provisions, one can see that the National Refugee Act only establishes the guidelines of RSD in Brazil, reserving an important role to UNHCR. One of the few impositions of the National Refugee Act regarding RSD is that the decisions on RSD requests are to be made by CONARE, which is a collective deliberative body, as will be further explained below.

Building upon these guidelines, the Brazilian government, UNHCR, and Brazilian civil society have developed a tripartite enterprise regarding RSD*** which reflects the idea that, for the protection of refugees to be integral, it has to involve the international community, the state, and civil society. RSD procedure in Brazil begins, as stated above, with the asylum seeker's request for refuge to the competent authority. This authority is the Federal Police, which will formalize the request into a Declaration Term (*Termo de Declaração*). This document contains the civil qualification of the asylum seeker (name, nationality, name of parents, birthdate) as well as the main reasons for which the asylum seeker left his or her country of origin and is asking for refugee status in Brazil. The date of the

---

nationality to seek in a different country."

[11] The text of the National Refugee Act in English is cited based on the information available on the UNHRC Refworld web site, online: <http://www.unhcr.org/cgibin/

texis/vtx/refworld/rwmain?page=country&docid=3f4 dfb 134&skip= &category =LEGAL&coi=BRA&rid=4562d94e2>.

*** The current procedure for RSD in Brazil is spelled out on CONARE Normative Resolution 18, of 2014, and differs in minor ways from the one described in this text. This normative also formalizes a broader inclusion of civil society in RSD procedures.

Declaration Term is deemed to be the date of the beginning of the procedures.

In order to systematize the procedures, CONARE has established a standard Declaration Term to be followed by the Federal Police throughout the country.[12] Each adult asylum seeker should have an individual statement taken and written down in a Declaration Term. Children are encompassed in their parent's document. After having this document issued, the asylum seeker is instructed that he or she has to continue with the proceedings in order to be recognized as a refugee in Brazil. If the asylum seeker remains six months or more without responding to the requests of the proceeding or abandons it, the procedure is archived without having its merits analyzed.[13]

The step following the issuance of the Declaration Term is the completion of a more thorough standard questionnaire.[14] This step normally takes place at the refugee centres directed by civil society organizations. Nowadays there are two refugee centres in Brazil, directed by Caritas Arquidiocesana do Rio de Janeiro and Caritas Arquidiocesana de São Paulo. If the asylum seeker is located in a place where there is no refugee centre, the questionnaire is to be filled in at the Federal Police Department.[15]

After the questionnaire is filled in, it is sent to CONARE and the asylum seeker is granted authorization to have a provisory identification issued. This document is the Provisional Protocol (*Protocolo Provisório*).[16]

The asylum seeker, then, has to go through two interviews. The first interview is conducted by a lawyer from civil society. In the past, this lawyer was appointed by the Brazilian Bar Association and worked in a partnership between UNHCR

---

[12] CONARE Normative Resolution 1, 27 October 1998, establishes the standard Declaration Term to be completed by the Federal Police Department on the occasion of the request for refugee status. Furthermore, it states that this document shall be sent to the General Coordination of CONARE, with a copy to the Caritas Arquidiocesana, aiming the fulfillment of the questionnaire in order to make possible the analysis of the refugee solicitation.

[13] CONARE Normative Resolution 11, 29 April 2005, provides for the publication of the notification established by article 29 of Law 9.474, 22 July 1997 (deadline for certain procedures and for attending to official notifications). This resolution revoked CONARE Normative Resolution 7, 6 August 2002. If CONARE has already issued a negative decision and the asylum seeker can not be found in order to receive the notification, the decision shall be published by the official press for the purpose of establishing the deadline for appeal.

[14] CONARE Normative Resolution 2, 27 October 1998, establishes the standard questionnaire for refugee status request, which shall be completed by the asylum seeker at the headquarter of the Caritas Arquidiocesana and sent to the General Coordination of CONARE in order to continue with the procedures. In a location where there is no Caritas representation, the completion of the questionnaire shall be arranged by the Federal Police Department and the questionnaire sent to CONARE along with the Term of Declaration. Although there is no provision for the language in which the questionnaire is to be available, it is available in Portuguese, English, French, and Spanish. An asylum seeker who does not speak any of these languages can be aided by a translator, who is not part of the regular staff of the institutions enrolled in the process.

[15] CONARE Normative Resolution 9, 6 August 2002, establishes the place for completion of the questionnaire for requesting refugee status in the localities in which there is no representation of Caritas Arquidiocesana.

[16] CONARE Normative Resolution 6, 26 May 1999, provides for the concession of a protocol to asylum seeker. Once the asylum seeker has the Provisional Protocol, he or she is entitled to have a labour license and a document relevant for financial purposes called the Register of Natural Persons (*Cadastro de Pessoas Físicas*, or CPF); so that he or she can begin to integrate into Brazilian society more fully.

and the two mentioned refugee centres. Nowadays, the refugee centres hire the lawyers themselves and UNHCR assists their work by funding their salaries and providing technical support.

The interview is conducted individually and whenever possible in the language of the asylum seeker. When an interpreter is required, the interpreter is instructed about the confidentiality of the proceedings. The second interview is conducted by a representative of CONARE and follows the same rules as the first interview. As mentioned above, CONARE is a collective deliberative body. It has both governmental and non- governmental members and the UNHCR has "voice-no-vote" status.

The government representatives come from the Ministry of Justice, the Ministry of Foreign Affairs, the Ministry of Health, the Ministry of Labour and Employment, the Ministry of Education and Sports, and the Federal Police. The representative of the civil society comes from an NGO that is involved in the assistance and protection of refugees. Nowadays this seat is occupied by Caritas Arquidiocesana de São Paulo, with Caritas Arquidiocesana do Rio de Janeiro being the alternate.

CONARE is presided over by the Ministry of Justice and has a general coordinator that assists its work by organizing the RSD cases to be decided in a plenary meeting with all its members. The general coordinator operates under the umbrella of the Ministry of Justice and is also in charge of the administrative issues regarding refugees, such as the expedition of status declarations, travel authorizations, and authorizations for the issuance of identification documents. After the two interviews have taken place, there is a meeting by a Preliminary Analysis Group (*Grupo de Estudos Prévios*) to assess the merits of the case. This step grew out of practice, with the perception that it would be impossible for CONARE to have in-depth analysis of each case in its bimonthly plenary meetings. In order to have each case considered thoroughly, the Preliminary Analysis Group was established. It convenes before CONARE's plenary meeting and does a preliminary analysis of the case, taking into consideration the findings of the civil society's and government's interviews.

The Preliminary Analysis Group consists of CONARE's general coordinator, a representative of the Ministry of Foreign Affairs, a representative of the Federal Police, a representative of UNHCR, and a representative of the civil society organization who has a seat in the CONARE. With the pre-analysis executed, the cases go to the CONARE's plenary to be decided. In the plenary each member is entitled to one vote, and decisions are made by majority. If the decision is positive, the asylum seeker is recognized as a refugee in Brazil. If the decision is negative, there is the possibility of an appeal.[17] This appeal is also an administrative procedure, which has to take place within fifteen days after the asylum seeker is

---

[17] CONARE Normative Resolution 8, 6 August 2002, provides for notification of the request of the refugee status. If the asylum seeker can not be found after six months from the date of the CONARE decision to receive the notification, the negative decision of the refugee status request shall be published in the official press.

notified of it, in order to be timely.

The appeal is analyzed by the Minister of Justice, who gives the final decision on RSD in Brazil. If he changes CONARE's decision, the person is recognized as a refugee; if he does not, the person is subject to the general foreigner's regimen[18] and is not a refugee in Brazil.

After being recognized as a refugee by CONARE or the Minister of Justice, the refugee has to present herself or himself to the Federal Police Department in order to be registered as a refugee. Before registration, the refugee has to sign a Term of Responsibility (*Termo de Responsabilidade*), a standard form which was established by CONARE's Normative Resolution 3.[19] According to this term, the refugee agrees to observe the rules, laws, and provisions aimed at the maintenance of public order and the respect of the rights and duties established by Brazilian law, and attests his or her awareness of being subject to Brazilian civil and criminal law. The refugee also assumes the responsibility of collaborating with Brazilian authorities and humanitarian agencies that assist refugees in Brazil.

The refugee states that he or she is aware of the conditions that may result in the loss of refugee status: (i) proof of falsity during the RSD process; (ii) omission of facts that, if known, should result in a negative decision; (iii) acts against the national security or public order; (iv) leaving Brazilian territory without previous authorization from the Brazilian government.

In regard to the need for authorization to leave Brazilian territory, CONARE's Normative Resolutions[20] establish the conditions for obtaining an authorization to travel abroad. The refugee shall submit a solicitation to CONARE stating the duration, destination, and reasons of the trip. If necessary, the refugee can ask for a Brazilian passport issued to foreigners, according to provisions of the Foreigners Statute (Law 6.815, 19 August 1980). ****

The principle of family unity does not operate only when all family members become refugees at the same time. Rather, in Brazil, it can be equally applied to cases where a family unit has been temporarily disrupted through the flight of one or more of its members. CONARE's Normative Resolution 4[21] provides for the extension of refugee status through the application of the family unity principle and establishes a standard form of Term of Family Unit Request. According to this

---

[18] The Statute of Foreigner (Law 6.815, 19 August 1980, establishes the legal situation of foreigner in Brazil, and creates the National Council of Immigration). Decree 86.815, 10 December 1981, rules the Law 6.815/80, which establishes the legal situation of foreigner in Brazil and creates the National Council of Immigration and stipulates other provisions.

[19] CONARE Normative Resolution 3, 27 October 1998, establishes the standard form Term of Responsibility which has to be signed by the refugee before his or her register into the Federal Police Department. The competent authority shall provide an interpreter if necessary so the refugee has knowledge of the content of the Term.

[20] CONARE Normative Resolution 5, 11 March 1999, provides for authorization to travel to abroad. CONARE Normative Resolution 12, 29 April 2005, provides for authorization for a refugee to travel abroad; for issuing of a Brazilian passport to a refugee foreigner, when necessary; and for processing of the loss of refugee status because of leaving Brazilian territory without authorization.

**** In 2017 Brazil adopted Law 13.445, the new law on migration in the country.

[21] CONARE Normative Resolution 4, 11 March 1999, establishes the extension of refugee status through the application of the family unit principle.

resolution, refugee status can be extended to family members (spouse, "ascendant" and "descendant," as well as other elements of the family group who depend economically on the refugee[22]), once they are located in the national territory.

Finally, in the spirit of the establishment of durable solutions for refugees living in Brazil, CONARE's Normative Resolution 10[23] ruled on the situation of the refugee who achieves permanent status. In general, the resolution states that even with permanent status, refugee status is continued. As can be noted by the above description, some of these procedures have been formalized by resolutions of CONARE, but some relevant aspects derive only from practice, as, for instance, the participation of civil society.[*****] This has both positive and negative aspects, as, on the one hand, it enables constant improvement, and on the other hand, it may lead to suppression without prior notice of developments that may be seen as guarantees to the refugees. It is important to note, however, that since redemocratization, the trend of refugee law and protection in Brazil has been to evolve, which may minimize this last concern.

Analyzing RSD in Brazil

Having reviewed RSD procedure in Brazil in the previous section, this section will proceed to analyze it in order to extract lessons, either for its improvement or for the improvement of RSD in general. This analysis is threefold. First it is important to consider RSD in Brazil from an internal standpoint, considering the National Refugee Act, the practice of RSD, and the context in which it occurs. Secondly, the analysis should be made in comparison to the international standards of RSD, i.e. to international refugee law. And finally, bearing in mind that international refugee law is part of a wider system of the protection of the human person (alongside international human rights and international humanitarian law), the analysis of RSD in Brazil should take into consideration whether or not it is in keeping with the most protective standards.

RSD in Brazil in light of the internal context

First of all the adoption of the National Refugee Act in 1997 must be considered in the context of the redemocratization of Brazil and promulgation of the Federal Constitution in 1988, which considered the primacy of human rights and the concession of political asylum to be guiding principles for Brazil in its international relations (article 4, II and X). This is a key issue because the geographic limitation was suspended just after the Federal Constitution's promulgation, starting the

---

[22] For the purpose of the resolution, "dependents" must be understood as: the spouse; the single son/daughter, under twenty-one years old, including those adopted, or older than twenty-one years old when they can not provide for themselves; ascendant; and sisters/brothers, grandsons/ granddaughters, great-grandson/great-granddaughter, nephew/niece, only if they are orphans, single, and under twenty-one years old, or of any age when they can not provide for themselves. The situation of economic dependency of a person older than twenty-one years who cannot provide for her/himself has to be related to physical and mental health and must be declared by a doctor. The minor children whose parents are detained or have disappeared must be considered in the same situation as orphans.

[23] CONARE Normative Resolution 10, 22 September 2003, provides for the situation of the refugee who achieves permanent status.

[*****] As mentioned, CONARE Normative Resolution 18 formalizes a broader participation of the civil society (specifically on the Preliminary Study Group).

process of developing an internal RSD process in Brazil, which was consolidated in 1997.

Brazil's National Refugee Act is modern and consistent with international standards on refugee protection, being considered as a model to South American countries since the time of its adoption.[24] It is interesting to observe that some countries, inspired by the Brazilian legislation, issued their own internal rules on refugees, providing for specific situations such as the recognition of refugee status based on reasons of gender, as in the case of Argentina. In Brazil, this aspect has been considered in the broad concept of membership in a particular social group. Asylum seekers can apply to receive refugee protection all over the country with no cost to them at all.[25] The decentralization and cost-free nature of the procedure are points to be commended in RSD in Brazil.

The RSD procedure is normally fast: an asylum seeker's request for refugee status usually takes six months to be analyzed by CONARE.[******] In the meantime, asylum seekers receive permission to work, although their language, background experience, and social discrimination are obstacles that they may face in trying to find jobs. It is important to highlight that RSD procedures in Brazil were developed for examination of claims on an individual basis. This has been satisfactory given that the number of asylum seekers in Brazil is not relatively large,[26] but the situation could be different in the case of a mass influx of refugees. It would be desirable to create prevention mechanisms in order to avoid a humanitarian crisis in such a situation. However, in RSD in Brazil, there is no procedure for determining eligibility for refugee status on a group basis, rather than through individual screening, when there might be a mass influx or when prevailing conditions might have substantially the same effect upon a large population.

Brazil faced a challenging situation during 2006, when an impressive number (by Brazilian standards) of asylum seekers from Lebanon asked Brazil for protection as refugees.[27] On that occasion, CONARE decided not to consider the sur place refugee condition of some individuals who were in Brazilian territory when the conflict started, giving a misguided interpretation to that situation. Besides that, because of many fraudulent requests, CONARE decided to apply a "fast-track" procedure for requests by people from Lebanon. This solution, however, did not consider international standards, especially the ExCom Conclusion 30 (XXXIV) of 1983 on the problem of manifestly unfounded or

---

[24] Supra note 8.

[25] Only when recognized they will have to pay the required amount in order to have a refugee identification document issued. Currently a judicial provisional measure suspends this payment if the foreigner states her or his economic condition.

[******] This has changed considerably in recent years, with cases pending sometimes for over 4 years. Brazil has 85.000 pending requests for refugee status as of March 2018.

[26] According to CONARE, during 2007 Brazil received fewer than 500 requests for refugee status, and as of June 2008, Brazil hosted 3,513 refugees.

[27] For details, see the position of Caritas Arquidiocesana de São Paulo on asylum seekers from Lebanon: Caritas Arquidiocesana de São Paulo, *Documento entregue na Reunião do CONARE de 23.03.2007* [Legal position presented at CONARE'S meeting of March 23, 2007], Posição da Caritas Arquidiocesana de São Paulo sobre Solicitantes de Refúgio Libaneses [Caritas Arquidiocesana de São Paulo position on asylum seekers from Lebanon].

abusive applications for refugee status or asylum, which states:

> *(e) Recognized the substantive character of a decision that an application for refugee status is manifestly unfounded or abusive, the grave consequences of an erroneous determination for the applicant and the resulting need for such a decision to be accompanied by appropriate procedural guarantees and therefore recommended that:*
>
> *(i) as in the case of all requests for the determination of refugee status or the grant of asylum, the applicant should be given a complete personal interview by a fully qualified official and, whenever possible, by an official of the authority competent to determine refugee status.*

In the case described above, one can see that the fast-track or emergency approach developed by CONARE took into consideration only the interest of the Brazilian government. However, at the other end of the spectrum, one sees that CONARE has used an emergency approach in other circumstances, mainly in order to give a fast response in resettlement cases needing immediate protection.

The fast-track procedure, however, is not ruled by law in any of the cases. This can be regarded as a problem as there is no legal guarantee of the continuity of the procedure in the resettlement cases in the case of a change of government and of public policies in the future. Besides, the fast-track procedure can mean a different treatment for the asylum seeker who arrives in Brazil and asks for refugee status and for the resettled refugee, as the fast track is applied positively almost exclusively to the latter. The fact that RSD procedure is based mainly on an administrative structure has positive and negative aspects. The expertise of CONARE could have more results if, in fact, the members of CONARE were experts in refugee protection, with advanced knowledge of international and comparative rules. It is true that there has been an effort at capacity building; however, it continues to be limited since there is no attention to the broad system of international law. To determine refugee status, one must consider the inclusion and exclusion clauses, which requires knowledge of other areas of international law, such as international humanitarian law, international criminal law, and international human rights law. Keeping this limitation in mind, the possibility of judicial review of the RSD decisions is important. In the Brazilian system, there is no legal rule about appeal to the Judiciary in causes related to formal aspects of RSD or to the final decision of the administrative procedure (CONARE and the Minister of Justice). It must be observed that CONARE's decision— either negative or positive—is limited to stating the recognition or the non-recognition of the condition of "refugee."

There is no satisfactory motivation of the decisions. This fact per se denies a basic principle of public administration, and affects the asylum seeker's defense in the case of an appeal, as he or she does not know with certainty the reasons why his or her refugee status request was denied, as the main motivation in the refusal is that the case did not meet "refugee criteria." In this matter it is important to note that, in the few cases that were brought to the Judiciary, this organ said that the statement that the case did not meet "refugee criteria" was enough motivation.[28]

---

[28] For instance the decision of the Superior Court of Justice (Superior Tribunal de Justiça) in: Agravo Regimental no Agravo Regimental do Mandado de Segurança 12.212/DF, cited in Liliana L. Jubilut, O

Although the Federal Constitution guarantees access to the Judiciary[29] in the case of violation or threat to a right, as this is not manifestly stated in the National Refugee Act, few cases are proposed for the consideration of the Judiciary. The result is a precarious judicial jurisprudence on refugee issues in Brazil and unsatisfactory knowledge of the international standards by the members of the Judiciary. In most of the cases in which the Judiciary was called to rule on RSD related issues, it referred to CONARE's decision, justifying this action by highlighting the technical expertise of this body, without proceeding to a new analysis of the merits of the case.[30] Initiatives of training and developing capacity as well as diffusion of international refugee law should be acknowledged, as, for instance, the first course on international refugee law, established in 2007 for university teachers and public attorneys in Rio de Janeiro.[31] Recognition of participation by civil society as a full member of the CONARE was innovative:

> *Another distinguishing characteristic of CONARE compared to similar organs in the region is that civil society, represented by an NGO that works with refugees, is not only present but is also entitled to vote. In other countries, these three trends (a representative of a non-governmental organization which works with refugees and is entitled to vote) are not present simultaneously. For example, in Argentina and Uruguay civil society is not represented; in Paraguay the representative of the NGO cannot vote and in Bolivia civil society is represented by the church and by Universidad Mayor de San Andres but there is no mention of the fact that these organs work or have to work with refugees.*[32]

Nonetheless it was a reflection of the state of rules based on human rights established by the Federal Constitution of 1988 and the history of refugee protection in Brazil. In fact, if one adopts a more cynical point of view, one could say that the government did not want to assume the entire responsibility for refugees, leaving the practical concern related to the actual reception and integration to the historical experts on the issue—UNHCR and civil society.

Despite the causes that influenced the tripartite design of RSD in Brazil, it presents positive aspects that can not (and should not) be denied. The participation of civil society balanced the state's concern about national security with the insertion of human concerns into decision making. However, as commented, the participation of civil society has a limited role given that (i) its functioning is not part of the positive law, (ii) an interview of the asylum seeker by CONARE is

---

Direito Internacional dos Refugiados e sua aplicação no ordenamento jurídico brasileiro [International refugee law and its application in the Brazilian legal order], supra note 1 at 103. (Agravo Regimental is a special appeal according to specific court regulations only available for Superior Courts. Mandado de Segurança is the writ of security or the writ of mandamus.)

[29] Federal Constitution 1988, article 5, XXXV: "the law shall not exclude from review by the Judiciary any violation of or threat to a right."

[30] For instance the decisions of the Superior Court of Justice in: Agravo Regimental do Mandado de Segurança 12212/ DF; Habeas corpus 36033/DF; and Habeas corpus 32622/DF, cited by Liliana L. Jubilut, *O Direito Internacional dos Refugiados e sua aplicação no ordenamento jurídico brasileiro*, [International refugee law and its application in the Brazilian legal order], supra note 1 at 103.

[31] Liliana Lyra Jubilut and Silvia Menicucci de O. S. Apolinário (organizers). I Course on International Refugee Law, held in December 2007 at the Centre of Human Rights, Department of Law, PUC-Rio.

[32] Supra note 7 at 33.

required, and (iii) in CONARE's plenary meeting it has only one vote.

In addition, the organizations of civil society that are engaged in refugee protection have no institutional common basis to unite them. When they speak up, they mainly do so separately. So, the current initiative to create a national council on refugees (the Brazilian Refugee Council) that unites the legitimized organizations that work with refugee issues assumes a huge relevance. Once established, the Brazilian Refugee Council will have the ability to enhance the position of civil society in CONARE and in the Brazilian government as a whole, and to aid in demanding that the rights of refugees and asylum seekers be fulfilled, that this population's interests be represented in general public policies, and that specific public policies be created respecting the plurality of human beings and the rights of foreign people in conformity with article 5 of the Brazilian Federal Constitution of 1988. The lack of legal provision on the cooperation of government and civil society ends up generating double efforts and a logistic cost to the asylum seekers related to completion of all the required forms. This cost does not seem to represent a problem to someone with a regular economic condition; however, to an asylum seeker struggling to integrate, it can be insurmountable, notwithstanding the fact that RSD should be free of all costs (direct and indirect).

To sum up, the positive aspects of RSD in Brazil, from the internal point of view, are: participation of civil society (the most important and singular aspect of RSD in Brazil); decentralization; freedom from cost; and democratization of the political dialogue and future endeavours. The negative aspects are: non-legal provision of the exercise of the participation of civil society and the limited role reserved to it; inequality of RSD depending on the place of solicitation (presence or lack of civil society assistance); logistic cost; double efforts; confusion of responsible actors in the perspective of the asylum seeker who does not know the system and therefore has difficulty in grasping the tripartite enterprise; non-legal provision of mass influx procedure or of an emergency approach; non-legal provision of financial assistance; and co-optation of civil society and individual role played by the civil society actors.

Consistency of RSD in Brazil with International Refugee Law

Because Brazil is a state-member of the Refugee Convention and its 1967 Protocol, the analysis of the conformity of RSD with international standards will be based on Part Two of the Handbook on Procedures and Criteria for Determining Refugee Status under the 1951 Convention and the 1967 Protocol relating to the Status of Refugees, directed to the procedures for the determination of refugee status.[33] In view of the situation of different procedures established by

---

[33] HCR/IP/4/Eng/REV.1 Reedited, Geneva, January 1992, UNHCR 1979. The UNHCR also developed a handbook on procedural standards for refugee status determination under UNHCR's mandate, in which it considers general issues, reception and registration in RSD operations, adjudication of refugee claims, processing claims based on the right to family unity, notification of RSD decisions, appeal of negative RSD decisions, UNHCR refugee certificate, procedures for file closure / re-opening, procedures for cancellation of refugee status, and procedures for cessation of refugee status. See "Procedural Standards for Refugee Status Determination under UNHCR's Mandate," <http:// www.unhcr.org/publ/ PUBL/ 4316f0c02.html>.

states and of the unlikelihood that all states bound by the Refugee Convention and the 1967 Protocol would establish identical procedures, ExCom, at its twenty-eighth session in October 1977, recommended that procedures should satisfy certain basic requirements. These basic requirements, which reflect the special vulnerability of the asylum seeker and which would ensure that the applicant is provided with certain essential guarantees, are the following:

a. The competent official (e.g., immigration officer or border police officer) to whom the applicant addresses himself or herself at the border or in the territory of a Contracting State should have clear instructions for dealing with cases which might come within the purview of the relevant international instruments. The official should be required to act in accordance with the principle of non-refoulement and to refer such cases to a higher authority;

b. The applicant should receive the necessary guidance as to the procedure to be followed.

c. There should be a clearly identified authority, wherever possible a single central authority, with responsibility for examining requests for refugee status and taking a decision in the first instance.

d. The applicant should be given the necessary facilities, including the services of a competent interpreter, for submitting his or her case to the authorities concerned. Applicants should also be given the opportunity, of which they should be duly informed, to contact a representative of UNHCR.

e. If the applicant is recognized as a refugee, he or she should be informed accordingly and issued with documentation certifying his or her refugee status;

f. If the applicant is not recognized, he or she should be given a reasonable time to appeal for a formal reconsideration of the decision, either to the same or to a different authority, whether administrative or judicial, according to the prevailing system.

g. The applicant should be permitted to remain in the country pending a decision on his or her initial request by the competent authority referred to above, unless it has been established by that authority that his or her request is clearly abusive. He or she should also be permitted to remain in the country while an appeal to a higher administrative authority or to the courts is pending.

As considered before, Brazil has developed a procedure specifically on RSD that conforms to the standards listed above. However, some observations must be made. Concerning the qualification of the personnel engaged in these procedures there is still a long way to go in order to achieve the ideal level of necessary knowledge and understanding of an applicant's particular difficulties and needs.

The National Refugee Act and CONARE's resolutions do not require expert professionals to deal with refugee issues. There are no interpreters who have been through special training. In most cases, a refugee who already has a satisfactory knowledge of Portuguese assists with translation during the interview phase of the RSD procedure when there is difficulty related to language understanding. Furthermore, there is a difference of reception procedure if one considers the presence of refugee centres in the locality in which the applicant requests refugee status. Usually the asylum seeker will find facilities (Portuguese course, medical treatment, and others) and assistance in Caritas Arquidiocesana do Rio de Janeiro and Caritas Arquidiocesana de São Paulo, which leads to the conclusion that the asylum seeker who is located in a city in which there is no Caritas representation will be in a more vulnerable situation than applicants who can rely on Caritas,[********] including guidance through all the steps of the RSD procedure and the possibility of being interviewed by a lawyer provided by this organization.

Despite the existence of flaws, one can see an effort on the part of UNHCR and of CONARE to develop capacity regarding refugee issues in the Federal Police Department, which, as mentioned, has an important role in RSD in Brazil. An example of this effort was the creation of seminars for Federal Police members on procedures and criteria on RSD held in eight different cities (São Paulo, Santos, Guarulhos, Curitiba, Foz do Iguaçu, Paranaguá, Manaus and Tabatinga) during 2007.[34] There are plans to turn this initiative into a continuous effort, always focusing on cities that are ports of entry to Brazil or that have a considerable number of refugees. The ExCom also expressed the hope that all States Parties to the Refugee Convention and its 1967 Protocol would give favourable consideration to UNHCR participation in such procedures in appropriate form.[35] As mentioned before, UNHCR has an important role in the Brazilian RSD procedure; nonetheless it does not have the right to vote during the CONARE plenary sessions.

RSD in Brazil and the most protective rules

The National Refugee Act is in general a modern legal instrument. However, as expected of a consensus achieved in a post-dictatorship period and with a foreign status law from 1985 (before redemocratization), it is made up of general provisions. When the "law operator" has to apply the rule to the concrete case, there are many difficulties due to the lack of provisions for special cases or to reluctance to apply human rights rules to cases of asylum seekers and refugees, when they are children, elderly, sick, victims of torture, etc.

In light of this, if one considers the most protective rules, RSD in Brazil has a long way to go, in order to be satisfactory. The following comments illustrate some aspects of this. First, respect for due process is far from ideal: (i) experience shows that it is extremely difficult to change a decision of CONARE, (ii) there is no procedure of obligatory revision of the CONARE decisions, and (iii) the guarantee of the contradictory is also minimized. On the other hand, CONARE has in the past permitted lawyers to attend its plenary meetings, but this is not the regular situation. There is a common understanding in this body that RSD is not an adversarial procedure and, in consequence, there is no need of a lawyer. This

---

[********] RSD procedures have since become more decentralized in Brazil. However, it remains true that asylum seekers who can count on UNHCR partners and/or NGOs are better assisted throughout the procedure.

[34] In the cities of São Paulo, Santos, and Guarulhos the seminar was offered with the support and participation of Caritas Arquidiocesana de São Paulo.

[35] Such participation is based on article 35 of the Refugee Convention and the corresponding article 11 of the 1967 Protocol, which provide for co-operation by the Contracting States with the High Commissioner's Office.

situation contributes to the non-technical character of the CONARE decisions and also to a lack of motivation of the decision, which as seen has not so far being regarded by the Judiciary as a reason for ruling against CONARE's decision.[36]

Secondly, regarding complementary protection[*********], one can see that RSD in Brazil is broader than the universal rules, as the National Refugee Act provides for the recognition of refugee status based on gross violations of human rights. This provision enables RSD to focus not on individual fear of persecution but rather on the situation in the country of origin, and, therefore, enables people coming from a situation of gross and generalized violation of human rights (as for instance from a situation of internal conflict) to be recognized as refugees.

Furthermore, although Brazil does not have a mechanism of temporary protection, CONARE's Normative Resolution 13 of 23 March 2007 provides for the reference of special situations by CONARE to the National Council on Immigration. According to this resolution, the requests for refugee status that can not fulfill the requirements of eligibility under Law 9.474/1997 shall be analyzed by the National Council on Immigration in order to grant a permanent status based on humanitarian conditions.[*********]

In this sense one can see that complementary protection is advancing in Brazil, and may make up, in some cases, for the feeble due process guarantees that are in place. Concerning the protection of vulnerable groups, there are some cases that give rise to special problems in establishing the facts during the RSD procedure, and because of this, have to count on special legal provisions in order to prevent discrimination and different treatment of similar situations. These are mentally disturbed persons and unaccompanied minors.

In determining refugee status the subjective element of fear and the objective element of it being well-founded need to be established. Mental or emotional disturbances impede a normal examination of the case. A mentally disturbed person may, however, be a refugee, and while that person's claim therefore cannot be disregarded, it should call for different techniques of examination, especially a formal statement of medical advice. Untrue statements by themselves are not a reason for refusal of refugee status and it is the examiner's responsibility to evaluate such statements in the light of all the circumstances of the case. If there is an attested case of legal incapacity (according to the Brazilian Civil Code), a legal representative should be nominated for this person. This has not been the case of RSD in Brazil, where there is no special provision on the rules of a case involving a person with a mental illness. In some cases, when Caritas is enrolled in the procedure, the asylum seeker can count on special assistance (as for instance

---

[36] The decision of the Superior Court of Justice in: Agravo Regimental no Agravo Regimental do Mandado de Segurança 12.212/DF cited in Liliana L. Jubilut, *O Direito Internacional dos Refugiados e sua aplicação no ordenamento jurídico brasileiro*, [International refugee law and its application in the Brazilian legal order], supra note 1 at 103.

[*********] Complementary protection is used in this text in the sense of "extra" protection, as the individuals protected in this maner are deemed refugees and to be protected by International Refugee Law.

[*********] Since 2012 Brazil has humanitarian visas (of entry and of stay) to Haitians and Syrians which can be regarded as temporary protection mechanisms.

medical treatment before the interviews).

However, the extent of such assistance is not nearly enough, a situation which is far from desirable. There is no special provision in the legally binding international refugee instruments regarding the refugee status of persons under age. The same definition of a refugee applies to all individuals, regardless of their age. When it is necessary to determine the refugee status of a minor, problems may arise due to the difficulty of applying the criteria of "well-founded fear" in the case. If a minor is accompanied by one (or both) of his or her parents, or by another family member on whom the minor is dependent and who requests refugee status, the minor's own refugee status will be determined according to the principle of family unity. However, there is still the problem of evidence of paternity considering the need of child protection against trafficking.

The handbook of the UNHCR[37] says that the question of whether an unaccompanied minor may qualify for refugee status must be determined in the first instance according to the degree of the minor's mental development and maturity. However, in Brazil, the Civil Code and judicial procedures and rules demand that a legal representative be nominated in order to preserve the rights of the unaccompanied minor (under eighteen years old) and to act as a guardian. The international standards stipulate that, in the absence of parents or of a legally appointed guardian, it is for the authorities to ensure that the interests of a minor applicant for refugee status are fully safeguarded.

The problem is that the judicial procedure required to nominate a guardian demands a lot of time, with the result that the minor suffers the insecurity of being in a non-regular status in Brazil, since the minor can not appear alone before the Department of Federal Police in order to make the initial declaration (Term of Declaration). A special procedure shall be determined by law so the best interests of the minor are preserved.

In relation to minors, there are also some difficulties concerning the lack of a birth certificate, which is required by some authorities in order to provide access to education and health treatment services, and also concerning the risk of stateless condition. In fact, stateless cases are not considered in all their aspects and application of the relevant international agreements.

RSD in Brazil—lessons learned?

From the above, it seems that the most relevant lesson that RSD in Brazil can teach is the importance of having a strong presence of civil society in the proceedings, as this may balance the state's concern with national security as well as help to improve integral protection. However, civil society contributes to the creation of protection links that are too personally based. It is necessary that achievements related to health, education, shelter, etc. assume a legal character in order to provide legal security and a permanent status to the facilities and services.

Civil society is an important actor in defending inclusion of asylum seekers and refugees in general public policies and programs, and also in attributing character

---

[37] Handbook on Procedural Standards for Refugee Status Determination under UNHCR's Mandate.

of positive law to some of the assistance practices directed to guarantee the rights of children, elders, victims of torture and sexual violence, traumatized persons, etc. Once legal provisions are in place, it is easier for government actors and civil society to prove their violation, hence strengthening the protection of asylum seekers and refugees.

A second lesson that should be highlighted is the importance of having a technical body with knowledge of international law in general, and international refugee law in particular, in charge of RSD. However, there should also be some measure of judicial review in order to rectify mistakes and improve refugee protection. Also in relation to RSD procedure it seems important to have the most transparent system possible and to have the most protective guarantees in place, regularized by law so that they can not be withdrawn due to political shifts.

Lastly, one cannot highlight enough the importance of training all the actors involved in RSD procedures, especially those in charge of the first approach, in general the staff of the Federal Police Department (Immigration Branch of the Police), and also the staff of NGOs and of the judiciary. Only with training will there be awareness of the rights and duties of refugees and asylum seekers, as well as of the special characteristics of this population and the need to have special procedures in place so that they can have their rights really respected.

Conclusion

Although Brazil has a long way to go in RSD, the basis for dialogue is already in place. It must be consolidated in order to allow for the tripartite structure involving the UNHCR, the Brazilian government, and civil society to be successful in guaranteeing integral protection to refugees and asylum seekers.

The tripartite structure is a model to inspire RSD in other countries given that it permits dialogue and analysis of the problems from different perspectives and the integration of various social protection nets. But it is not enough in itself. These social arrangements of refugees' and asylum seekers' protection must be converted to fundamental rights, so they can be demanded if not respected or implemented, with each participant being receptive to new perspectives and preserving their functional original roles.

The role of civil society in RSD is paramount as it adds a "democratic aspect" to RSD in Brazil, and could stress the humanitarian concerns of the individual cases in order to minimize the national security and labour competitive arguments brought by some government sectors.

The government should keep in mind its international obligations, arising not only from international refugee law but from international law in general, especially humanitarian assistance obligations that are required not only by law but also by any standard of legitimacy.

Lastly, UNHCR has to live up to its role as "guardian" of international refugee law, remembering that the law is only there to protect the people it was designed to assist, so that political and/or economic considerations should be kept to a minimum in light of the humanitarian plea of refugees.

The design of the tripartite RSD is definitely a "best practice" in terms of RSD and refugee protection, but its results must go from the local/subjective to the national/objective (positive law) level, and then become a model to be mutatis mutandis duplicated in other countries.

JUBILUT

RESETTLEMENT IN SOLIDARITY: A NEW REGIONAL APPROACH TOWARDS A MORE HUMANE DURABLE SOLUTION (2011)

Liliana Lyra Jubilut[*] and Wellington Pereira Carneiro[**]

1. Introduction

In an age of closed borders and increasing challenges in forced migration due to the economic crisis and security fears, a new approach to a traditional durable solution has emerged in Latin America: resettlement in solidarity.[1] Proposed during the celebration of the 20th anniversary of the Cartagena Declaration in 2004, and in light of the Colombian refugee crisis, resettlement in solidarity has at its core the idea that States in the region should create or deepen existing resettlement programmes with a focus on aiding Colombia's neighbouring countries (mainly Ecuador and Costa Rica) by receiving resettled refugees from within the region. The idea was adopted in the Mexico Plan of Action (MPA)[2] and has been translated into practice in Brazil, Chile, Argentina, and Uruguay. It has also been debated and supported by States outside of the region, such as the United States (US), Canada,

---

[*] Liliana Lyra Jubilut holds a PhD and a Master Degree in International Law from Universidade de São Paulo, and an LLM in International Legal Studies from New York University School of Law. She is a Professor at Faculdade de Direito do Sul de Minas and has been working as a lawyer, researcher and consultant with refugees and asylum seekers in Brazil for 12 years.

[**] Wellington Pereira Carneiro is a Brazilian lawyer, who is serving as an United Nations (UN) staff member in Sudan. He is a PhD candidate in History of International Relations at the Universidade de Brasília, holds a Master in International Human Rights Law from Oxford University, and an LLM from the University Drujby Narodov. The author worked as the Protection Officer of United Nations High Commissioner for Refugees (UNHCR) Brazil from 2004 to 2010.

Note: This article has been written using a pragmatic approach, building on the experience of the writers with refugee protection in Latin America, and, therefore, doctrinal references are limited. The opinions expressed are exclusively from the authors and do not represent those of the institutions in which they are or were engaged. The authors would like to thank everyone who contributed data and arguments used in this article, especially UNHCR Brazil and Comitê Nacional para Refugiados (CONARE)

[1] This article uses the term "resettlement in solidarity" as this translation of the original *reassentamento solidário* seems to be more in line with the proposed new concepts of the Mexico Plan of Action than the generally used term of "solidarity resettlement".

[2] The text of the MPA is available at: http://www.acnur.org/biblioteca/pdf/3016.pdf (in Spanish); or at: http://www.acnur.org/biblioteca/pdf/3453.pdf (in English; version used for this article) (last visited 15 May 2011). The MPA refers to a regional approach that takes "into account the socio-economic conditions prevailing in the countries of asylum [. . .]. This requires devising new strategies to achieve self-sufficiency and local integration, both in urban centers as well as border areas, as well as the strategic use of resettlement, in a framework of regional solidarity". MPA, 6.

and Norway through twinning agreements and other initiatives.

Resettlement in solidarity is an idea in progress that, if successful, can lead to both a new approach to refugee protection in light of acute refugee crises, and to a new model of dialogue among States and among actors involved in refugee protection. An analytical assessment of its main ideas is therefore in order. Examination of the on-going practice is important to ascertain whether, in the future, this new regional solution can be effective in establishing a more humane approach to resettlement. This is relevant in so far as International Refugee Law, as Human Rights Law, is founded on the principle of human dignity. Hence, to be effective, resettlement has to be analysed both in light of its actual results and its adequacy to uphold the most protective standards of human dignity.

In light of this, this article describes resettlement in solidarity in order to assist in the assessment of whether or not this new regional approach will lead to a more humane durable solution and contribute to refugee protection globally. In order to fulfil this task, this article will present a case study of resettlement in solidarity in Brazil, as this country proposed and pioneered the implementation of this new regional approach to resettlement. Section 2 provides an outline of the theoretical and doctrinal background that led to the Brazilian proposal, followed by a description of the concept of resettlement in solidarity in Section 3, and an assessment of its main merits and shortcomings, so far, in Section 4.

2. The backdrop of the concept of resettlement in solidarity

2.1. Colombia's refugee crisis[3]

The Colombian crisis is very complex, given that it is a multifaceted conflict that subsists through its own dynamics. Although the initial triggers and factors are no longer the main concern in terms of resolving the conflict, it is generally agreed that the Colombian conflict originated in the confrontation between the conservative and liberal parties over the sharing of power in the country.[4] Both political forces have engaged in military confrontations several times throughout the 200 years of Colombia's history of independence. The most serious explosion of political violence occurred during the period known as *La Violencia* between April 1948 and 1958, followed by a popular uprising called *Bogotazo* that virtually destroyed the capital city. Violence erupted between political factions and, in the following 10 years, an estimated 200,000 people lost their lives.[5]

That period of Colombia's history marked the appearance of armed militias that were initially constituted as self-defence structures in the countryside villages to face organized political violence. These militias are at the origin of the guerrillas existing today, although the latter no longer retain any resemblance with the former. Around 1964, 100 armed groups were estimated to be active in Colombia, especially in the coffee producing areas. With the appearance of drug cartels in the late 1970s

---

[3] The information on Colombia's history and the refugee crisis in this country are based on UNHCR sources. See UNHCR, International Protection Considerations on the International Protection of Colombian Refugees and Asylum Seekers, Geneva, UNHCR, Mar. 2005, available at: http://www.unhcr.se/Pdf/protect/Colombia_policy.pdf (last visited 26 Jan. 2011).

[4] D. Bushnell, *Colombia, Una Nación a Pesar de sí Misma*, Bogota, Editorial Planeta, 2007, 140.

[5] Ibid., 287.

and early 1980s, the Colombian Government was weakened due to generalised corruption, intimidation, and selective killings. Between 1982 and 1998, there were several attempts to negotiate a peace agreement.[6] However, peace talks were usually followed by an escalation of violence. As a result, any attempt to transform the guerrilla organizations into political parties were struck down. Selective killings exterminated the majority of the members of these newly formed political organizations. Such killings also targeted members of the new political parties created by the guerrilla organizations. These processes widely failed to keep the doors open to peace, due to wide scale violence. Moreover, and more seriously, this inspired the widespread assumption that there was no possibility of non-violent political participation in Colombia.

In 2002, Alvaro Uribe Vélez came to power with an ambitious plan to militarily win the conflict. An initial offensive generated lower levels of violence with the withdrawal of armed groups. It was followed by the demobilisation of paramilitary groups and the retreat of the main guerrillas to their traditional strongholds, mainly in the jungle areas of the southern and eastern provinces. Despite all these measures, the humanitarian crisis did not improve. Reports commenting on the thousands of persons who remained abducted in the country illustrate this situation.

Against this background, the number of refugees and internally displaced persons (IDPs), that were collateral effects of the crisis since its inception, continued to increase: by 2007, they reached the alarming number of 3 million, surpassed only by Sudan in 2009.[7] Furthermore, the enhanced security situation in urban areas has been accompanied by a deteriorating situation in rural areas, which reflected in the profile of refugees. Besides this, there was a constant blurring between combatants and non-combatants during the conflict, in clear violation of the principle of distinction under International Humanitarian Law.

As a result, the Government adopted the policy of "one million friends", which was meant to recruit one million informers. This initiative was actually based on a practice that was common to the guerrilla groups and paramilitaries. These measures had dire consequences for the civil population and deepened the refugee crisis.

In addition to (i) the number of refugees, (ii) the changing profile of the refugee population, and (iii) the precarious situation of the civil population, a fourth factor was perceived in the Colombian refugee crisis: the permeable nature of the borders meant that the violence reached the refugees and asylum seekers in some neighbouring countries. This new trend, combined with the other factors of the Colombian refugee crisis, made it necessary to find new and regional approaches to refugee protection in the region. The crisis was no longer local and, as it became a regional concern, a regional approach was needed to deal with it.

---

[6] Ibid., 249.

[7] According to data of UNHCR in, *2009 Global Trends: Refugees, Asylum-Seekers, Returnees, Internally Displaced and Stateless Persons*, Geneva, UNHCR, 15 Jun. 2010, available at http://www.unhcr.org/cgi-bin/texis/vtx/home/opendocPDFViewer.html? docid¼4c11f0be9&query¼global%20trends (last visited 15 May 2011)

2.2. The perspective of Cartagena

A regional approach to refugee protection is not a novelty in Latin America. In fact, it seems to be a part of the history of protecting persecuted people in the region in so far as: (i) a regional custom of granting asylum was recognized in International Law due to the practice of States[8] and their commitment to asylum;[9] and (ii) a regional concept of the refugee definition was proposed in the early 1980s. This regional concept was established in the Declaration of Cartagena – the result of a 1984 meeting hosted by the Colombian Government in the city of Cartagena and that included representatives of several Governments and civil society organizations. The aim was to elaborate an original and pragmatic concept to renew the international protection regime in Latin America, keeping with the peculiarities of the region.[10] The Declaration of Cartagena was adopted and established a new regional refugee definition.

The Declaration of Cartagena emerged in the context of the conflicts that seriously affected Central America at the end of the 1970s and early 1980s. The civil wars in Nicaragua, El Salvador, and Guatemala resulted in the displacement of thousands of people.[11] Against such a background, the Declaration expanded the universal definition of refugees by allowing people fleeing from gross and generalised violations of human rights to be recognized as refugees. The concept was inspired by the enlarged refugee definition in the 1969 Organization of African Unity *Convention Governing the Specific Aspects of Refugee Problems in Africa* and also by the 1969 *American Convention on Human Rights*. Such regional approaches to refugee protection are justified, on the one hand, by the fact that 80 per cent of refugees are hosted by neighbouring countries[12] and, on the other hand, by the specificities of the regional situation which indeed call for regional, rather than universal, responses. Hence, pragmatism seemingly marked the construction of the concept of Cartagena, embraced by the majority of refugee systems across Latin America.[13]

---

[8] See, for instance, International Court of Justice, Haya de la Torre Case (Colombia v. Peru), Judgment, ICJ Reports 1951.

[9] As seen, for instance, with the Montevideo Treaty on International Penal Law, 3 Jan. 1889; the Convention on Asylum, Havana, 6th International Conference of American States, 20 Feb. 1928 (entry into force: 21 May 1929); the Convention on Political Asylum, Montevideo, 7th International Conference of American States, 26 Dec. 1933 (entry into force: 28 Mar. 1935); the Treaty on Asylum and Political Refuge, Montevideo, 4 Aug. 1939; the Declaration of Rights and Duties of Man, Bogotá, 9th International Conference of American States, 2 May 1948; and the Convention on Diplomatic Asylum, Caracas, 10th International Conference of American States, OAS, Treaty Series, No. 18, 29 Dec. 1954.

[10] For more on the Declaration of Cartagena and of the peculiarities of the American region on Refugee Law and protection see, F. Piovesan & L.L. Jubilut, "Regional Developments: Americas", in A. Zimmermann (ed.), *The 1951 Convention Relating to the Status of Refugees and its 1967 Protocol – A Commentary*, Oxford, Oxford University Press, 2011, 205–224.

[11] On the subject of Central American conflicts in the 1980s see, for instance, W.I. Robinson, *Transnational Conflicts: Central America, Social Changes and Globalization*, London, Verso, 2003.

[12] UNHCR, *2007 Global Trends: Refugees, Asylum-Seekers, Returnees, Internally Displaced and Stateless Persons*, Geneva, UNHCR, 2 Jun. 2008, available at: http://www.unhcr.org/4852366f2.pdf (last visited 15 May 2011).

[13] According to UNHCR, as of 2007, 11 of the 20 States that have adopted the MPA have included the regional definition of Cartagena in their national laws. UNHCR, *Plan de Acción de México: El impacto de la Solidaridad Regional*, Geneva, UNHCR, 2007, 11 and 16, available at: http://acnur.org/t3/fileadmin/scripts/doc.php?file¼biblioteca/pdf/5484 (last visited 16 May 2011). However, this number seems to have increased since. According to the UNHCR website for the Americas, 13 countries have adopted the concept of Cartagena in their national legislation: Argentina, Belize, Bolivia, Brazil, Ecuador, El Salvador, Guatemala,

Nevertheless, although the Cartagena Declaration is known for its enlarged refugee definition, this perception falls short of explaining the concept of Cartagena. In fact, it is not simply an extension, as it does not introduce new criteria within the individualised conventional refugee definition. Rather, it is mainly based on the objective situation and the social and political environment of the country of origin. Recognition as a refugee, therefore, occurs regardless of the individual attributes of the person in need of protection (such as religion or ethnicity) unlike in the traditional universal criteria applied since 1951. The Cartagena concept is, thus, closely linked to International Human Rights Law, and International Humanitarian Law, as it aims to protect the fundamental rights of human beings from a potentially threatening situation. Life, security, and liberty are expressly mentioned as rights to be protected from chaos or generalised violence. It is also related to the political situation of the country of origin, thereby requiring a continuous reflection on such contexts.[14]

Against such a background, it became clear that the region is willing to: (i) enforce the spirit of Cartagena, (ii) advance International Refugee Law and protection, and (iii) restate previous commitments in order to make them effective in facing the new challenges of forced migration and refugee crises. All of these characteristics are in place in the concept of resettlement in solidarity, which can thus be described as a reflection of the spirit of Cartagena: Latin American countries are required to respond to the challenges of humanitarian crises by finding humane solutions.

3. The foundations of the concept of resettlement in solidarity

In light of the plight of refugees and IDPs in Colombia and the more humane approach to refugee protection demanded by the spirit of Cartagena, a new approach to resettlement has started to emerge.[15] This new approach builds on the idea of burden-sharing that appears in connection with the "re-birth" of resettlement as a durable solution. It was also conceived on the basis of solidarity between countries, especially with those facing massive arrivals of Colombian refugees.[16] An understanding of these foundations is important for appraising the

---

Honduras, Mexico, Nicaragua, Paraguay, Peru, and Uruguay. UNHCR, *Países que Incorporan Cartagena en la Legislación Nacional*, Geneva, UNHCR, 2008, available at: http://www.acnur.org/ paginas/index.php ?id_pag¼42317&id_sec¼ (last visited 15 May 2011).

[14] In general, the processes of reflection of Cartagena culminate with regional meetings every 10 years.

[15] The MPA reflects the wide support and consensus achieved by Latin American countries on the objectives of the MPA including resettlement: "To this end, four sub-regional preparatory meetings were held in San Jose, Costa Rica (12–13 August), Brasilia, Brazil (26–27 August), Cartagena de Indias, Colombia (16–17 September) and Bogota, Colombia (6–7 October), in which the refugee situation in each region was analyzed. As the outcome of each gathering, a report was adopted by consensus." MPA, 5.

[16] A survey conducted by UNHCR Ecuador in 2007 indicated that there would be around 135,000 Colombians in need of international protection in Ecuador. Therefore, with the enhanced registration programme, a simplified procedure, and roving registration operations around the country registered until Apr. 2010, 27,600 new refugees. This figure added to the refugees recognized under ordinary procedure which led Ecuador to host a population of around 53,000 registered refugees in Apr. 2010, when the first phase was concluded. From these, 98 per cent were Colombians. On the other hand, in the beginning of 2010, Costa Rica counted around 18.1 thousand refugees mostly Colombians, as well as of Jan. 2009. See UNHCR, 2011 UNHCR Country Operations Profile – Ecuador, UNHCR, 2011, available at: http://www .unhcr.org/cgi-bin/texis/vtx/page?page¼449e492b66 (last visited 16 May 2011); and UNHCR, 2011 Regional Operations Profile – Latin America, UNHCR, 2011, available at: http://www.unhcr.org/cgi-bin/texis/vtx/

changing attitude of developing countries in Latin America in relation to the Colombian humanitarian crisis.

3.1. The " re-birth" of resettlement

Since its inception, UNHCR has established three durable solutions for the protection of refugees: local integration, repatriation, and resettlement.[17] Resettlement was an important durable solution in the aftermath of the Second World War and is today again practised by many States as the favoured solution. Against this background, it is noteworthy that "the decision to resettle a refugee is only made in the absence of other options – local integration or repatriation".[18] UNHCR has established resettlement as a strategic tool to deal with refugee crises. This trend can be noticed, for instance, in the Convention Plus initiative that lists "the strategic use of resettlement as a tool of protection".[19] UNHCR considers resettlement as:

> [. . .] *a vital protection tool and an international responsibility-sharing mechanism, but [it] also can be a key element in comprehensive solution strategies. It aims to provide protection to refugees whose life, liberty, safety, health or other fundamental human rights are at risk in their country of asylum. Comparatively, resettlement benefits a small number of refugees; in 2008, less than 1 per cent of the world's refugees directly benefited from resettlement.*[20]

This "re-birth" of resettlement has been evident in UNHCR's efforts since the late 1990s to find new or emerging countries of resettlement.[21] It has also played a fundamental role for the resettlement in solidarity initiative in Latin America, given that Brazil first became a country of resettlement before proposing a new approach to this durable solution.[22]

3.2. The principle of solidarity

The feeling of solidarity is positively valued in all major creed systems[23] and since 1945 has achieved a prominent position in International Law. From the Peace of Westphalia in 1648 to the end of the Second World War, the main norms of

---

page?page¼49e492456 (last visited 16 May 2011).

[17] UNHCR has been working with this three-pronged approach for a long time as a way to fulfil its tasks; as mentioned in UNHCR, General Information Paper, UN Doc. HCR/50B/1/82, Nov. 1982, 14. The MPA reframes the classic durable solutions formulation as: the "Solidarity Cities" Programme for Self-Sufficiency and Local Integration (MPA, 9); the Integrated "Borders of Solidarity" Programme (MPA, 10) and the Regional "Solidarity Resettlement" Programme (MPA, 11).

[18] S. Labman, "Resettlement's Renaissance: A Cautionary Advocacy", *Refuge*, 24(2), 2007, 36.

[19] UNHCR, *Convention Plus at a Glance*, Geneva, UNHCR, 2005, available at: http://www.unhcr.org/403b30684.html (last visited 15 May 2011).

[20] UNHCR, *2008 Global Trends: Refugees, Asylum-Seekers, Returnees, Internally Displaced and Stateless Persons*, Geneva, UNHCR, 16 Jun. 2009, 11, available at: http://www.unhcr.ch/uploads/media/2008_Global_Trends.pdf (last visited 16 May 2011).

[21] J.H. Fischel de Andrade & A. Marcolini, "A Política Brasileira de Proteção e Reassentamento de Refugiados: Breves Comentários sobre suas Principais Caracteríticas" [The Brazilian policy of protection and resettlement of refugees: brief notes on its main characteristics], *Revista Brasileira de Política Internacional*, 45(1), 2002, 168–176.

[22] L.L. Jubilut, "International Refugee Law and Protection in Brazil: A Model in South America?", *Journal of Refugee Studies*, 19(1), 2006, 22–44.

[23] J. Moses, *Unidade: Os Princípios Comuns a Todas as Religiões* [Oneness: Great Principles Shared by All Religions], Rio de Janeiro, Sextante, 2009.

International Law were norms of co-existence. With the changes brought along after this conflict, norms of cooperation have started to emerge especially in relation to global concerns and goods (such as international security and the environment) and shared values (such as human rights).[24] This new international order based on solidarity has thus gained momentum and is arguably considered nowadays as a principle of International Law:

> *While maintaining its political nature the notion of solidarity has become a principle proper to the international legal order because it has given rise to the creation, modification or confirmation of rights and obligations, and this to varying degrees and a wide range of modalities. Solidarity has evolved, gradually and not without difficulty, from an ideological principle of law into a principle of existing law. It has evolved from the realm of justice into the domain of law.*[25]

In the field of International Refugee Law, solidarity is paramount. It even constitutes the core of the responsibility assumed by the international community towards refugees. Recently, solidarity has gained further relevance in the refugee protection field, altering the former prevailing idea of burden-sharing. This change is one of the MPA's main innovations and contributions to International Refugee Law.

The term responsibility sharing is accordingly used *in lieu* of burden-sharing – a concept that "against the background of increasing restrictions worldwide on asylum in the 1990s, [. . .] has been revived and has begun to gain currency".[26] This change represents much more than a simple shift in semantics but rather a transformation of how refugee protection and refugees are perceived: not as a problem and a situation of sharing refugees, but as a responsibility for protecting the victims of violations of human rights.

Burden-sharing calls for collective actions in light of refugee emergencies and can thus be a positive departure from purely unilateral national responses. However, it also brings along – even if indirectly – the negative notion that the refugees are themselves a "burden".[27] This new concept of responsibility sharing appears rather to be linked to the idea of solidarity:

> *Solidarity is linked to the idea of everyone's responsibility for the privation or needs of any individual or social group. It is the transposition, in the arena of the political*

---

[24] L.L. Jubilut, "Os Fundamentos do Direito Internacional Contemporâneo: da Coexistência aos Valores Compartilhados" [The fundaments of contemporary international Law: from coexistence to shared values], *Anuário Brasileiro de Direito Internacional*, 9(2), 2010, 203–219.

[25] K. Wellens, "Solidarity as a Constitutional Principle: Its Expanding Role and Inherent Limitations", in R.St.J. MacDonald & D.M. Johnston (eds.), *Towards World Constitutionalism: Issues in the Legal Ordering of the World Community*, Leiden, Martinus Nijhoff Publisher, 2005, 776–777. The arguments in favour of international solidarity as a principle of International Law are also deepened in light of, for instance: (i) the appointment by the United Nations of an independent expert on human rights and international solidarity; (ii) resolutions of the United Nations Commission on Human Rights on the topic; and (iii) resolutions of the United Nations Human Rights Council on the topic. In the case of International Refugee Law, solidarity is mentioned as a principle, for instance, in the fifth, eighteenth and twenty-ninth paragraphs of the Preamble of the MPA.

[26] A. Suhrke, "Burden-Sharing during Refugee Emergencies: The Logic of Collective versus National Action", *Journal of Refugee Studies*, 11(4), 1998, 396.

[27] See for instance, P.H. Schuck, "Refugee Burden-Sharing: A Modest Proposal", *Yale Journal of International Law*, 22, 1997, 243.

*society, of the **obligatio in solidum** of the Roman private law. The ethical fundament of this principle is found in the idea of distributive justice understood as the needed compensation of goods and advantages between social classes with the socialization of the normal risks of the human existence.*[28]

In Latin America, this new discourse seems to have had an even stronger echo. The idea is not only a move from the concept of burden-sharing to that of responsibility sharing, but a deepening of States' commitment to refuge protection by creating a resettlement *in solidarity*. By emphasising on solidarity, the region highlights its respect for the humanitarian aspects of a refugee crisis. It furthermore reinforces the responsibility of States to assist in the protection of refugees and human rights.

4. The building of the concept of resettlement in solidarity

4.1. The proposal – The Mexico Plan of Action[29]

Since its re-democratisation, Brazil has aimed to improve its human rights and refugee protection records and has even been regarded as being a model in this field in South America.[30] Given such renewed commitment coupled with the re-opening of the UNHCR office in Brazil in March 2004, and the aforementioned "re-birth" of resettlement, the Government and UNHCR reached an agreement to re-organize the resettlement programme (which had existed since 2000) within the framework of the new concepts and initiatives in progress in light of the celebration of the 20th anniversary of the Cartagena Declaration. In August 2004, a preparatory meeting for the event that would officially celebrate the 20th anniversary of the Cartagena Declaration was held in Brasília (Brazil).[31] It was attended by members of civil society and representatives of the Governments of Argentina, Bolivia, Brazil, Chile, Paraguay, Peru, and Uruguay. During the meeting, Brazil launched the proposal which would become the resettlement in solidarity initiative.[32] This proposal built on (i) the regional tradition of refugee protection in Latin America, (ii) the "re-birth" of resettlement, and (iii) the principle of solidarity. In light of the Colombian refugee crisis, representatives of the Brazilian Government, supported by the representative of UNHCR Brazil,[33] hence proposed the creation of a regional resettlement programme to receive resettled refugees from other countries in the region. Any Latin American country could thus become a resettlement country for Latin American refugees that were recognized as such in another country of the

---

[28] F.K. Comparato, *A Afirmação Histórica dos Direitos Humanos* [The historical affirmation of human rights], São Paulo, Saraiva, 2003, 64, [authors' translation].

[29] For the MPA, see above footnote 2.

[30] For further information in relation to the resettlement program in Brazil and to the history of refugee protection in Brazil see, Jubilut, "International Refugee Law", 22–44.

[31] MPA, 4.

[32] MPA, 11: "In the preparatory meeting held in Brasilia (26–27 August 2004), the Government of Brazil proposed the creation of a regional resettlement programme for Latin American refugees, in the framework of international solidarity and responsibility-sharing. This initiative opens the possibility for any Latin American country, at the opportune time, to participate and to receive refugees who are in other Latin American countries." For the Brazilian proposal see L.P.T.F. Barreto, *Discursos Doutor Luiz Paulo Teles Ferreira Barreto no Seminário sobre Cartagena*, Speech on the Seminar on Cartagena, 2004 [on file with the authors].

[33] The idea of resettlement in solidarity was then defended by Luiz Paulo T. F. Barreto (the representative of Brazil in the meeting – who later became Minister of Justice in Brazil and is the President of CONARE) and by Luis Varese (the representative of UNHCR in Brazil at the time).

region.[34]

The aim of the proposal was twofold: (i) to establish a protection strategy to the spilled-over consequences of the Colombian conflict, and (ii) to offer durable solutions to refugees in the bordering countries of Colombia, already approximating hundreds of thousands.[35] Resettlement was also based on the principle of non-discrimination,[36] meaning that preference would be given to refugees from the region without, however, closing the doors to other refugees. Indeed, migration controls led to a high concentration of refugees in bordering countries as, with a Colombian passport, it was very difficult to travel anywhere in the world. Therefore, the options to seek asylum were very limited, making crossing the border into a neighbouring country the quasi-only alternative.[37] In some countries, such as Spain, with historical ties to Hispanic America, there were relatively small numbers of Colombian refugees. However, in Ecuador, Costa Rica, and Venezuela, the size of the population of concern was already over 200,000.[38] The number of recognized refugees in Ecuador and Costa Rica were respectively of 10,000 refugees at the time of the proposal.[39] The magnitude of the crisis is exemplified by the fact that, in relation to Ecuador with a population of 13 million people, the number of Colombians could have increased the population by 2 per cent in about a five-year period.

The Brasília meeting concluded that in Latin America there was a constant willingness to find solutions for refugee problems in a regional framework. A reformulation of the concept of burden-sharing represented an innovative step in order to avoid the perception of refugees as a burden.[40] Taking into account the international context, this change in wording had an expressive symbolic meaning.

Moreover, the resettlement in solidarity proposal combined the needs of individuals seeking protection and the social and security concerns of neighbouring countries, thereby introducing a viable and more humane solution to a huge humanitarian crisis. It provided a new hope for finding a durable solution in the face of first countries of asylum overwhelmed by massive arrivals. The resettlement in solidarity idea appeared, thus, not only as a viable alternative to the resettlement dilemma in the region but also as an improvement of the international protection

---

[34] MPA, 10.

[35] *Ibid.*

[36] "Latin American countries agree upon the importance of establishing resettlement policies that include a framework of principles and eligibility criteria, with due regard for the principle of non-discrimination. Furthermore, based on the experience of Brazil and Chile as emerging resettlement countries, they appeal to the international community to support the strengthening and consolidation of these initiatives, in order to improve and replicate them in other countries of Latin America." *Ibid.*

[37] Arguably, the new situation of migration controls in the world is clearly reflected in the situation of the Colombian conflict. In some embassies in Bogota, candidates for a visa may have to wait for more than a year for a regular interview, which led some countries to offer special procedures for potential asylum seekers, opening a quasi-exception to the territoriality of refugee procedures.

[38] UNHCR, Bureau for the Americas, "Resettlement", *Refview*, No. 3, Geneva, UNHCR, Jul. 2006, 5, available at: http://www.unhcr.org/cgi-bin/texis/vtx/home/opendoc PDFViewer.html?docid¼45b9d4b62 &query¼ REFVIEW (last visited 15 May 2011).

[39] These figures correspond to the approximate number of refugees by 2004. By early 2010 these figures had increased to 53,000 in Ecuador and around 18,000 in Costa Rica.

[40] See, for instance, para. 17 of the Preamble of the MPA, 2.

regime by widening the narrow humanitarian space in the world.

4.2. The Mexico Plan of Action

Following the preparatory meetings, the Mexico Declaration and the MPA became a reality in November 2004.[41] The Mexico Declaration simply reaffirms the commitment to the principle of international protection and vindicated the so-called "spirit of Cartagena". In this context, Latin American countries chose a humanitarian initiative, instead of closing their borders, or establishing more rigid migration controls. This may be explained by the fact that Latin America did not feel as threatened by terrorism as northern countries. Furthermore, with millions of their citizens living as immigrants abroad, it could neither support the price of setting tighter security border controls. This is not to say that there was no concern about migration and security but rather that the region opted to combine the State's and the refugee's needs in a new approach to refugee protection.

The MPA is comprised of two main components: 1) a protection component; and 2) a durable solution component which, in turn, is divided in three main elements, namely cities of solidarity, borders of solidarity, and resettlement in solidarity.[42]

In relation to the protection component, positive developments have been noted. During the Central American refugee crisis that inspired the Cartagena Declaration, Latin American countries supported the initiative but had a very limited operational role in protecting refugees. Indeed, they had no proper legal framework and some had not even acceded to the 1951 Geneva Convention Relating to the Status of Refugees at the time.[43] For example, Mexico received a large number of refugees from the Guatemalan conflict (about 80,000 people) in the 1980s,[44] but only ratified the 1951 Convention and its Protocol in 2000.[45] However, since then the various countries in the region have set up new legislation and eligibility mechanisms.

Moreover, twining initiatives – especially with regard to the strengthening of the national commissions in charge of refugee status determination (RSD) and instruments of complementary protection – have also been established in the region through, for instance, humanitarian visas, protection of victims of torture, and new

---

[41] See, UN General Assembly, Office of the United Nations High Commissioner for Refugees, UN Doc. A/RES/60/129, 24 Jan. 2006, para. 5: "Notes with interest the Mexico Plan of Action to Strengthen International Protection of Refugees in Latin America, endorsed by States participating in the meeting commemorating the twentieth anniversary of the Cartagena Declaration on Refugees convened in Mexico City on 15 and 16 November 2004 [. . .]".

[42] The two components are respectively in the MPA's chapter 2 and chapter 3. See MPA, 6 and 9.

[43] Geneva Convention Relating to the Status of Refugees, 189 UNTS 150, 28 Jul. 1951 (entry into force: 22 Apr. 1954), amended by the Protocol Relating to the Status of Refugees, 606 UNTS 267, 31 Jan. 1967 (entry into force: 4 Oct. 1967).

[44] According to L.O. Monasterio, *Guatemalan Refugees in Mexico: A Happy Ending*, Department of International Legal Affairs, Office of legal Cooperation, Organization of American States, 2005, available at: http://www.oas.org/juridico/English/ortize.html (last visited 16 May 2011).

[45] According to UNHCR, *States Parties to the 1951 Convention relating to the Status of Refugees and the 1967 Protocol*, Geneva, UNHCR, 2011, available at: http://www.unhcr. org/3b73b0d63.html (last visited 16 May 2011).

forms of legal residence.**** More recently, the region also adopted the Brasília Declaration reaffirming its commitment to enhancing Refugee Law and protection.[46]

Therefore, the objectives of doctrinal developments and institutional strengthening constituting the protection component of the MPA responded to the needs of these countries to address an increasing influx through their own means. The UNHCR was thus able to start relinquishing the operational role that it had for the previous 20 years when the Cartagena Declaration was drafted.

Alongside these positive developments in protection, enormous advancements were made in relation to the durable solution components: borders of solidarity, cities of solidarity, and resettlement in solidarity. The borders of solidarity was made up of two main concepts. On the one hand, it concentrated on the refugee population by establishing that: (i) safeguards to asylum seekers have to be in place in the borders, and (ii) border officials have to be trained in a way to ensure access to adequate RSD procedures and respect for human rights – so as to avoid, for instance, sexual harassment and corruption.[47] On the other hand, it focused on the population of the areas receiving refugees.[48] This approach was clearly a departure from the dominant views around the world regarding the security-refugee dilemma, where borders security is traditionally linked to tighter controls. In a context where armed militias were infiltrating neighbouring countries, it was a very innovative and daring approach.

The cities of solidarity objective basically had the aim of improving refugees' local integration in urban settings. It stemmed from clear recognition that the humanitarian crisis in Colombia was different from that of Central America in the 1980s when the majority of refugees had a rural background. Ideas such as establishing new partnerships with local Governments and civil society entities and recognizing people and institutions that helped refugee protection with awards were part of this initiative. The resettlement in solidarity objective was an explicit call to transform Latin America in general, and South America in particular, into the biggest and most promising emerging resettlement area in the world.

Brazil took this proposal to the Mexico Meeting as one of the most important conclusions of the preparatory meeting in Brasília and it was incorporated into the MPA. The outcome of the resettlement in solidarity idea was very tangible. Chile and Brazil had received small contingents of Colombian refugees and took the lead in committing to accept larger caseloads. In the same year (2004), the arrival of 75 refugees in Brazil clearly surpassed the number of previous arrivals. Although it constituted a small number in comparison to the numbers accepted by traditional resettlement countries (or of the general number of refugees in need of resettlement), it was a remarkable increase both in relation to previous numbers in

---

**** Complementary protection is currently used to mean practices that grant protection to persons facing humanitarian needs but that are not encompassed by the protection of the institute of refuge.

[46] The Brasilia Declaration on the Protection of Refugees and Stateless Persons in the Americas, 11 Nov. 2010, available at: http://www.unhcr.org/4cdd3fac6.pdf (last visited 15 May 2011).

[47] MPA, 10: Integrated "Borders of Solidarity" Programme.

[48] MPA, 1: "[. . .] the commitment of Latin American countries to keep their borders open in order to guarantee the protection and security of those who have a right to enjoy international protection".

the region and with regards to the scope of resettlement in those countries.[49] Also, shortly after the meeting in Mexico, Argentina signed a resettlement agreement with UNHCR. By June 2007, after three years of the MPA, Paraguay and Uruguay joined the resettlement in solidarity regional initiative.[50]

4.3. The Quito Meeting – the age of reason

Following the practice of meetings to analyse the implementation of the regional refugee protection initiatives, a meeting on resettlement in solidarity was held in Quito in February 2006, less than two years after the resettlement in solidarity initiative of the MPA.[51] The Quito Meeting enabled identifying the obstacles faced by participant countries, thereby calling for practical and realistic adjustments of the Mexico Meeting.

Developing countries realised that the costs of resettlement were very high, which made immediate funding from national sources a complex task. Some Latin American countries, especially in the Southern Cone, have had their *per capita* incomes increased and were experiencing sustained economic growth, thereby gradually no longer falling into the category of poor countries receiving international aid. However, they had no tradition of being international donors. With very extensive social programmes in place to reduce poverty, securing local resources was thus very competitive. As poverty reduction was a clear priority, they realised that finding resources to support the resettlement in solidarity initiative on their own was difficult.

Donor countries, such as the US, Canada, and Norway agreed to fund the initial efforts to establish sustained resettlement programmes, through an initiative called "twinning arrangements", with the view to create a favourable environment to future ownership. Capacity building was indeed an urgent need.

Thus, the twinning agreements with traditional resettlement countries were one of the successful proposals to improve both knowledge and the capacity of governmental officials to implement resettlement policies and programmes. Besides identification of the limitations for fundraising, the obstacles posed by the public health systems and fragile labour markets of the resettlement countries led to a more restrictive approach on resettlement selection criteria. However, developing countries underlined that integration prospects could not be taken as a decisive criterion for resettlement, as they were not that different in Brazil or Argentina in comparison to those in Ecuador or Costa Rica.[52]

---

[49] Statistical data obtained through consultations with UNHCR Brazil. See Table 2 for more statistical information.

[50] This fact is acknowledged by the Brasilia Declaration on the Protection of Refugees and Stateless Persons in the Americas, see above footnote 46, para. 11: "Underlining the creative and innovative character of the regional solidarity resettlement programme, implemented by Argentina, Brazil and Chile, joined by Uruguay and Paraguay, [. . .]", [original emphasis].

[51] Primera Reunión sobre Reasentamiento Solidário en América Latina, 2–3 Feb. 2006, Quito, Ecuador.

[52] Quito Meeting, Summary of the debates: UNHCR, *Reasentamiento Solidário en Acción: Políticas Programas y Necesidades: Oportunidades de Cooperación*, Quito, UNHCR, 2–3 Feb. 2006, available at: http://www.acnur. org/t3/fileadmin/scripts/doc.php? file¼biblioteca/ pdf/4057 (last visited 16 May 2011). "La experiencia de reasentamiento en la región ha revelado algunas dificultades, entre las cuales muchos participantes señalaron la integración de los refugiados en el país de reasentamiento". *Ibid.*, 2

This rebuttal of the integration prospects approach to resettlement also differentiates the resettlement in solidarity idea from some traditional resettlement programmes. In June 2007, another evaluation meeting took place in Buenos Aires.[53] Results were encouraging as the humanitarian community was at the forefront of, perhaps, the first successful emerging resettlement experience in developing countries. It was definitely possible to expand resettlement opportunities to the developing world, but it required a special approach as this experience accumulated a new know-how on creating conditions to this effect. Resettlement programmes could be much cheaper but had to be well-structured in order to avoid protracted situations and tensions with refugees.

5. Resettlement in solidarity in Brazil[*****]

5.1. Emerging resettlement countries: the beginning of resettlement in Brazil

As seen above, UNHCR recently gave a new boost to resettlement by trying, on the one hand, to establish it as a strategic tool in the Convention Plus initiative, and, on the other hand, to establish partnerships with countries not having a previous history of receiving refugees.[54]

These initiatives were a direct result of the post-Cold War period, which can be said to have been the most challenging for UNHCR and for the States Parties to the 1951 Convention as the number of refugees doubled in slightly more than 10 years. The figure of approximately 9 million refugees in 1989 multiplied to 22.5 million in 2003.[55] The increasing number of refugees and their need for protection challenged the whole international community, particularly those countries committed to refugees' resettlement.

The existing resettlement opportunities could never cover the annual demands for resettlement. This gap is continuously growing, in light of the multiple crises which mark the world, and combined with security fears from States that led to the closing of frontiers, resettlement in many cases (as for instance in the crisis in Afghanistan, the Balkans, and the Great Lakes in the mid-1990s) is the only possible solution.

During a meeting of the Working Group on Resettlement, some countries, particularly the Nordic States, requested that UNHCR increase and diversify the resettlement opportunities for refugees so as to ease the burden on traditional resettlement countries, as well as to meet the increasing demand.[56] The outcome

---

[53] Segundo Encuentro sobre Reasentamiento Solidário en las Américas, Jul. 2007, Buenos Aires, Argentina.

[*****] A more recent and updated description and analysis of resettlement in solidarity in Brazil will be available in 2018 in: L.L. Jubilut and A. C. G. Zamur, Brazil's Refugee Resettlement: power, humanitarianism and regional leadership. In: Adèle Garnier, Liliana Lyra Jubilut and Kristin Bergtora Sandvik (Eds.). *Refugee Resettlement: Power, Politics and Humanitarian Governance*. Oxford/NY: Berghahn Books, 2018, forthcoming.

[54] Fischel de Andrade & Marcolini, "A Política Brasileira de Proteção".

[55] S. Ogata, The Turbulent Decade: Confronting the Refugee Crisis of the 1990s, New York, W.W. Norton, 2005.

[56] Migration Policy Institute, Study on The Feasibility of Setting Up Resettlement Schemes in EU Member States or at EU Level, against the Background of the Common European Asylum System and the Goal of a Common Asylum Procedure, Study by the Migration Policy Institute on behalf of the European

was the establishment of a Trust Fund for Enhancing Resettlement Activities in January 1997, with the main objective of financing pilot projects in nontraditional resettlement countries. The project forged the expression "emerging resettlement countries" and launched negotiations with several countries to participate in this initiative.[57]

The criteria for the selection of these countries were very pragmatic and simple, but were essential for the success of the initiative, as the countries needed to: (i) not be a refugee producing country; (ii) have signed and implemented the international legal instruments on refugee protection; (iii) have a UNHCR presence in the country; and (iv) appear to offer some local integration prospects. In Africa the following countries were considered by UNHCR for selection: South Africa, Côte d'Ivoire, Ghana, Togo, Senegal, Benin, and Burkina Faso. The latter was the first to sign an agreement with UNHCR, followed by Benin. These two countries in Africa were, in the end, the ones that received resettled refugees.[58] Outside Africa, negotiations were held with four new resettlement countries: Iceland and Ireland in Europe, and Brazil and Chile in Latin America.

At the same time, in July 1997, Brazil enacted its national Refugee Act. This renewed commitment to respect International Human Rights Law transformed Brazil into a resettlement country due to the provisions of Articles 45 and 46.[59]

At this time, however, there was no agreement for the resettlement of refugees in Brazil. An agreement to this end was signed in 1999 despite the fact that UNHCR was not present in the country, as the local office had been closed in 1998 and the programme in Brazil was under the supervision of the Regional Office in Buenos Aires.

No refugees were resettled in Brazil until 2002, when a group of 22 Afghans arrived and were established in the Southern State of Rio Grande do Sul. In the following year, a group of 16 Colombians arrived, marking the beginning of a very careful and modest pilot resettlement programme. This caution can be justified by the fact that the resettlement programme occurring contemporaneously in Africa was marked by problems and shortcomings. By August 2003, 46 per cent of the cases resettled in Burkina Faso and 32 per cent of those resettled in Benin had left the country. Overestimation of integration prospects, the lack of a reception structure, and an excessive level of assistance, much higher than the average

---

Commission, 2002, 12, available at: http://www.unhcr.org/refworld/docid/439570104.html (last visited 16 May 2011).

[57] See, S. Sperl & I. Bradisteanu, *Refugee Resettlement in Developing Countries – The Experience of Benin and Burkina Faso, 1997-2003: An Independent Evaluation*, UNHCR Evaluation and Policy Analysis Unit and Resettlement and Special Cases Section, Doc. EPAU/2004/04-Rev.1, Apr. 2004, available at: http://www.unhcr.org/ 40cd76a8a.html (last visited 16 May 2011).

[58] Within this framework 16 refugees were resettled in South Africa with the resources of the trust fund, but the experience was not considered successful. Between 1997 and 2003, 226 refugees were resettled in Burkina Faso and Benin.

[59] Brazilian Refugee Act, Lei 9474/97, 22 Jul. 1997, Arts. 45 and 46 (Art. 45: "Resettlement of a refugee in other countries shall reflect, whenever possible, the free will of the refugee"; Art. 46: "Resettlement of a refugee in Brazil shall be planned, with the coordinated participation of state bodies and, whenever possible, of non-government institutions, identifying areas of cooperation and determination of responsibilities"). The English text of the Brazilian Refugee Act is available at: http://www.unhcr.org/refworld/pdfid/ 3f4dfb134.pdf (last visited 16 May 2011).

national income, led to dependency and frustration with local integration.[60] These shortcomings led to a complete re-evaluation of the project.

In 2003, the problem of assistance was also identified. As an additional burden to the programme in Brazil, the Afghans were coming from protracted refugee situations that, by themselves, raised special concerns in terms of integration strategy. In addition, they were given access to a level of assistance that could never be achieved in a normal self-reliant situation where they would be dependent on the local wages and services of a developing country. The programme was thus re-evaluated leading to the conclusion that the levels of welfare and assistance in traditional, industrial resettlement countries should not be automatically transferred to developing countries.[61] The lesson to be learned from these experiences seems to be that material assistance, in a developing country, should be kept at such a level that would not undermine the prospect of self-reliance, taking into consideration the specificities of the local situation.

Most Afghan refugees resettled in Brazil requested voluntary repatriation after the Taliban regime was removed. Despite the difficulties, it was considered an appropriate durable solution. Two families were well integrated and remained in Brazil. Conversely, the small group of Colombians resettled in Brazil, despite having endured a long struggle for self-reliance, successfully integrated with just three cases of repatriation or irregular secondary movement. In light of this, combined with the fact that the Colombian conflict was escalating (with about one million Colombians leaving the country between 2003 and 2005) and given Brazil's commitments to International Refugee Law, the programme was expanded alongside with the resettlement in solidarity initiative that was adopted. Therefore, it transformed Latin America into a region where resettlement was practiced with a humanitarian *façade*.

5.2. The beginning of resettlement in solidarity in Brazil

From the beginning, the consolidation of Latin American developing countries as resettlement countries had to compete with the attraction of traditional resettlement countries. Refugees had indeed a clear preference for industrialised countries due to economic opportunities therein. In light of the traditional reasons for resettlement – i.e. legal or physical protection, health needs, survivors of torture or other forms of violence, women-at-risk, family reunification, unaccompanied minors, elderly refugees, and refugees with no prospective of integration[62] – Brazil

---

[60] 60 D. McKeever, *Identifying Gaps in Protection Capacity Burkina Faso*, Geneva, UNHCR, Strengthening Protection Capacity Project, Jul. 2005, available at: http://www.unhcr.org/ 4305e8102.html (last visited 15 May 2011). The independent Evaluation Report of the Resettlement Pilot Project was completed in Apr. 2004. This Report concludes that the Pilot Project cannot be considered a success, for a number of reasons. The Report highlights the failed local integration and precarious economic situation of many of the refugees resettled to Burkina Faso. By Mar. 2005, only 39 of the 75 resettled refugees remained in Burkina Faso, the rest having left the country of their own accord. See *ibid.*, 48.

[61] We owe this argument to the kind contributions of Luis Varese and Karin Wapechowsky, respectively Desk Officer in 2003, and resettlement project coordinator in Porto Alegre in 2007.

[62] W.P. Carneiro, "A Declaração de Cartagena de 1984 e os Desafios da Proteção Internacional dos Refugiados, 20 Anos depois" [The 1984 Cartagena Declaration and the challenges of the international protection of refugees, 20 years later], in C.A.S. da Silva & V.M. Rodrigues (eds.), *Refugiados* [Refugees], Nuares, Centro Universitário Vila Velha, 2005, 68–72.

embraced physical and legal protection needs, family reunion, and women-at-risk criteria as the most suitable to begin resettlement in developing countries. A programme for the reception of women-at-risk also represented an attempt to specialise the resettlement initiative allowing for the establishment of clear priorities with a suitable reception structure. As noted by Nogueira and Marques, "[i]t is estimated that 20% of the resettled refugees in the country are women heads of household."[63]

Moreover, many resettlement applicants in Ecuador and Costa Rica faced clear security problems, fearing the long "tentacles" of the armed groups from Colombia. Therefore, the possibility of immediate relief was favoured in the choice of destination country over economic prospects in developed States.[64]

Few refugees preferred to stay in Latin America for cultural reasons or because of the challenge of learning another language. Unlike Argentina or Chile, refugees willing to be resettled in Brazil also had to face a considerable cultural challenge. Being the only country in the Americas with Portuguese as the official language and the *lingua franca*, Brazil could not even offer the language advantage, and the cultural proximity was quite relative. Nevertheless, the racial and cultural diversity of Brazil was attractive to refugees facing discrimination such as Afro-Colombians or persons with indigenous backgrounds.[65]

Therefore, based on the discussions about the challenges of emerging resettlement countries from the Quito Meeting, Brazil established the urgent resettlement procedure in December 2004 by which it aimed to specialise in physical security cases. The objective was to set up an immediate and efficient fast-track procedure that would make the country more attractive to certain applicants with acute physical security concerns.[66] According to this procedure, after a screening by UNHCR, a presentation by electronic means to CONARE – the organ vested with the responsibility to accept, in first instance, refugees in Brazil – is made and a decision has to be taken by its members within three working days. The lack of a response would mean acceptance of the case.

The fast-track procedure exists alongside the normal resettlement procedure in which the case is debated in one of the regular meetings of CONARE, after a UNHCR staff member, a CONARE official, and a representative of a civil society organization in charge of the reception of the resettled refugees have interviewed the prospective candidates (Table 1).

---

[63] M.B. Nogueira & C. Marques, "Brazil: Ten Years of Refugee Protection", *Forced Migration Review*, 30, 2008, 57.

[64] CONARE concluded that it had to specialise on high security cases, and issued a regulation for the fast-track procedure in which a decision should be made in three working days.

[65] W.P. Carneiro & J.M. Collar, "Reflexões sobre a Questão Racial e Refúgio no Sistema Brasileiro", in V.M. Rodrigues (ed.), *Direitos Humanos e Refugiados*, Vila Velha, UVV, 2006, 9–34.

[66] As in most cases regarding refugee protection in Brazil, in general, and resettlement in solidarity, in particular, the decision was adopted in one of CONARE's meetings. These meetings are registered through CONARE but do not result in public official documents.

Table 1. Resettled refugees in Brazil by type of procedure

	Normal	Fast-track	Family reunification	Dossier	Total
2002	23	0	0	0	23
2003	16	0	0	0	16
2004	75	0	0	0	75
2005	57	27	1	0	85
2006	36	16	0	0	52
2007	71	41	1	43	156
2008	11	8	0	0	19
2009	19	11	4	0	34
2010	7	21	0	0	28
2011	15	0	0	0	15
Total	330	124	6	43	503

Source: Data obtained with UNHCR Brazil. Data updated until 31 January 2011.

Table 2. Resettled refugees in Brazil by country/nationality[a]

	Afghanistan	Colombia[b]	Ecuador	RDC	Palestine	Cuba	Jordan	Iraq	Guatemala	Lebanon	Stateless	Total
2002	23	0	0	0	0	0	0	0	0	0	0	23
2003	0	15	0	1[c]	0	0	0	0	0	0	0	16
2004	0	71	3	0	1[d]	0	0	0	0	0	0	75
2005	0	81	4	0	0	0	0	0	0	0	0	85
2006	0	50	2	0	0	0	0	0	0	0	0	52
2007	0	42	2	0	99	2[e]	1	4	2	1	3	156
2008	0	16	3	0	0	0	0	0	0	0	0	19
2009	0	28	2	0	4	0	0	0	0	0	0	34
2010	0	25	3	0	0	0	0	0	0	0	0	28
2011	0	15	0	0	0	0	0	0	0	0	0	15
Total[f]	23	343	19	1	104	2	1	4	2	1	3	503

[a] According to CONARE the numbers are: 23 resettled refugees from Afghanistan (all arrived in 2002), 318 from Colombia (with arrivals as follows: 14 in 2003, 64 in 2004, 67 in 2005, 47 in 2006, 39 in 2007, 17 in 2008, 30 in 2009, 25 in 2010, and 15 in 2011), one from Costa Rica (that arrived in 2003), 28 from Ecuador (10 arrived in 2004, three in 2005, five in 2006, two in 2007, three in 2008, two in 2009, and three in 2010); one from the Democratic Republic of Congo (that arrived in 2003), 104 Palestinians (one arrived in 2004, 102 in 2007, and one in 2009), one from Jordan (arrived in 2007), one from Iraq (arrived in 2007), two from Guatemala (arrived in 2007), one from Lebanon (arrived in 2007), and three stateless (arrived in 2007); which amounts to a total of 483 resettled refugees. Data updated until 31 January 2011. [b] Mainly coming from Ecuador and Costa Rica. [c] Living in Costa Rica prior to arrival. [d] Living in Cuba prior to arrival. [e] Family Reunification. [f] The total number shown represents resettled refugees in Brazil not considering the ones that have been repatriated.

Source: UNHCR Brazil. Data updated until 31 January 2011.

The fast-track procedure enabled the reception of urgent cases in very short periods, representing an important innovation in terms of refugee protection. From 2002 to February 2010, 480 refugees have been resettled in Brazil according to

UNHCR,[67] of whom 328 were Colombians[68] (Tables 2 and 3). In January 2011 another 15 Colombians arrived, totalling 503 resettled refugees.

Table 3. Colombian resettled refugees in Brazil

	Resettled	Repatriated/left the country/deceased	Total
2003	15	2	13
2004	71	8	63
2005	81	11	70
2006	50	6	44
2007	42	11	31
2008	16	0	16
2009	28	0	28
2010	25	0	25
2011	15	0	15
Total	343	38	305[a]

Data updated until 31 January 2011, Ecuadorian children and family members are not included in this statistics.
Source: Data obtained with CONARE (number of returns and deaths) and UNHCR Brazil (number of resettled refugees). [a] If only CONARE's numbers are taken into account, the current number of Colombians resettled in Brazil would be 280. Given that CONARE acknowledges 602 Colombian refugees in the country, Colombian resettled refugees would represent 46.5 per cent of this population (as of 31 December 2010).

From this contingent, the fast-track procedure was used to resettle 124 people (104 Colombians), which means 36 per cent of all resettled Colombian refugees, reflecting a successful application of the procedure and a real alternative to the urgent physical security cases. More recently, another type of procedure – by *dossier* – has been established for situations where it is more difficult to conduct *in situ* personal interviews and when refugees are not in need of fast-track examination, as in the case of Palestinian refugees.[69]

At first, integration in developing countries raised challenges. One of the particular challenges was when Brazil first went from receiving small groups of resettled refugees in a pilot project – hence treated on an individual case-by-case basis – to welcoming bigger groups, thus requiring a more general intervention of public policies to address integration issues. Some public policies on poverty

---

[67] It is important to highlight that the number of resettled refugees recognized by UNHCR differs from the number adopted by CONARE. This is due to the fact that CONARE works with the number of refugees that have officially applied, entered Brazil as resettled refugees, and are still living in the country, whereas UNHCR works with numbers, including all refugees once resettled in the country regardless of their current status. Besides these and the differences in methodology adopted by each organ, another difficulty that makes the data on resettled refuges in Brazil controversial is the fact that until recently there was not a comprehensive and systemic way of assessing this information which resulted in the need for researchers to come up with their own methodology and to count each case individually instead of relying on the official data. As one of the aims of the paper is to describe the resettlement in solidarity initiative in its plenitude and given that the writers had access to each individual case recorded, the paper will work with the highest numbers, but will bring CONARE's numbers when they differ from the adopted data in footnotes. According to CONARE the total number of resettled refugees is 483 of which 421 are currently living in Brazil.

[68] 305 according to CONARE.

[69] 305 according to CONARE.

reduction, social assistance, and income generation that could benefit refugees were implemented with federal funds but managed by local authorities, such as municipalities and Federal States. This reality demanded local promotion initiatives to grant refugees access to social programmes and benefit from existing public policies for vulnerable groups intertwined with the cities in solidarity initiative of the MPA. With a small refugee community of 4,359 refugees (according to CONARE, as of 31 December 2010) in a country of over 190 million, the widespread lack of knowledge regarding the real refugee situation in Brazil frequently represents an obstacle to accessing public services or programmes.

Local authorities frequently lack the required know-how to address refugees' needs. However, due to the decisive intervention of civil society, a huge network of solidarity is gradually and continuously being formed in the receiving regions, developing an appropriate reception structure that will enable growing numbers of resettled refugees to be received and integrated. By June 2007, it was calculated that over 80 enterprises, Government departments, NGOs, social clubs, churches, educational institutions, and individuals in 22 towns in five States (from a total of 27) were actively involved in different aspects related to the reception of refugees in Brazil.[70]

The results also demonstrated a sharp enhancement in the first three years of the solidarity resettlement programme with: (i) 19 per cent of refugees having their own house, covering mortgages, or property; (ii) 6 per cent of refugee families covering their own rental fees; (iii) 77 per cent of working age refugees involved in income generating activities; and (iv) only around 10 per cent being motivated to repatriate, due to the improvement of the security situation in urban areas in Colombia.[71]

In the course of the resettlement in solidarity initiative in Brazil, a change in the social profile of refugees from Colombia has been noticed.[72] This change is related to the dynamics of the conflict. While during the years 2003–2005 the majority of refugees were professionals from urban areas, a sharp change took place in 2006–2007, shifting to refugees from semi-rural or rural areas of lower class and mainly from the southern areas. This shows the importance of a dynamic programme that can be tailored to the changing needs of refugees.

In May 2007, the resettlement in solidarity initiative in Brazil, which was initially conceived as a regional programme, took a significant and challenging step forward: Brazil agreed to receive a group of over 100 Palestinians who had been stranded for four years in a refugee camp in the desert of Jordan.[73] They escaped from targeted persecution by militia groups against Palestinians in Iraq, as they were perceived as being favoured by the former regime. The procedure of resettlement for this group was done, as aforementioned, by dossier.

---

[70] Nogueira & Marques, "Brazil", 57.

[71] Data obtained through consultations with UNHCR Brazil in 2009.

[72] We owe this argument to Sanchez, Walter Alt in Quito (during the Quito Meeting).

[73] The group of Palestinians comprised persons with other nationalities or stateless persons, but because they all arrived in the scenario of the closing of Palestinian refugee camps they are loosely referred to as Palestinians.

In August 2007, the number of resettled Palestinians had grown due to the process of family reunification. But it was particularly in September of that year that a dramatic increase in the number of resettled Palestinians occurred, with a wide mediatisation. Integration of these refugees from outside the region, with a different cultural background than that of the Colombians, constituted a real challenge. But Brazilian authorities firmly stuck to the humanitarian agenda as a priority in refugee issues and as the basis of resettlement in solidarity.

Furthermore, the Brazilian initiative inspired other countries of the region, mainly Chile, thereby expanding the resettlement in solidarity initiative to other humanitarian crises outside of the region.[74] The resettlement of Palestinians had an important effect on the programme in general and on the resettlement of Colombians in particular in Brazil. A very particular, culturally diverse, and difficult caseload overwhelmed the reception capacity, which meant a sharp decrease in the new arrivals of Colombians for two years as the resettlement of Palestinians proved to be more challenging than expected. However, the previous targets started to be resumed in 2009–2010.

Despite some difficulties in the local integration of the Palestinian refugees, which are gradually and still being addressed, the willingness of Brazil to receive them represented a huge step in transforming Brazil – and Latin America – into a reliable resettlement region.[75] The humanitarian community is, perhaps, at the forefront of a successful emerging resettlement experience in a developing country.

5.3. Analysis of resettlement in solidarity in Brazil

Overall, the resettlement in solidarity in Brazil can be seen as a successful new approach to a traditional durable solution as it provided: (i) an alternative for refugees in need of resettlement; (ii) a unique foundation based on humanitarian grounds and solidarity; (iii) an inspiration for a regional approach to a regional refugees crisis; (iv) a balanced approach between State' concerns and individuals' needs; and (v) a practical implementation of the spirit of Cartagena. The shortcomings of the programme arise not from its inception but from its implementation as it is an idea in progress. The analysis of these difficulties may assist in improving resettlement in solidarity in general.

By comparing the resettlement of Colombian and Palestinian refugees in Brazil, some lessons can be drawn, both positive and negative, although all analysis should be considered as simply preliminary considerations given the short existence of the programme to date. It seems that receiving smaller groups may render the initiative more successful as the challenges of local integration can be better addressed and personalised social assistance can be put in place. It also appears that the experience of dispersing the resettled refugees throughout Brazil (as in the case of the

---

[74] Chile, shortly after the Brazilian initiative in 2007, conducted a mission and resettled a group of around 100 Palestinians. For more information on the work of UNHCR in Chile and mentions of the resettlement program see, for instance, UNHCR Chile, *El Trabajo del ACNUR en Chile*, Santiago de Chile, UNHCR, undated, available at: http://www.acnur.org/ t3/fileadmin/scripts/doc.php? file¼t3/21uploads/ tx_refugiadosamericas/ El_trabajo_del_ACNUR_en_Chile (last visited 16 May 2011).

[75] Recently Brazil has declared that it is willing to accept refugees from the on-going conflict in Libya. See "ONU pede para Brasil acolher refugiados", *Correio do Brasil*, 4 Jul. 2011, available at: http://correiodobrasil. com.br/onu-pede-para-brasil-acolher-refugiados/ 263458/ (last visited 11 Jul. 2011).

Colombians) is more successful, and may even raise more solidarity from the receiving communities. It is interesting to notice that the dispersion solution was thought to be in line with the multi-faceted characteristics of the Colombian crisis. Given the different actors of persecution, it would indeed have been unwise to place refugees who could have different relations with these actors involved in the conflict in the same area.

On the other hand, it was not done in the same proportion in the case of the Palestinians – which were resettled in two regions with a high concentration in one city in each region – due to the fact that they had been living together in the camps in Jordan. But, in the end, it proved less effective in terms of integration. This begs the question of whether dispersion should be appraised on the basis of receiving communities' integration capacities, rather than from the perspective of refugees' background.

Another lesson to be learned is that cultural proximity (even if not similarity) may render the initiative more or less successful, especially in terms of integration and self-reliance. The difficulties in the integration of the Palestinian refugees are in this sense illustrative. Furthermore, it is important that, through the selection process, the situation of the country of asylum is clearly communicated to the refugees. Indeed, expectations should be minimized so as to meet the reality, thereby avoiding frustration, resentment, and an unwillingness to adjust to the new country. It is also relevant that, as pointed out by UNHCR, when deciding on the criteria for emerging resettlement countries, local integration prospects have to exist. Thus, a minimum level of industrialization and development is required of the resettlement country.

Table 4. RSD of Colombians in Brazil

	Asylum requests made	Asylum requests granted	Percentage
1999	2	2	100.00
2000	32	11	34.38
2001	11	10	90.91
2002	80	35	43.75
2003	28	10	35.71
2004	29	19	65.52
2005	114	85	74.56
2006	78	56	71.79
2007	83	24	28.92
2008	35	16	45.71
2009	57	36	63.15
2010	41	15	36.58

Data updated until 31 December 2010. *Source*: CONARE.

Furthermore, resettlement in solidarity should co-exist with other forms of protection, including RSD in the receiving country, acting thus both as a first country of asylum and a resettlement country. If this is not the case, protection will not be enhanced but merely shifted and the benefit of the initiative will be lost.

Brazil has been engaged in both forms of protection. On the one hand, it has played a leading role for resettlement in solidarity. On the other hand, it has also continuously accepted Colombian refugees as the first country of asylum in the same (or even higher) proportion than before the resettlement programme was established (Table 4).

In any case one should not minimise the paramount change that resettlement in solidarity has already brought to refugee protection. Solidarity has led countries to resettle on a humanitarian basis, distancing themselves from considerations as to local integration's prospects or cultural proximity. Hence, not only is the rhetoric changing, but also the practice of refugee protection heading towards a more humane approach.

6. Conclusion

Resettlement in solidarity is a new Latin American approach to the traditional universal durable solution of resettlement. This novel approach has only existed since 2004 but can greatly contribute to International Refugee Law and protection. While further consolidation is needed, the Brazilian experience as a pioneer of the initiative allows for important lessons to be drawn. On the one hand, it shows that there is still a need to enhance the level of professionalization of partners and municipal agents. A more effective approach to public policies should also be introduced, so that the integration prospects of a higher number of resettled refugees may be improved. The lessons learned from the existing programmes should thus be taken into consideration for further developments.

Funding is also a challenging and pressing issue, but the political will to enhance protection in Latin America is in place and should be further developed. On the other hand, however, the experience in Brazil shows that it is possible for new countries of resettlement to emerge. Such a conclusion thus calls for three main remarks.

First, middle-income countries such as Brazil, Argentina, and Chile may offer new possibilities to provide international protection. Moreover, as far as they lie distant from conflict zones, they may constitute durable solutions providers instead of temporary protection havens. Second, the more focused strategy of resettlement in solidarity allows for a quicker and more effective response to an acute refugee crisis.

Third, and perhaps most importantly, resettlement in solidarity can pave the way to a more humane approach to resettlement. This is due to two main factors. First, it can establish a new model of dialogue among States and actors involved in refugee protection based on the concept of solidarity. As a result, the paradigm of "burden-sharing" may lose its former prevalence in this field. Second, by focusing on both the needs of individuals and the concerns of States, resettlement in solidarity can actually become a viable tool in refugee protection. In light of the above, it is important to promote this initiative and its implementation with the aim of strengthening the refugee protection regime in due respect with human dignity.

ENHANCING REFUGEES' INTEGRATION: NEW INITIATIVES IN BRAZIL (2010)

Liliana Lyra Jubilut[*]

Brazil's commitment to refugee law and protection since the mid-1950s resulted in the passing of a bill on refugees in 1997 (Law 9474). This not only broadened protection for refugees by including gross violation of human rights as a criterion for refugee status but also created an administrative procedure for refugee status determination (RSD) and established the basis for refugee protection and integration in Brazil. This third task is undertaken by the Brazilian government, UNHCR and civil society together. Bringing social actors other than the government into the fold is regarded as a positive aspect of refugee protection and integration in Brazil, providing for a more holistic commitment to the cause of refugees. The government is, however, the most relevant actor in refugee protection, given that the National Committee for Refugees (CONARE), which has responsibility for RSD, votes by simple majority and is composed of six representatives of government and only one representative of civil society.

Civil society, on the other hand, has led the way in supporting the integration of refugees in Brazil, providing, through direct work or partnership, up to 60% of the total budget for refugee integration in the country. This highlights the fact that in the first 10 years of modern refugee protection in the country, the focus of the government seems to have been on eligibility rather than on integration. This trend, however, has started to change since the 10th anniversary of the 1997 law.

Since 2007 the Brazilian government has begun to devote attention both to refugee protection (through maintaining procedures on RSD that uphold international standards) and refugee integration, and has started to establish public policies on refugees. The federal government is looking into the insertion of refugees in existing public policies in Brazil; where this is not possible, it is considering the creation of specific public policies for refugees.

Concern for the economic and social rights of refugees has now extended to the local government level where there have been new initiatives to improve refugee protection through integration.

---

[*] Liliana Lyra Jubilut (lljubilut@gmail.com) has been working as a lawyer, consultant and researcher with refugees in Brazil for 11 years.

State Committees on Refugees

One of these initiatives has been the creation of State Committees on Refugees, in the states of São Paulo and Rio de Janeiro. These two states have the two most relevant centres for refugee protection in the country, given that the two UNHCR implementing partners for local integration are in these cities and assist over 90% of the refugees in Brazil.[1]

The first State Committee on Refugees was established in São Paulo in April 2008, presided over by the Secretary of Justice and the Defence of Citizenship. It brings together representatives from several other ministries – Economy and Planning, Housing, Assistance and Social Development, Employment and Work Relations, Education, Health, Institutional Relations, Culture, and Public Security – and from UNHCR, local UNHCR implementing partners and State defence attorneys. At the end of 2009 Rio de Janeiro established its State Committee with similarly wide representation.[2]

So far, the State Committee in São Paulo has acted in three different situations: on an issue of public security involving resettled refugees in the countryside, on a health issue concerning a hospital and resettled refugees, and by including 102 refugees and asylum seekers in its State work programme. It is clear from the Committee's actions to date – i.e. involving groups of refugees but not the whole refugee population – that the Committee does not want to micro-manage individual cases but has yet to adopt public policies that will benefit the whole refugee population in the State. It is important that the Committee has started to act in specific cases that were brought to its attention but it is essential that broader public policy issues be its main concern in future actions.

At the municipal level, a committee was set up in the city of São Paulo involving organs of the City hall, under the coordination of the Municipal Commission on Human Rights, and civil society to debate public policies for refugees and immigrants there. This is an important example of local government acting to protect refugees.

These initiatives on refugee integration and on public policies for refugees in Brazil appear to be rooted in three factors. Firstly, in recent years Brazil has begun to be concerned with development and economic and social rights for its native population and this focus seems to have spread to refugees as well.

Secondly, in light of the growing urbanisation of the world's refugee population, UNHCR has started to work towards securing the rights of refugees in urban settings and is therefore highlighting the need for a more comprehensive integration and protection of refugees in urban settings such as in Brazil.

Lastly, the focus on refugee integration has been one of the main axes of the Mexico Plan of Action under the Cities of Solidarity initiative.[3] The main goal of this initiative is to promote access to basic services in health, education,

---

[1] UNHCR also has implementing partners for resettlement and for protection.

[2] For information regarding the representation in Rio de Janeiro's Committee, see Decreto 42182 of December 2009.

[3] http://www.acnur.org/biblioteca/pdf/3453.pdf.

employment and housing – all best achieved through public policies.

It is important to highlight, however, that the State Committees for Refugees should not be seen as an end in themselves. Rather, they work as a catalyst for the creation of public policies to help ensure full protection of refugees in Brazil, guaranteeing both their civil and political rights and their economic and social rights.

REFUGEE POPULATION IN BRAZIL: THE QUEST FOR INTEGRAL PROTECTION (2008)[*]

Liliana Lyra Jubilut[**] and **Silvia Menicucci de Oliveira Selmi Apolinário**[***]

1. Introduction

Brazil is commonly considered a model for the reception and protecting of the refugee population[1] in South America[2] due to its advanced refugee law, which involves government agencies, civil society entities and organs of the international community.

This evaluation may be reasonable when using as parameter the minimum standards stipulated by International Refugee Law, embodied, above all, by the 1951 Convention on the Status of Refugees (1951 Convention), the 1967 Protocol on the Status of Refugees (1967 Protocol), and regional instruments, such as the Cartagena Declaration of 1984. However, since the reception and protection of the refugee population are integral parts of International Human Rights Law[3], principles based on the protection of human dignity,[4] improvements, aiming at an integral protection, must be implemented.

---

[*] This text was translated from Portuguese to English by Victor Augusto Mendes, and revised by Rosilandy C. C. Lapa. A final revision was performed by the authors.

[**] PhD and Master in International Law from Universidade de São Paulo and LL.M in International Legal Studies from New York University School of Law. Professor of International Law at the Faculdade de Direito do Sul de Minas. She is a Consultant for the Creation of the Brazilian Council for Refugees and was a lawyer at the Refugee Center of Caritas Arquidiocesana de São Paulo in partnership with UNHCR and the Brazilian government.

[***] PhD and Master in International Law from Universidade de São Paulo. She is a professor of International Law at the International Relations course at UNICEUB, and coordinator of Apex-Brasil's Legal Unit. She was a lawyer at the Refugee Center of Caritas Arquidiocesana do Rio de Janeiro in partnership with UNHCR and the Brazilian government.

[1] Refers to the "refugee population" as the set of persons who have sought refuge and are awaiting a decision regarding their application (applicants or asylum seekers) and persons who have already had their refugee status recognized (refugees).

[2] For more details on the subject, see: JUBILUT, 2006, p. 22-24 and FISCHEL; MARCOLINI, 2002, p. 37-39.

[3] The expression "international protection of Human beings" is used as the set of norms and values ensured by International Human Rights Law, International Refugee Law, International Humanitarian Law and International Criminal Law. In this sense, it refers to the broader set of rules emanating from human dignity, and aimed at ensuring the most protective scenario for the human being.

[4] The article is based on the teachings of Hannah Arendt by which human dignity is a given, while human rights are construed from it. See LAFER, 1999, p. 134.

Based on this premise, this article aims to describe the protection and reception of the refugee population in Brazil, in order to verify which aspects can and should be changed so as to obtaining integral protection: a protection that guarantees not only the rights stipulated by International Refugee Law, but also the human rights of refugees and asylum seekers, in line with International Human Rights Law and the Brazilian legal system itself.

2. Historical aspects of the reception and institutionalization of the protection of the refugee population in Brazil

The universal international system for the protection of refugees emerged after World War II as a direct response to the consequences of this conflict, regarding the displacement of persons. In 1950, the United Nations High Commissioner for Refugees (UNHCR), which sponsored the 1951 Convention and the 1967 Protocol, was established in the form of a subsidiary organ of the General Assembly of the United Nations (UN). These universal documents establish minimum standards of protection, being up to States to enforce them and, whenever possible, to expand them.

In light of this, the commitment of States and its reflection on their internal legal systems are essential to ensuring protection for the refugee population. In Brazil, despite being linked to formal standards, there has been some engagement since 1958, when Brazil joined the UNHCR Executive Committee, and subsequently ratified and incorporated both the 1951 Convention and the 1967 Protocol[5] .[6]

By the end of the 1970s, UNHCR had established an *ad hoc* office in Brazil. However, the Brazilian government recognized it as an international body only in 1982. The negative position of the Brazilian government for more than a decade made it very difficult for the international community to act, in Brazil, in favor of the refugee population. In this period of non-recognition, Brazil (yet under an undemocratic regime) served only as a transit territory for Latin American refugees. It did not provide protection or permitted the settlement of them in its territory. During this phase, some 20,000 Argentines, Bolivians, Chileans and Uruguayans were resettled in Australia, Canada, Europe and New Zealand.[7]

Since the beginning of the reception and protection of the refugee population in Brazil, civil society entities have been playing an important role in providing direct assistance to them. Because of the work of these entities, it was possible to extend protection in Brazil, even if indirectly and in specific contexts, for instance by the sheltering of 150 Vietnamese refugees, some Cuban refugees and 50 Baha'i families which were received between 1975 and 1980 and 1986 respectively as foreign residents.[8]

In 1989 and 1990, in the wake of redemocratization, Brazil expanded its commitment to the refugee cause by denouncing reservations it had made to the

---

[5] The 1951 Convention was adopted in 1961 and the 1967 Protocol in 1972.

[6] For more details on the reception and protection of the refugee population in Brazil, see. JUBILUT, 2007.

[7] See FISCHEL DE ANDRADE; MARCOLINI, 2002, p. 169.

[8] See JUBILUT, 2007, p. 173.

1951 Convention. The Inter-ministerial Ordinance n. 394 was adopted in 1991 to regulate the procedure for recognition of refugee status. This procedure formally predicted the participation of the international community, through the UNHCR, and the Brazilian government. It also allowed for the participation of civil society that continued to provide direct assistance to the refugee population.[9]

In 1992, inspired by the Cartagena Declaration, Brazil began to adopt the criteria of a "gross and generalized violation of human rights" for the recognition of refugee status,[10] which allowed the protection of Angolans who fled the civil war in their country, and made up for a long time the largest percentage in terms of nationality of recognized refugees in Brazil.

In 1997, continuing the trend of advancing the protection of refugee in the domestic level, initiated with the redemocratization, Brazil adopted Law 9.474 of July 22, which defined the mechanisms for the implementation of the 1951 Convention and consolidated the protection of the refugee population. Since then, this is the domestic legislation that enforces the protection measures towards the refugee population.

3. Protecting the Refugee Population in Brazil: Procedures of Refugee Status Determination and Resettlement

Law 9.474 of 1997 became a landmark in the protection of the refugee population in Brazil and consolidated relevant changes in Brazil's protection of refugees. It set the rights and duties of both individuals and of the Brazilian State.

From this legal instrument, one can see that the reception and protection of refugees may occur in Brazil through two ways: 1) when Brazil is the first country of asylum and protection, that is, when the refugee status determination is carried out by the Brazilian government or 2) when Brazil resettles refugees already recognized as such by other States or by UNHCR.[11] As the procedures in each situation are distinct, they will be considered in two different sections.

3.1. Brazil as the first host country and protection

Most of the refugees in Brazil[12] had the country as their first place of refuge. This means that their refugee status determination was performed in Brazil, and that their situation met the legal criteria (both national and international) for the recognition of refugee status.

According to the 1951 Convention, for a person to be recognized as a refugee s/he must: 1) have a well-founded fear of persecution; 2) on the basis of race,

---

[9] "In general terms, the procedure for granting refuge was as follows: UNHCR conducted an interview with asylum seekers and based it on an opinion recommending whether or not to grant refuge in that case. This opinion was sent to the Ministry of Foreign Affairs, which gave its opinion on this and sent it to the Ministry of Justice, which issued the final decision. ". JUBILUT, 2007, p.175.

[10] The gross and generalized violation of human rights was enshrined in art. 1, item III of Law 9.474 / 97. When applied, it shifts the focus from the analysis of the request for refuge from individual persecution to the objective situation of the applicant's country of origin.

[11] Depending on its status, UNHCR may recognize "mandated" refugees.

[12] Of the 3956 refugees in Brazil, 3579 had their status originally recognized in Brazil and 377 were resettled, making them more than 90% of the total. Data updated as of January 14, 2009 and obtained in consultation with the National Committee for Refugees (CONARE).

religion, nationality, political opinion or membership of a social group; 3) lack international protection, which means that the objective situation of his/her country of origin or of habitual residence must give rise to the need for international protection, i.e. the person cannot be included in the cessation clauses; and 4) merit international protection, that is, s/he cannot have acted in contrary to International Law and, therefore, cannot fall under exclusion clauses which include war crimes, crimes against humanity or crimes against peace, or have committed serious crime or acted in contrary to the principles and purposes of the United Nations.

In addition to these requirements, the 1951 Convention allowed States to choose to recognize as refugees only persons who fulfilled all these conditions due to events occurring in Europe before January 1, 1951. Such possibilities became known as the geographical and temporal limitations.

The inclusion of such reservations denotes the constant understanding by States that refugee status is a time-limited issue: as the 1951 Convention targeted the refugee population as a result of World War II, States felt that they could limit the definition to cover only this group. Such an understanding, however, proved to be wrong.

Because of the continued emergence of refugees, the 1967 Protocol was adopted to specifically remove the temporal limitation permitted by the 1951 Convention. Therefore, the best universal international protection is the one set forth by the 1951 Convention reviewed by the 1967 Protocol.

By adopting Law 9.474 of 1997, Brazil incorporated the rules of the universal international system into its national definition of refugees, and also, as mentioned, expanded protection by including the gross and generalized violation of human rights as a reason for the recognition of refugee status.[13]

In addition to establishing the definition of refugee to be applied in Brazil, Law 9.474 of 1997 set the bases for the administrative procedures for refugee status determination.

The first innovation in this sense was the creation of a collective deliberation body, within the scope of the Ministry of Justice, the National Committee for Refugees (CONARE),[14] with competence to: analyze requests for refugee status and recognize said status at first instance, determine *ex officio* or at the request of the competent authorities the loss of refugee status at first instance,[15] guide and coordinate the necessary actions for effective protection, assistance and legal

---

[13] Regarding the issue and, above all, the differences between the Brazilian definition and universal international definition, see JUBILUT, 2006, p. 31 et seq.

[14] The Internal Rules of the National Committee for Refugees can be found at: BARBOSA; HORA, 2007, p. 148-152.

[15] Art. 39, item IV of Law 9.474 / 97 determines that the exit from the national territory without prior authorization of the Government Brazil will lead to the loss of refugee status, in addition to other possibilities, namely: renunciation to the status, proof of falsity of reasons given for the recognition of refugee status or the existence of facts that, had they been known at the time of recognition, would have resulted in a negative decision, and exercise of activities contrary to national security or public order. The case of exiting the country without prior authorization from the Brazilian government has been the subject of Resolution 5 of CONARE paragraph 5, of March 11, 1999, subsequently revoked by Resolution 12, of April 29, 2005, which regulates international travel authorization for refugees, the issuance of Brazilian passports for refugees, when necessary, as well as procedures for losing refugee status due to unauthorized international travel.

support for the refugee population; and approve normative instructions clarifying the implementation of Law 9.474 of 1997.

Each of the following entities has a representative, who, together, make up the CONARE:[16] Ministry of Justice, which presides over it, Ministry of Foreign Affairs, Ministry of Labor, Ministry of Health, Ministry of Education and Sports, Federal Police Department and a nongovernmental organization that is dedicated to assistance and protection of the refugee population in the country, which is currently Caritas.**** UNHCR is an invited member of CONARE meetings, with "voice no vote" status.

The General Coordinator of CONARE is responsible for preparing the case docket for deliberation and the agenda of the meetings. CONARE can meet with a quorum of four members with the right to vote, acting by a simple majority. In the event of a tie, the vote of the President of CONARE shall be considered decisive. Thus, in practice, once the agenda has been defined, the "group of preliminary studies" (formed by CONARE's General Coordinator, representatives of UNHCR, the Ministry of Foreign Affairs, Federal Police and civil society) meets to assess requests in order to speed up the effective decision-making at the plenary session that formally recognizes refugee status or denies the request.[17]

The direct membership of civil society and UNHCR's participation in CONARE are evidence of the tripartite character of refugee status determination in Brazil. This is a second innovation in procedural terms, and seeks to ensure a more holistic approach to protection since the reception of refugees and refugee seekers is made by Brazil as a whole and not only by the Brazilian government. This characteristic is verified not only in the decision-making moment, but also throughout the procedure and reception of the refugee population in Brazil.

In general terms, the procedure for the recognition of refugee status***** begins with the asylum seeker presenting him/herself to the competent authority - the nearest Federal Police from the asylum seekers' location- to express his/her wish to apply for refugee status. The process is free and deemed urgent. A statement is taken and formally marks the establishment of the procedures. It should be emphasized that irregular entry into the national territory does not impede the request for refuge.[18] UNHCR should be informed of the request for refugee status and may offer suggestions to facilitate its progress.[19]

The asylum seeker provides statements regarding the circumstances of his/her entry into Brazil and the reasons why s/he left his/her country of origin or of habitual residence. The asylum seeker then fills out, with the assistance of an

---

[16] The representatives mentioned are designated by the President, from indications by the organs and the entity that compose it. (Law 9.474 / 97, art. 14, § 2).

**** Since the publication of this article there are also invited members at CONARE as the *Defensoria Pública da União* and the *Ministério Público Federal.*

[17] For further analysis of CONARE's actions: LEÃO, 2007, p. 148-152.

***** Since the publication of this article CONARE has adopted Normative Resolution 18 that details (and, in some instances, changes) the procedure of refugee status determination in Brazil and institutionalizes some practices, such as the one referring to the group of preliminary studies.

[18] See art. 8 of Law 9.474 / 97.

[19] See art. 18 sole paragraph of Law 9.474 / 97. See Resolution 18 for changes in procedures.

interpreter if necessary, a questionnaire for the request of recognition as a refugee, indicating full identification, professional qualification, degree of education of the applicant and members of his/her family group, as well as the formal report of the circumstances and facts that substantiate the request for refuge, including indication of pertinent evidence.

Law 9.474 of 1997 establishes that the registration of the formal request declaration[20] and supervision of the fulfillment of the request for refuge must be carried out by qualified employees and in conditions that guarantee the secrecy of the information. In practice, there will be a difference if the process starts before the Federal Police in Rio de Janeiro or in São Paulo or in other cities of the country, since Rio de Janeiro and São Paulo are headquarters of Caritas Arquidiocesana do Rio de Janeiro and Caritas Arquidiocesana de São Paulo,[21],****** which assist the applicant during the process, at the Refugee Reception Centers. Thus, when the refugee counts on these Refugee Centers, s/he receives a more effective support. In order to address such situation, Caritas Arquidiocesana in Rio de Janeiro and São Paulo and UNHCR seek to build and expand a network of solidarity, involving entities outside the Rio-São Paulo axis, so that refugee applicants have effective support wherever they are located in Brazil.*******

After receiving the request for refuge and a declaration of CONARE, the Federal Police issues a protocol in favor of the applicant and his/her family group that is with him/her in the national territory. This will be recorded in the protocol of the asylum seeker and in the name of those responsible for those under the age of fourteen.[22],******** This protocol authorizes the legal stay of the applicant and his/her relatives in Brazil until the final decision of the process. Based on this protocol and observing its period of validity, the Ministry of Labor issues a provisional work permit for the exercise of remunerated activities in the country at

---

[20] CONARE's Resolution 1 of October 27, 1998, established the model for the Declaration Statement to be completed by the Federal Police during the initial retreat request. The resolution states that the said term should be referred to the General Coordination of CONARE, with a copy to the appropriate Archdiocesan Caritas, aimed at completing the questionnaire will enable the examination of the application.

[21] The Normative Resolution of CONARE No 2 of 27 October 1998, sets the model questionnaire to be completed by the asylum seeker. The resolution determines that the questionnaire is to be completed at the headquarters of the respective Caritas Archdiocese and subsequently forwarded to the General Coordination of CONARE, for the relevant procedures which must issue a statement certifying that the foreigner requested refuge, allowing him/her to obtain the protocol to be issued by the Federal Police. The amendments introduced by Resolution 9 of August 6, 2002, sets that in districts where there are no headquarters of Caritas, the filling must be made at the Federal Police Department and forwarded along with the formal statement of the request.

****** See Resolution 18 for changes in procedures

******* Since the publication of this article, refugee status requests have been decentralized in Brazil, even though São Paulo and Rio de Janeiro remain the main centers.

[22] CONARE's Resolution 6 of 26 May 1999 concerns the granting of the to the protocol to asylum seeker. It is understood that the Federal Police will issue a protocol on behalf of the applicant and his/her family group which is on national territory, following a declaration provided by the General Coordination of CONARE. The period of validity of the protocol is ninety days, extendable for equal period, until the final decision of the process.

******** Resolution 18 also changed the validity of the protocol to 1 year. More recently Decree 9.277 of February 5, 2018, determines the protocol entitles the asylum seeker to the *Documento Provisório de Registro Nacional Migratório* (Provisional Document of National Migratory Registry) which is valid for the duration of the procedure in CONARE.

the request of the asylum seeker.

While the process related to the request for refuge is pending, applicants are subjected to the legislation regarding foreigners - Law 6,815, of August 19, 1980 (known as the Foreigners Statute)********* -, respecting the specific provisions set forth by Law 9.474 of 1997. Interestingly, the request for refugee status suspends, until a final decision on it, any pending extradition proceedings, based on the same facts justifying recognition of refugee status, as well as any administrative or criminal proceedings due to an illegal entry .[23] Therefore, the request must be communicated to the agency in which the process or procedure is conducted.

Subsequently, the competent authority shall proceed with the actions requested by CONARE, and shall inquire into the facts, whose knowledge is convenient for a just and prompt decision, while respecting the principle of confidentiality. After this instruction, the competent authority shall prepare a report which shall be sent to the General Coordinator of CONARE for the inclusion of the case in the agenda of the next meeting. If the applicant does not follow up within six months to any of the legal procedures that aim at the final decision of the request or does not comply with the summons addressed to him/her, his request for refuge will be subject to refusal by CONARE. The rejection shall be published in the *Diário Oficial da União* – the official newspaper.[24]

Any person that intervenes in refugee status request proceedings shall keep professional secrecy relating to the information to which they shall have access in the course of their duties.

Article 26 of Law 9.474 of 1997 is of extreme relevance as it states that the decision to recognize refugee status is considered a declaratory act and must be duly substantiated. Once the decision has been taken, CONARE notifies the applicant and the Federal Police of appropriate administrative measures. In the case of a positive decision, the refugee is registered with the Federal Police and must sign a responsibility term[25] and request its identity card, which carries, expressly, the recognized refugee status.

The recognition of refugee status impedes the continuation of any request for extradition based on the facts underlying the recognition of refugee status.[26] Nor

---

********* On November 2017, a new migration law (Law 13.445) entered into force in Brazil. This is the new normative on migrants in Brazil.

[23] See Arts. 10:34 of Law 9.474 / 97.

[24] CONARE' s Resolution 7 of August 6, 2002, came to regulate the adoption of procedures and compliance with official notifications and requests of presence, and was revoked by Resolution 11 of April 29, 2005, which had, as its aim, to provide for the publication of the notification provided for in art. 29 of Law 9.474 / 97, that is, to establish the start of the appeal period in question, where the person concerned is not found. The resolution established that will be subject to rejection by CONARE without merit analysis, the request for recognition of refugee status of an asylum seeker that does not comply with any legal proceedings aimed at the final decision on the application within six months, or who does not attend to the calls made to it.

[25] CONARE's Resolution 3 of 27 October 1998 established the template for the Responsibility Term that must precede refugee status registration at the Federal Police. There is the provision that the competent authority shall use an interpreter in cases where the applicant does not speak Portuguese, aiming to fully enable awareness of the term's content.

[26] The Supreme Court voted for the constitutionality of Law 9.474 / 97 regarding the possibility of the recognition of refugee status precluding extradition, justifying such a stance as it believes that given that

can a refugee who is regularly registered be expelled from the national territory, except for reasons of national security or public order. If an expulsion is performed, it cannot be to a country where the life, liberty or physical integrity of the refugee may be at risk, and can only be done when there is certainty of his/her admission to a country where there are no risks of persecution. The recognition of refugee status also implies the archiving of administrative and criminal procedures and procedures due to irregular entry into Brazil.

The specific bases of a negative decision by CONARE must be provided on its notification to the asylum seeker.[27] A right of appeal to the Minister of Justice, within a period of fifteen days from the receipt of the notification, is available. During the evaluation of the appeal, the applicant and his/her family members may remain in the national territory as asylum seekers.

The decision of the Minister of Justice shall not be subject to appeal in the administrative sphere, and shall be notified to CONARE, for the knowledge of the applicant, and to the Federal Police, for appropriate measures. If there is a final refusal of recognition of refugee status, the applicant will be subjected to the general law for foreigners in Brazil and transfers to their country of nationality or habitual residence, while the circumstances that endanger his/her life, physical integrity and freedom remain may not occur, except in cases where s/he has committed a crime against peace, war crime, crime against humanity, heinous crime, has participated in terrorist acts or drug trafficking, or is found guilty of acts contrary to the purposes and principles of the United Nations.

Notwithstanding the refusal in the administrative process, access to justice should be guaranteed to all persons in Brazilian territory. So, an asylum seeker might go to Courts of Law to access whether the decision was in accordance with the provisions of Law 9.474 of 1997, as, given that the recognition of refugee status is a declaratory and not constitutive act, there may be a violation of a right of the applicant if the request is refused.

In addition to the procedure described above, there is also the possibility of extending refugee status to the spouse, the ascendants and descendants, as well as other members of the family group that depend economically on the refugee, provided that they are in the national territory. Refugees must therefore seek the Federal Police to formalize the request for refugee status, by means of a statement, when their relatives arrive in Brazil.

CONARE's Resolution 4, dated of March 11, 1999, determined that the effects of refugee status could be extended as a family reunion, and considers as dependents for this purpose: the spouse; unmarried children under 21 years of age, natural or adoptive, or older when they cannot provide for themselves; grandchildren, grand-grandchildren or nephews, if orphaned, unmarried and under

---

refuge and extradition are executive competence in Brazil there would be no violation of the separation of powers. See BRAZIL, BRAZIL 2001 and 2007.

[27] Resolution 8 of August 6, 2002 dealt with the rejection notification of the application for refugee status recognition. It was determined that the rejection of the application for recognition of refugee status of an asylum seeker that within six months from the date of the decision of CONARE is not found to receive proper notice is to be published in the official newspaper.

21 years of age, or of any age when they cannot afford to support themselves.[28] A minor whose parents are in prison or missing is deemed an orphan. Attached to said Resolution is the form for family reunification.

Lastly, there is still an incipient temporary protection mechanism, established by CONARE's Resolution 13 of March 23, 2007, which provides for referral of special situations by CONARE to the National Immigration Council (*Conselho Nacional de Imigração* -CNIg). According to this resolution, the cases of request for refuge that do not comply with the eligibility requirements of Law 9.474 of 1997 can be analyzed by the CNIg and be granted permanence authorization, based on humanitarian conditions. It is not, therefore, a mechanism that can be requested by the foreigner himself, demanding the initiative of CONARE.

3.2. Brazil as a resettlement country

The international refugee protection system is based on three "durable solutions": 1) local integration; 2) repatriation; and 3) resettlement.

Local integration is the "adaptation of the refugee to the society of the host country which granted refuge".[29] In this regard, the Brazilian legal order provided for the possibility of refugees obtaining permanent residency. CNIg's Normative Resolution of August 21, 1997, provides that the Ministry of Justice, safeguarding national interests, may grant permanent residency to a foreigner who is a refugee or asylee, who can prove that s/he meets one of the following requirements: 1) have resided in Brazil for at least six years as a refugee or asylee; 2) is a qualified professional and in hire by an institution installed in the country, in which case the Ministry of Labor should be heard; 3) is a professional with recognized capacity by a relevant body in his/her area; and 4) is established with a business resulting from equity investment that satisfies the CNIg's regulatory resolution objectives regarding the granting of a visa to a foreign investor.[30] The possibility of naturalization, in turn, is subordinated to the precepts existing in the Brazilian Constitution of 1988 (CF/88) and the Foreigners Statute.[31]

Repatriation is the refugee's return to his/her country of origin or of habitual residence once the risks to his/her life, safety, freedom or physical integrity have ceased, that is, once the risks of persecution have ceased.

Resettlement, on the other hand:

> *Can be understood in two ways: at the beginning of UNHCR's activities it was the practice of transferring refugees from one State to another and could even be from their State of origin directly to the host State, i.e. the actual transfer of a refugee to a country*

---

[28] The evaluation of the dependent's condition that cannot provide for their own meet the criteria of physical and mental order and must be declared by a physician.

[29] JUBILUT, 2007, p.154 (free translation)

[30] CONARE's Resolution 10, of September 22, 2003 came to provide for the situation of refugees holders of permanent residency, stating that the stay does not require the assignment or the loss of refugee status, as well as other provisions regarding the issuance of identity documents and issuance of Brazilian passport refugee in permanent situation. See the new migration law for changes in these possibilities.

[31] Art. 34 of the Convention 51 requires States to facilitate as far as possible, the assimilation and naturalization of refugees, struggling especially to accelerate the naturalization process and reduce as far as possible the charges and costs of such proceedings. See the new migration law for changes in these possibilities.

of asylum; nowadays it is the transfer of individuals already recognized as refugees but who have not adapted to the host country (also called asylum country or first country), to another State, which is denominated third country, which meets more adequately the needs of these individuals.[32]

UNHCR functions as the interlocutor in the resettlement process, trying to secure the needs of individuals and seeking the necessary cooperation from States that accept to receive resettled refugees, since resettlement is not a right of individuals.

Brazil accepted the challenge of becoming a resettlement country in 1999, when it celebrate a Framework Agreement for the Resettlement of Refugees with UNHCR, based on Article 46 of Law 9.474 of 1997. Since then, the resettlement project in Brazil has been in implementation.[33]

The first group of resettled refugees in Brazil was composed of Afghans who arrived in the country in 2002 and were received in Porto Alegre. Nearly half of the resettled refugees returned to Afghanistan in 2003 by choice, and the pilot project was assessed as having positive outcomes.

In 2004, a new phase of resettlement began in Brazil, when, at the commemorations of the anniversary of the Cartagena Declaration, Brazil proposed the idea of resettlement in solidarity, which is a humanitarian approach to resettlement with a regional focus. The proposal would be to assist States in the region that were hosting large numbers of refugees from the Colombian conflict, and to select refugees for resettlement based on humanitarian criteria.

This proposal became part of the regional initiative of the Mexico Declaration and Plan of Action to Strengthen the International Protection of Refugees in Latin America[34] and to guide resettlement in Brazil. And with it, there was an increase in the number of resettled refugees received by the country and the entities involved in hosting them in partnership with UNHCR and the Brazilian government. Currently there are three entities that work with refugees resettled in Brazil: the *Associação Antonio Vieira* (in Rio Grande do Sul), *Caritas Brasileira – Regional São Paulo* (in São Paulo) and the *Centro de Direitos Humanos e Memória Popular* (in Rio Grande do Norte).[35]

In 2008, there were further changes to the initial project, with the arrival of a large group of Palestinians, an estimated taken considering the average number of refugees received by Brazil. The resettlement of the Palestinians has shown that despite the regional focus proposed for resettlement, the Brazilian project remains attentive and supportive of the universal challenges and has sought to accommodate refugees in need of international protection, thus fulfilling its

---

[32] JUBILUT, 2007, p.154. (free translation)

[33] For details on resettlement in Brazil, see JUBILUT, 2007, p. 199 et seq.

[34] Adopted during the Commemorative Meeting of the Twentieth Anniversary of the Cartagena Declaration on Refugees, held in Mexico City, Mexico, on 15 and 16 November 2004.

[35] Besides the two partners in the reception of people seeking refuge in Brazil (Caritas Arquidiocesana do Rio de Janeiro and Caritas Arquidiocesana de São Paulo) and the three resettlement partners, o *Instituto Migração e Direitos Humanos* is also UNHCR's partner and Brazilian government in protecting and reception to refugees in Brazil.

humanitarian responsibilities.

4. In search of integral protection for the refugee population in Brazil

Having presented the history and the current characteristics of the reception and protection of the refugee population in Brazil in the previous items, this paper now turns to analyzing how they can be deepened, in order to reach integral protection for the refugee population in Brazil.

4.1. International Refugee Law as a protective branch for the international protection of human beings

The doctrine identifies three branches of the international protection of human beings: International Human Rights Law, International Humanitarian Law and International Refugee Law. From a compartmentalized view, based on diverse historical origins, international doctrine and practice are moving towards normative interaction among these three branches of Public International Law, despite their differences in terms of means of implementation, supervision or control in certain circumstances.[36] Thus, it is increasingly difficult to deny complementarity between the aforementioned branches, which are guided by the same purpose - the protection of human beings in any and all circumstances.

The causes that motivate requests for refugee status constitute, in essence, violations of human rights enshrined in international treaties, especially in terms of their civil and political status. At the Latin-American level, the Cartagena Declaration reaffirms this understanding by establishing in its third conclusion, with reference to the OAU Convention and the doctrine used in the reports of the Inter-American Commission on Human Rights, that the definition or concept of refugee recommended for use in the region is the one that in addition to the elements of the 1951 Convention and the 1967 Protocol, also consider as refugees:

> [...] *persons who have fled their countries because their life, security or freedom have been threatened by widespread violence, foreign aggression, internal strife, massive violation of human rights or other circumstances that have seriously disrupted the public order.*

In the same way, as the process of requesting refuge occurs in relation to a State, it must observe due process guarantees provided for in human rights instruments. Whether or not refugee status is recognized, the asylum seeker does not cease to be a subject of human rights and must be respected in his/her dignity. Thus, before, during and after the request for refuge, the asylum seeker cannot be deprived of human rights - civil, political, economic, social and cultural - to which s/he is entitled to, under the terms established by International Law, due only to his/her human condition.

In this perspective, art. 48 of Law 9.474 of 1997 is of extreme importance when it provides that:

> *The provisions of this Law shall be interpreted in accordance with the 1948 Universal Declaration of Human Rights, the 1951 Convention Relating to Status of Refugees, the 1967*

---

[36] See CANÇADO TRINDADE; PEYTRIGNET; SANTIAGO, 2004 and JUBILUT, 2007, p. 51 et seq.

*Protocol Relating to Statute of Refugees and all provisions of applicable international instrument on the protection of human rights to which the Brazilian Government is bound.*In this sense, the obligation that refuge in Brazil be considered from a standpoint of international protection of human rights, in line with all the human rights treaties ratified by the Brazilian State and with the internal norms related to these rights, is established, given that only in this way, it will be possible to ascertain integral protection to the refugee population in Brazil.

Regarding the relationship between the international and domestic spheres and the acceptance by Brazil of the jurisdiction of the Inter-American Court of Human Rights, it should be mentioned that the Inter-American Human Rights System has a rich jurisprudence relating to the protection of the refugee population, demonstrating the relationship between International Refugee Law and International Human Rights Law.[37]

In the Constitutional Court vs. Peru case,[38] for example, the Inter-American Court of Human Rights stated that the listing of minimum guarantees of due process (art. 8.2. of the American Convention) must be respected in any State act concerning the determination of the rights of individuals[39] and is not restricted only to criminal proceedings, which explains, therefore, its application in refugee status determination procedures.

Importantly, in terms of the relationship between the protection of the refugee population and human rights, a focus on refugee status determination procedures is not enough, as it is also necessary that the link also exists at the time of durable solution (voluntary repatriation, local integration, resettlement), thus ensuring the respect for all human rights and not only the rights specifically granted to refugees.

As a result, the analysis of integral protection of the refugee population in Brazil will be made in the next two items, initially considering refugee status determination procedures and subsequently, especially considering economic, social and cultural rights, whose realization is a critical factor at the time of the durable solution, requiring the planning and implementation of specific public policies for refugees.

4.2 Refugee status determination procedures in Brazil and human rights

The analysis of refugee status determination procedures in Brazil, described in this article from the standpoint of the international protection of human beings, allows for the identification of a few issues of particular importance regarding the respect of human rights of the refugee population.

In this regard, one should pay more attention, for example, to the asylum seeker's right to be assisted by an interpreter during the refugee status determination procedure. In practice, although there is a legal provision in this regard in Brazil, it is verified that the translation is often precarious, made by a recognized refugee who knows the language of the applicant, which is far from the

---

[37] See INTER-AMERICAN COURT OF HUMAN DERECHOS, 2007 and COMISION INTER-AMERICAN HUMAN DERECHOS, 2006.

[38] INTER-AMERICAN COURT OF HUMAN DERECHOS 2001.

[39] Art. 14 I of the Universal Declaration of Human Rights of 1948 states that "Every man, persecution of the victim has the right to seek and to enjoy asylum in other countries."

ideal provided by the Law. This same concern applies after the recognition, at the signing of the abovementioned responsibility term, since this document contains information of extreme relevance to the refugee that, if not observed, can cause the loss of the refugee status. One such example is the need of prior authorization for any travels abroad.

Another issue is the motivation of the decision mentioned in Law 9.474 of 1997, which should be included in the notification of both the approval and the rejection of the request for refuge. The notification given by CONARE, in general, only indicates that the application was accepted based on art. 1 of Law 9.474 of 1997 or that it was rejected because it did not comply with the provisions of the Law or, more recently, that there is no credibility or that there is not a well-founded fear of persecution. Even if one considers the need for confidentiality, this type of motivation does not allow for the petitioner, when his request is rejected, to bring an appropriate appeal to the Minister of Justice, or even before the Judiciary.

Moreover, in this regard, an express provision in Law 9.474 of 1997 for access to the Judiciary, to inquire about the eligibility of the request for refuge could allow for cases of refusal of refugee status to be analyzed more frequently by Courts; since the refugee population is unaware of the Brazilian legal system and, in particular, the constitutional provision of art. 5, XXXV of the Brazilian Constitution of 1988, that guarantees everyone's access to justice .[40] In addition, this would encourage reflection among lawyers on the coherence between protective norms of refuge and human rights, allowing for fairer decisions.

Law 9.474 of 1997 was generic when considering asylum seekers. Thus, there are no specific procedures pertaining to refuge for cases where applicants are minors, elderly, mentally ill, disabled, or victims of torture, cruel or inhumane treatment, among other situations of greater vulnerability. This mismatch with the trend of specification of human rights subjects would not be a failure of the legislation if the whole procedure were guided by an integral protection approach, based on the international obligations provided for by universal and regional instruments regarding specific protection in the case of women; children involved

---

[40] "Regarding the Brazilian case it turns out that it is scarce regarding the issue of refugees, with only 18 judgments on the issue. In the cases of the Supreme Court, they are varied in nature: 1) there is a case that deals with a negative decision in the refugee status determination procedure - Mandate 24304 / DF, 04/09/2002; 2) two cases concerning the application for a prohibition of expulsion on the basis of the person being a refugee - Habeas Corpus 69268 / DF of 05/22/1992 and Habeas Corpus 71935 / SC of 27/10/94; 3) nine cases concerning the request for an extradition fence claiming the refugee status of the person to be extradited - Extradition 232 of 09/10/1961, Extradition 419 / ES of 04/24/1985, Extradition 524 / PG of 31 / Second issue of order in extradition 785 / ME of 13/09/2001, Complaint 2069 / DF of 06/27/2002, Agravo Regimental in the records of the Extradition 783 / ME of 06/26/2002, Habeas Corpus 83501 / DF of 10/29/2003, Declaratory Embargoes in Extradition 785 / ME of 27/3 / 2003-; 4) and three cases that deal with the relaxation of the prison for extradition when a request for refuge is made - Habeas Corpus 81127 / DF of November 28, 2001, Second extradition issue 783 / ME of 11/28/2001, Second question Of order in extradition 784 / ME of 11/28/2001. The judgments of the Superior Court of Justice are three (Agravo Regimental of the Security Order 12212 / DF, Habeas corpus 36033 / DF and Habeas corpus 32622 / DF), and denote, on the one hand, the ignorance of the refugee issue (by referring to the application for recognition as a refugee as a request for recognition as a "fugitive" or referring to the Brazilian law on refugees as Law 4,947 of 1997, when the correct is Law 9.474 of 1997) and, on the other hand, tend to always go in favor of the decisions of the National Committee for Refugees [CONARE] even when finding that the motivation for refusal of recognition of refugee status is "laconic". See JUBILUT, 2007, p. 102-103, 195.

in armed conflicts and children in general; victims of torture; cruel and inhuman treatment; and disabled people.

To ensure respect for the human rights of the persons mentioned above, it is essential that the *Defensoria Pública* is involved in the procedures, to facilitate within the Judiciary the necessary measures to ensure representation of minors, elderly, and mentally ill when needed. It is also necessary to begin exploring the possibilities for reparations by the States that inflicted the violations, when this does not endanger the integrity of the refugee population itself. The involvement of the *Defensoria Pública* embodies art. 16 of the 1951 Convention which establishes that refugees must have free and easy access to the courts, and enjoy the same treatment as a national in matters pertaining the access to courts, including legal aid and exemption from costs *cautio judicatum solvi*.

From all the above, one sees that as the minimum standards of International Refugee Law are present in the protection of refugees in terms of refugee status determination procedures in Brazil, it is now time for the next step: to incorporate the challenges brought by human rights in the seeking of a more holistic interpretation of the international protection of the human being in order to allow for integral protection of the refugee population in the country.

4.3. The protection of the refugee population in the sphere of economic, social and cultural rights

The relationship between economic, social and cultural rights and the refugee population can be analyzed from four perspectives: 1) the violation of these rights as motivation for the seeking of protection through refuge;[41] 2) the violation of said rights during displacement; 3) the protection of the refugee population in countries of asylum; and 4) the violation of these rights from the moment the refugees return to their countries of origin. The third perspective concerns the scope of this article, that is, how the protection of economic, social and cultural rights of the refugee population in Brazil is being addressed.

At the outset, it should be emphasized that human rights are not only citizens or nationals rights. Refugees also have the right to protection under International Human Rights Law, including economic, social and cultural rights. Art. 5 of the Brazilian Constitution of 1988 affirms that "all are equal before the law", without distinction of any kind, guaranteeing to Brazilians and foreigners residing in the country the inviolability of the rights to life, liberty, equality, security and property. Thus, the Brazilian constitutional legal regime protects both Brazilians and foreigners.

In addition, the Brazilian Supreme Court upheld the interpretation that, in accordance with the provisions of the caput of art. 5, foreigners living in the country are entitled to fundamental rights and guarantees.[42] The refugee population, thus, has the right, as well as all persons, to an adequate standard of living, food and shelter, as well as physical and mental health.

The 1951 Convention contains some, albeit limited, provisions relating to

---

[41] On this perspective, see FOSTER, 2007.
[42] See BRAZIL, 1996.

economic, social and cultural rights.[43] In light of this, the protection of these rights is not only a matter of humanitarian assistance, but is rather an international obligation assumed by Brazil, as it has ratified that international instrument and which is constitutionally obligated to guarantee human rights also to foreigners residing in its territory.

Article 7 of the 1951 Convention begins by stating that "subject to the most favorable provisions of this Convention, a Contracting State shall accord to refugees the regime it grants to aliens in general." In this sense, most of the provisions relating to economic, social and cultural rights in the 1951 Convention provide that a Member State shall accord to refugees the "most favorable treatment" granted to nationals of a foreign country "in the same circumstances".[44] Chapter III of the 1951 Convention deals with paid employment, including the situation of employees,[45] self-employed[46] and liberal professionals.[47]

Those refugees who are able to obtain a job must, under the terms of the 1951 Convention, benefit from the same treatment as nationals with respect to remuneration and other rights related to work, as well as social security, subject to the restrictions listed in art. 24. Freedom of association without political or lucrative purposes, and related to professional unions was guaranteed in art. 15 of Convention 51, and the "most favorable treatment" is granted.

In Brazil, as seen, the right to work is guaranteed to the refugee population, and the rights arising from an employment relationship and related to social security also are. However, in practice, the refugee population faces problems in order to work, either due to difficulties with the language, lack of experience or impossibility of proving previous experience, lack of qualification, social discrimination[48] or

---

[43] Under International Law, a person is considered a refugee for satisfying the definition provided in the 1951 Convention regardless of the domestic process of determining refugee status. But in practice, it appears that the refugees may be unable to have access to the rights under the 1951 Convention until they have been formally recognized as refugees by the domestic authorities of the countries of asylum. Domestic authorities generally consider that asylum seekers are not entitled to specific protections of the 1951 Convention.

[44] Art. 6 of the 1951 Convention explains that the phrase "in the same circumstances" implies that all the conditions that the person concerned would have to meet in order to exercise the right in question, if s/he were not a refugee, must be fulfilled by him/her, with the exception of conditions, because of their nature, that cannot be filled by a refugee.

[45] Art. 17 Convention b 51 stipulated that the restrictive measures imposed on aliens or the employment of aliens for the protection of the national labor market shall not apply to refugees who meet one of the following conditions: i) have three years of residency in the country ; ii) have a spouse who holds the citizenship of the country of residence; iii) having one or more children possessing the nationality of the country of residence; iv) Member States shall consider favorably the adoption of measures to assimilate the rights of all refugees with regard to wage-earning employment to those of their nationals and in particular for the refugees who have entered their territory pursuant a hand recruitment program of work or immigration schemes.

[46] Art. 18 of the 1951 Convention sets the "more favorable treatment" regarding the exercise of a profession self-employed in agriculture, industry, handicrafts, trade and the installation of commercial and industrial firms.

[47] Art. 19 of the 1951 Convention established the "more favorable treatment" to refugees lawfully staying in their territory who hold diplomas recognized by the competent authorities of the State of refuge wishing to pursue a profession.

[48] The issuance of work documents (CTPS) was regulated by CONARE's Resolution 7 of August 6, 2002, and the Circular Letter 103/2006 (CIRP / CGSAP / DES / SPPE / MTE). The Ministry of Labor sought to dispel the discrimination by the labor market and determined not to use the nomenclature "refugee" in the identification of labor documentation. See Barbosa; HORA, 2007, p. 60.

impossibility of exercising the original profession performed in the country of origin for not being able to prove training through the presentation of documents or for the language related difficulties to succeed in qualifying exams, notwithstanding the provisions of articles 43 and 44 of Law 9.474 of 1997. This scenario is exacerbated by the impact of the international financial crisis on unemployment rates.

The 1951 Convention continues to provide that the same treatment accorded to nationals should be accorded to refugees if there is a system of rationing of scarce products (Article 20); as regards primary education (Article 22 (1)); and in matters of public assistance and relief (Article 23). Treatment which is as favorable as possible and in any case no less favorable than that given to foreigners in the same circumstances should be given to refugees as regards accommodation, subject to the control of public authorities or regulated by Laws or regulations (Article 21). The same is also true with regard to education, in addition to primary education, and in particular in relation to access to studies, the recognition of study certificates, foreign diplomas and degrees, exemption from fees and the granting of scholarships (Article 22, 2).

The 1951 Convention contains no provision regarding the adequate standard of living or of physical and mental health and does not contain clear mandatory provisions regarding the role of the family. However, other international instruments, such as the International Covenant on Economic, Social and Cultural Rights, and the Protocol of San Salvador, based on the principle of non-discrimination, should not be forgotten.

In the Brazilian legal system, education is a right for everyone,[49] therefore, also of the entire refugee population. However, some children, due to lack of documents, such as birth certificates or its equivalent, face problems in accessing day care centers and schools, requiring the intervention of the Judiciary to exercise the constitutionally guaranteed rights. As far as university education is concerned there is no consistent public policy, and the access of refugees to higher education depends on *ad hoc* decisions of educational institutions.

In Brazil, social assistance aims to provide basic needs relating to the protection of family, maternity, childhood, adolescence, elderly and disabled persons, regardless of their contribution to social security schemes. Its foundation is human solidarity, which has in the State an instrument of action, aiming at the protection of person deprived of the means to survive with dignity.

Because of the causes of his/her flight, the involuntary nature of the displacement and, in most cases, the difficulties of the flight, when s/he is completely vulnerable, the asylum seeker usually arrives traumatized in the country where s/he seeks refuge, without financial resources or other means of subsistence. Because of the situation that led to the flight, the refugee may have lost or been forcibly severed from his/her family or community, which, in addition to emotional

---

[49] In accordance with Art. 205 of CF/88, education is everyone's right and A duty of the State and the family and should be promoted and encouraged with the cooperation of society, aiming at the full development of the person, his/her preparation for the exercise of citizenship and his/her qualification for job.

traumas, may also mean the loss of a provider. In general, the refugee does not speak the language of the country of asylum and may also face hostility from residents of the country arising from racial or other kinds of discrimination. In this way, s/he needs the support of social assistance.

Article 203 of the Brazilian Constitution of 1988 determines as follows:

> *Social assistance shall be rendered to whomever may need it, regardless of contribution to social welfare and shall have as objectives: I – the protection of the family, maternity, childhood, adolescence and old age; II – the assistance to needy children and adolescents; III – the promotion of the integration into the labour market; IV – the habilitation and rehabilitation of the handicapped and their integration into community life; V – the guarantee of a monthly benefit of one minimum wage to the handicapped and to the elderly who prove their incapability of providing for their own support or having it provided for by their families, as set forth by law.*

Thus, social assistance will be provided to those who need it, not excluding foreigners, let alone refugees.

Regarding the right to health, since health in Brazil is a universal right,[50] what is needed are policies to facilitate access to the system. *Ad hoc* actions subjected to political will and often due to supportive people in institutions can be identified, but they do not guarantee continuity if there is political change or if the person is transferred from the institution or even from the position previously occupied.

This is the case of the creation of what was called the *Centro de Referência para a Saúde dos Refugiados* (Reference Center for Refugees' Health) at the *Hospital dos Servidores do Estado do Rio de Janeiro*. There is no legal instrument creating such a Reference Center, nor determining the training policies of health workers. Such initiatives are due to the efforts of individuals involved within the institution and civil society. Notwithstanding the risk of discontinuity, it contributes to indicating the path of entry into the health system for the refugee population, which is not prohibited to any foreigner, according to the constitutional norms.

The refugee population is not homogeneous, which means that this group may have different practical experiences and varying problems in the countries of asylum. Angolans, Congolese, Colombians, Iraqis, Afghans, etc. certainly face different situations in everyday life in Brazil. However, there is a common problem shared by all, regardless of nationality, social origin or any other criterion: the refugee population faces practical problems in realizing their economic, social and cultural rights.

In Brazil, there are no refugee camps, in which case a specific and complex logistic should be in play for the realization of human rights. There is, as seen, a procedure that takes a certain time for the recognition of refugee status, the need to obtain the required documents for residency and work permit, and the need to learn the way of accessing the benefits to which one is entitled to as a refugee or as a human being. All these challenges are even more hampered by the lack of

---

[50] Art. 196 of CF/88 recognizes that health is everyone's right and a duty of the State, guaranteed through social and economic policies aimed at reducing the risk of disease and other health problems and the universal and equal access to actions and services for its promotion, protection and recovery.

knowledge of the language and other integration difficulties that can range from discrimination on the part of the community of the country of asylum, traumas suffered and their after effects, to the lack of knowledge by the State agents that foreigners are entitled to rights, and, in some circumstances, have specific rights.

It is important to emphasize that the current interpretation of the economic, social and cultural rights of the refugee population adopts the situation of the country of asylum as a standard of analysis of integration. It does not advocate for differential or better treatment for refugees than for nationals, but for equal treatment as provided for in the 1951 Convention.

In view of the normative reality and practice, it is necessary to implement public policies that allow the effective realization of the economic, social and cultural rights of the refugee population, either by their inclusion in existing policies, or by the tailoring of policies to allow for their inclusion or by the creation of new policies.

This concern, which was already being debated in the doctrine,[51] is gaining space in the governmental realm. There have been initiatives by CONARE to mobilize other federal agencies to ensure that Brazil's international obligations to the refugee population are fully respected and that their economic, social and cultural rights are guaranteed.

The same role of awareness-creating has been played by UNHCR and civil society, with emphasis on the work carried out in São Paulo. In less than a year, the *Comitê Estadual para Refugiados* (São Paulo State Committee for Refugees)[52] and the *Comitê Paulista para Imigrantes e Refugiados*[53] was established to facilitate the integration of refugees and, consequently, to ensure public policies that guarantee economic, social and cultural rights of the refugee population.

These initiatives demonstrate that, gradually, Brazil is moving towards integral protection of the refugee population, and that, even if it is far from ideal, at least there seems to be a governmental awakening to the theme and a desire to deepen the protection and reception of the refugee population in Brazil. There is a need for combined action between government institutions and civil society, taking into account the obligations assumed internationally by Brazil with regards to the international protection of human beings.

5. Conclusion

The quest for integral protection of the refugee population is a challenge that must be faced if the full protection of the inherent dignity of all human beings is to be ensured. It is a continuous process of analysis and a constant search for improvement that has a greater chance of being realized when the reception and

---

[51] See, for example, Milese; AMBROS, 2007.

[52] The *Comitê Estadual para Refugiados*, established on April 1, 2008, is a government agency of the State of São Paulo, composed of representatives of state departments and Caritas of São Paulo and the Brazilian Regional São Paulo, aimed at proposing and implementing public policies to aid the integration of the refugee population in São Paulo.

[53] The *Comitê Paulista para Imigrantes e Refugiados* was established on 5 February 2009 and aims to bring together and join efforts between government and civil society for information, the proposition and implementation of public policies aimed at vulnerable populations of refugees and immigrants in São Paulo.

protection processes encompass the government, the international community and civil society.

In this sense, Brazil seems to be moving in the right direction, as are the recent initiatives to debate and create public policies that include or are specific to the refugee population.

Despite this, the advances are still shy in terms of concrete results, which can be explained by: (i) the small number of refugees and asylum seekers in Brazil; (ii) the fact that the system of refugee protection hasn't been established for a long time; (iii) the fact that Brazil's concern to respect international standards for the protection of the human being is recent in its history; (iv) the distance of the Judiciary from refugee issues and the difficulties of seeking guarantees for the respect for refugees' rights; and (v) the perennial problem of lack of political will to secure rights without a return in terms of interests and direct gains.

Brazil has taken significant steps, yet it still faces major challenges in the quest for integral protection for the refugee population. It is necessary to promote decisions, policies and actions that point to the right direction, that is, in the sense of the greatest possible protection for people who can only rely on international solidarity and cooperation.

References

1951 CONVENTION on the Status of Refugees. Available at: <http://www.cidadevirtual.pt/acnur/refworld/refworld/legal/instrume/asylum/ conv-0.html>. Accessed on: 29 jun. 2009.

APOLINÁRIO, Silvia Menicucci O. S.; JUBILUT, Liliana L. Refugee status determination in Brazil: a tripartite enterprise [Sl]:. *Refuge*, Mar. 2009. (Mimeo).

BARBOSA, Luciano Pestana; HORA, José Roberto S. *A Polícia Federal e a proteção internacional dos refugiados*. Brasília, 2007.

BRAZIL. Constitution (1988). Constitution of the Federative Republic of Brazil. Available at: <http://www.planalto.gov.br/ccivil_03/constituicao/ constitutes% C3% A7ao.htm>. Accessed on: 29 jun. 2009.

BRAZIL. Law 6,815, of July 19, 1980. Defines the legal situation of the foreigner in Brazil, creates the National Immigration Council. Available at: <http://www.planalto.gov.br/CCIVIL/LEIS/L6815.htm>. Accessed on: 26 jun. 2009.

BRAZIL. Law 9474 of July 22, 1997. Available at: <http://www.planalto.gov.br/ CCIVIL / LEIS / L9474.htm>. Accessed on: 26 jun. 2009.

BRAZIL. Superior Justice Tribunal. Criminal proceedings. Habeas corpus. Fundamental rights and guarantees of the foreigner. Habeas corpus. 74 051 of the Federal Court of the State of Santa Catarina, Brasília, June 18, 1996. Available at: <http://www.stf.jus.br/portal/processo/ verProcessoAndamento. Asp? Number = 74051 & class = HC & codeClasse = 0 & origin = AP & resource = 0 & type Judgment = M>. Accessed on: 29 jun. 2009.

BRAZIL. Federal Court of Justice. Judgment. Extradition: Colombia: crimes related to the participation of the extradite - then priest of the Catholic Church - in military action of the Revolutionary Armed Forces of Colombia (FARC). Point of order ... Ext 1008 / CB - COLOMBIA. Full Court. Rapporteur: Min. Gilmar Mendes. Rapporteur (s) for Judgment: Min. Sepúlveda Pertence. Brasilia, 21 Mar. 2007. Available at: <http://www.stf.jus.br/ portal / jurisprudence / listarJurisprudencia. Asp? S1 = Ext.SCLA.% 20E% 201008.NUME. & Base = baseAccessories>. Accessed on: 29 jun. 2009.

BRAZIL. Federal Court of Justice. Judgment. Extradition. A point of order. Request for refuge. Suspension of proceedings. Law 9.474 / 97, art. 34. A point of order resolved in the sense that the request for refuge, formulated after the judgment on the merits of extradition, has the effect of suspending the proceedings, even when the judgment has already been published, preventing the appeal period from being passed. Ext 785 QO-Q / ME - MEXICO. Full Court. Rapporteur: Min. Néri da Silveira. Brasília, September 13. 2001. Available at: <http://www.stf.jus.br/portal/ jurisprudencia / listarJurisprudencia.asp? S1 = Ext-QO-QO.SCLA.% 20E% 20785. NUM. & Base = baseAcordaos>. Accessed on: 29 jun. 2009.

CANÇADO TRINDADE, A. A.; PEYTRIGNET, G. e SANTIAGO, J. R. de. *As três vertentes da proteção internacional da pessoa humana: Direitos Humanos, Direito Humanitário e Direito dos Refugiados.* São José da Costa Rica, Brasília: IIDH, Comitê Internacional da Cruz Vermelha e ACNUR, 1996.

FISCHEL DE ANDRADE, H. H; MARCOLINI, A. A política brasileira de proteção e reassentamento de refugiados: breves comentários sobre suas principais características, *Revista Brasileira de Política Internacional*, [S.l.], v. 45, n. 1, p. 168- 176, 2002

JUBILUT, Liliana L. *O direito internacional dos refugiados e sua aplicação no ordenamento jurídico brasileiro.* São Paulo: Método, 2007.

JUBILUT, Liliana L. *O procedimento de concessão de refúgio no Brasil.* Available at: <http://www.mj.gov.br/data/Pages/MJ7605B707ITEMIDA5 DA279AA51B46539284ED27C62FF31APTBRIE.htm>. Accessed on: 26 jun. 2009.

LAFER, Celso. *A reconstrução dos direitos humanos: um diálogo com o pensamento de Hannah Arendt.* 3. reimp. São Paulo: Companhia das Letras, 1999.

LEÃO, Renato Zerbini. *O reconhecimento dos refugiados pelo Brasil - Comentários sobre decisões do CONARE.* Brasília, 2007

MILESI, Rosita; AMBROS, Simone. *Políticas públicas para migrações internacionais: migrantes e refugiados.* 2. ed. Brasília, 2007.

NOGUEIRA, Maria Beatriz; MARQUES, Carla Cristina. Brazil: ten years of refugee protection. *Forced Migration Review*, [S.l.], n. 30, p. 57-58, Apr. 2008.

UNHCR. *Plan de Acción de Mexico.* Geneva, 2009. Available at: <http: // www. Acnur.org/pam/>. Accessed on: 29 jun. 2009.

HUMANITARIAN VISAS: BUILDING ON BRAZIL'S EXPERIENCE (2016)

Liliana Lyra Jubilut[*], Camila Sombra Muiños de Andrade[**] and André de Lima Madureira[***], [****]

Brazil's granting of humanitarian visas began in 2012 in favour of Haitians after the devastating earthquake that hit Haiti in 2010, and was extended in 2013 to benefit people affected by the conflict in Syria. The general national legislation on migration dates back to the period of dictatorship (from 1964 to the mid-80s) and, with its logic of national security, offers very limited possibilities of visas and of regular status for migrants. This changed a little in the late 1990s when a specific law on refugees was established, in what can be seen as a step towards accepting humanitarian grounds for staying in the country. Ever since, there have been debates focusing on changing the migration regime[*****] so as to allow for other humanitarian forms of entry and residency in the country but the only real achievement has been the introduction of ad hoc humanitarian visas for forced migrants, and even for this Brazil has been praised.

Haitians

In the aftermath of the 2010 earthquake Haitians wanting to migrate to Brazil faced two challenges: first, a regular tourist visa was required which many Haitians did not possess and, second, the routes to Brazil were risky, for instance because of the activities of human smugglers. In 2012, the Brazilian government decided to create an easier legal pathway for Haitians coming to Brazil and made it possible for humanitarian visas to be obtained at the Brazilian Embassy in Port-au-Prince, citing "the deterioration of the Haitian population's living conditions due to the

[*] Liliana Lyra Jubilut, Professor, Universidade Católica de Santos, www.unisantos.br, E-mail: lljubilut@gmail.com.

[**] Camila Sombra Muiños de Andrade, PhD candidate, Universidade de São Paulo, www.usp.br, E-mail: camilamuinos@gmail.com.

[***] André de Lima Madureira, MSc Human Rights student, London School of Economics www.lse.ac.uk and Member of the Research Group 'Human Rights and Vulnerabilities' of Universidade Católica de Santos, www.unisantos.br, E-mail: alimadureira@gmail.com.

[****] All the authors are part of PRIO's Brazil's Rise to the Global Stage (BraGS): Humanitarianism, Peacekeeping and the Quest for Great Powerhood project www.prio.org/Projects/Project/?x=1645

[*****] In 2017 Brazil adopted a new law on migration: Law 13.445.

earthquake in that country on January 12, 2010".

An initial quota of 1,200 visas a year and the limitation of visas only being issued in Port-au-Prince were later revoked. Any number of these visas could then be obtained and at any Brazilian consulate, even outside Haiti. It is important to note that the requirements for the humanitarian visas are less than for the regular tourist visa, requiring only a valid passport, proof of residency in Haiti and proof of good standing.

The visas were thus a way to facilitate the arrival of Haitians in Brazil, an innovative measure for making it easier to reach a safer country. But once in the country they did not have guaranteed migration status. In light of this, most Haitians sought refugee status, at which point they were granted temporary documentation and work permits. However, the Brazilian government's understanding was that environmental crises were not a valid reason for recognition of refugee status. The solution adopted was to refer the Haitians' refugee applications to the National Immigration Council (CNIg), which has the competence to rule on those cases considered 'special or not regulated'. CNIg granted permanent residency for humanitarian reasons to Haitians, with those Haitians who had a humanitarian visa having their migration status resolved faster. It is estimated that over 85,000 Haitians have entered Brazil since the earthquake.

Syrians

It is the Brazilian government's position that it is important for refugees to have access to procedures for applying for asylum, that it recognises the disproportionate burden that countries neighbouring conflicts may endure, and that the international community needs to take action as these are matters of international law.[1]

In light of this, in 2013 the National Committee for Refugees (CONARE) passed a resolution allowing for visas to be granted to people affected by the Syrian conflict with fewer requirements than for a regular visa.[2] Initially valid for two years, it was renewed in 2015 for a further two years.[3] [******] The resolution recognises that those who flee war and/or persecution are usually not able to fulfil the formal requirements for a Brazilian visa, such as presenting bank statements, invitation letters and a roundtrip airplane ticket. In this case, Brazilian embassies are exceptionally authorised to grant visas even when the travel document of the applicant is due to expire in less than six months and to issue a laissez-passer for those who do not possess a valid passport. However, family members of Syrian nationals who are in Brazil have not been able to get humanitarian visas for themselves. At the Brazilian diplomatic representations they have been instructed to apply for family reunification instead but as quite a few of the Syrians in Brazil are still asylum seekers, and not refugees, this demand in practice has resulted in

---

[1] Brazilian Ambassador at the High-level Meeting on Global Responsibility Sharing through Pathways for Admission of Syrian Refugees. Geneva, 30 March 2016.

[2] www.legisweb.com.br/legislacao/?id=258708

[3] www.legisweb.com.br/legislacao/?id=303612

[******] CONARE Normative Resolution 25 of September 14, 2017 extended the visas for another 2 years (i.e. until September 2019).

there being no way for family members to enter Brazil.[4]

The broad provisions of the resolution allow visas to be granted not only to Syrian nationals but also to people affected by the Syrian conflict so that minority groups such as the Palestinians and Kurds have also benefitted from the Brazilian humanitarian visa programme. Over 8,500 humanitarian visas have been granted in total[5] and 26% of all refugees in Brazil are now Syrian, at 2,298 forming the largest refugee group in the country.[6]

As in the case of Haitians, the humanitarian visas to people affected by the Syrian conflict serve as a way to facilitate travel to Brazil. Once they are in the country forms of regularisation of their migration status need to be sought.

Good, but how good?

UNHCR, the UN Refugee Agency, has praised Brazil for the use of humanitarian visas in the context of the Syrian conflict and urged other countries to take similar steps in order to facilitate regular migration channels for those affected by that conflict.

However, despite the humanitarian visas being a positive development in Brazil's migration regime, there are shortcomings. The first of these is the fact that Brazil's humanitarian visas are established through normative resolutions of administrative organs of the Executive. This means that they can expire, be amended or be revoked depending on the political will of the government. In late 2015, as the time of the expiration of the resolution on humanitarian visas for people affected by the Syrian conflict approached, there was a real risk that it was not going to be renewed. In the end it was, but uncertainty and legal insecurity are marks of both sets of visas.

A second issue is that the humanitarian visas were established and are applied in ad hoc situations based on nationality or specific contexts, that is, for specific groups of people. Thus there seems to be a violation of the principles of equality and non-discrimination. The question needs to be posed as to why migrants from similar situations are not benefiting from this form of protection.

Since both these shortcomings can be seen as adding flexibility to the implementation of the humanitarian visas, the model could appear palatable to states that might replicate it and would be able to tailor humanitarian visas to the groups and situations that they desire. However, it also adds legal uncertainty and reinforces the political nature of a humanitarian measure.

Thirdly, there is the fact that once in the country other forms of protection need to be sought. In the case of Brazil all forms of humanitarian protection lead in practice to a request for recognition of refugee status, causing severe inflation of the pressure on the system for dealing with refugees. However, there seems to be no contingency plan in the event that the people who are granted humanitarian visas are not recognised as refugees, or do not find another migration status in

---

[4] Interview with Larissa Leite, Protection Coordinator of the Refugee Center at Caritas Arquidiocesana de São Paulo.

[5] Brazilian Ambassador, as endnote 1.

[6] http://dados.mj.gov.br/dataset/comite-nacional-para-osrefugiados

Brazil.

Lastly, asylum seekers from the Syrian conflict who have been granted humanitarian visas were, for most of the period of the existence of the visas, recognized as refugees as a group on a prima facie basis, without going through individual refugee status determination. This practice could lead to the potential recognition of persecutors as refugees. Recently, however, individual interviews were reintroduced, as a simple correction of this problem.

There seem to be similarly obvious solutions to all the criticisms of the Brazilian humanitarian visas. If humanitarian visas are to become a more widespread step forward in advancing protection for humanitarian migrants, the Brazilian practice can be seen as a good starting point.

PART 2. REFUGEE PROTECTION IN LATIN AMERICA

REGIONALISM: A STRATEGY FOR DEALING WITH CRISIS MIGRATION (2014)

Liliana Lyra Jubilut[*] and Érika Pires Ramos[**]

The increasing scope, scale and complexity of population movements which are not covered by the existing mandates of international agencies or by states (and which in general affect several countries along a migration route) challenge the ability of individual states to respond and point to the need for joint strategies. In order to tackle the lack of legal protection or status of people involved in such movements, proposals have ranged from the expansion of existing systems and regimes – mainly an enlargement of the normative concept of refugee – to the creation of new legal concepts and institutions. Little though has been achieved, despite existing proposals in progress, among which two deserve mention.

First is the Draft Convention on the Protection of Persons in the Event of Disasters being developed by the UN International Law Commission which aims to regulate cooperation and assistance among affected and nonaffected states, establishing the duties to cooperate, seek assistance, consent to external assistance and offer assistance to people affected by disasters.[1]

The second is the Project for a Convention on the International Status of Environmentally Displaced Persons, drafted by research groups at the University of Limoges and other contributors (individuals and institutions), which proposes recognition of a specific legal status for a new category of migrants, that is, potential and actual victims of natural, environmental and technological disasters.[2] This proposal does not create new rights for the people affected nor an obligation on states to protect them but aims to adapt the protection of existing human rights to

---

[*] Liliana Lyra Jubilut, lljubilut@gmail.com, Professor of Law, Universidade Católica de Santos (UniSantos), Brazil.

[**] Erika Pires Ramos, erikaprs@gmail.com, Federal Attorney and co-founder of RESAMA South American Network for Environmental Migrations, Brazil.

[1] Draft Convention on the Protection of Persons in the Event of Disaster http://legal.un.org/ilc/reports/2012/english/chp5.pdf

[2] Proposed in 2008 by Centre International de Droit Comparé de l'Environnement (CIDCE), Centre de Recherche Interdisciplinaire en Droit de l'Environnement, de l'Aménagement et de l'Urbanisme (CRIDEAU) and Centre de Recherche sur les Droits de la Personne (CRDP) and others, and still under review. Projet de Convention Relative au Statut International des Desplacés Environnementaux, Second version (May 2010). http://tinyurl.com/CIDCE-Environmental-displaced

the specific condition of environmentally displaced persons.

The apparent lack of success of these and other initiatives seems to stem from the lack of willingness to adopt practical concepts of responsibility-sharing, the constant intertwining of the issue of migration (even forced displacement) with economic and security concerns, and the perception that this is a problem for which a one-time commitment will not suffice, as it requires political will for long-term endeavours and solutions.

An alternative route that could allow for new developments is a focus on regionalism. This strategy would not compete with existing efforts but would aim to complement them. Regionalism seems to be working in the field of IDPs in the absence of a global system, especially since the Kampala Convention. It has also worked in the Latin-American context of refugees through the expanded definition in the Cartagena Declaration,[3] as well as the regional approach to resettlement stemming from the periodical review of this document.[4] In 2012 the MERCOSUR Declaration of Principles on International Protection of Refugees highlighted the need for strengthening the regional humanitarian space, encouraging all states to adopt the wider definition of refugees from the 1984 Cartagena Declaration.[5]

In the same region, the institution of political asylum, recognised in international regional law since the 19th century and since the mid-20th century by the International Court of Justice as regional customary law, is another example of a regional initiative on migration. In light of the regional effects of crisis migration, regional solutions that are tailored to the specific scenarios may be politically more acceptable, and therefore more effective and easy to apply, than universally established formulae.

Indeed, it seems that regional solidarity – or at least the perception of regionally shared problems and situations – is more likely to succeed in the present world, giving time for the global system to come up with a comprehensive system of protection for migrants. Such a focus on regionalism would not jeopardise any international search for universal solutions but would enhance a rights-based approach to humanitarian situations.

That said, existing regional initiatives do not eliminate the need for adopting a global instrument and policy that set minimum general standards of protection for internally and externally displaced people and that, if necessary, provide access to international assistance but they can be a stepping stone towards them. In this sense, regionalism, especially in Latin America, emerges as a strategic option that can provide an open dialogue among states and non-state actors. It can, thus, stimulate cooperation to elaborate more coherent policies and legal frameworks to address common impacts on the countries of the region, as well as allow for the effective protection of these migrants.

---

[3] www.refworld.org/docid/3ae6b36ec.html

[4] www.refworld.org/docid/424bf6914.html

[5] Declaration of Principles on International Protection of Refugees. Unofficial English version at: http://tinyurl.com/Declaration-MERCOSUR-En

REGIONAL DEVELOPMENTS: AMERICAS (2011)

Flávia Piovesan[*] and Liliana Lyra Jubilut[**]

A. Introduction

Since the approval of its two main documents—the 1951 Convention and the 1967 Protocol—refugee law and protection have been enhanced mainly through regional developments. The Americas are a part of this trend given that, as a region, they have been vested with the purpose of deepening and broadening the refugee protection established by the universal system in theory and in practice.

In the early 1980s, the Cartagena Declaration on Refugees (Cartagena Declaration) was approved and in the following years it became part of several Latin American States' legislation on refugee protection. More recently, starting in 2004, a new regional approach to refugee protection emerged—the Mexico Plan of Action to Strengthen International Protection of Refugees in Latin America (MPA)[1]. In the meantime, the United States and Canada remain key States in receiving and protecting refugees. All of these developments coexist with the universal system, *i.e.* the 1951 Convention as altered by the 1967 Protocol.

In light of this, and as part of a collection about the 1951 Convention, this chapter aims to describe how the Americas have developed regional instruments to enhance refugee law and protection, analysing their improvements and shortcomings in a dialogue with the main universal document in the area. In order to do so, this chapter will present a description of how the region acted in the

---

[*] Flávia Piovesan, Professor of Constitutional Law and Human Rights at the Catholic University of São Paulo and in the Human Rights post-graduate programmes of the Catholic University of São Paulo, the Catholic University of Paraná, and the Human Rights and Development Programme of Pablo de Olavide University (Spain); Ph.D. in Constitutional Law from the Catholic University of São Paulo; visiting fellow of the Human Rights Program at Harvard Law School in 1995, returning to the programme in 2000 and 2002; human rights fellow at the Centre for Brazilian Studies, University of Oxford in 2005; visiting fellow at the Max Planck Institute for Comparative Public Law and International Law, in Heidelberg, in 2007–2008 and currently a Humboldt Foundation Georg Forster Research Fellow (2009–2011) at the Max Planck Institute for Comparative Public Law and International Law; member of the UN High Level Task Force on the implementation of the right to development.

[**] Liliana Lyra Jubilut, PhD and Master in International Law from Universidade de São Paulo; LLM in International Legal Studies from New York University School of Law; Professor at Faculdade de Direito do Sul de Minas.

[1] Contained in UNHCR, Mexico Declaration and Plan of Action to Strengthen the International Protection of Refugees in Latin America (2004), available at <http://www.acnur.org/biblioteca/pdf/3453.pdf>.

drafting of the 1951 Convention, followed by an analysis of its implementation and the broadening of the concept of refugees in the Cartagena Declaration, and then will examine the newest development in the region—the MPA.

B. The Americas and the 1951 Convention

I. *Travaux Préparatoires*

Despite having started at the beginning of the 20th century, refugee law and protection became an international universal system with the adoption of the 1951 Convention, following the Second World War. Although historically contextualized, given that this document aimed to solve the refugee crisis provoked by that conflict and its aftermath,[2] the 1951 Convention became the cornerstone of the universal system of refugee protection that exists to this day. This document ascertains the definition of a refugee; lists the rights of refugees and the obligations of the States who decided to accept its text; and establishes durable solutions for refugees.

The 1951 Convention determines that for a person to have refugee status, he or she has to (i) have well-founded fear of persecution; (ii) by reasons of race, religion, nationality, political opinion or membership in a social group; (iii) be outside his or her country of origin (or outside the country of his or her former habitual residence if he or she does not have a nationality), *i.e.* alienage; (iv) be in need of international protection (and therefore not be included in the cessation clauses); and (v) deserve international protection (*i.e.* not be incorporated in the exclusion clauses). If refugee status is ascertained one of three durable solutions—local integration, resettlement, or repatriation—should be sought.[3]

This document also establishes rights for refugees with a special focus on economic and social rights (such as education and social assistance). In this regard it is relevant to note the connection between human rights and refugee law, given that, besides the rights listed in the 1951 Convention, refugees are entitled to all the fundamental rights guaranteed by the human rights system.

Nowadays the prevailing view is that refugee law and protection are a part of international human rights law in its broader sense (*i.e.* international law on the protection of human beings); or at least that an alignment between the two is possible.[4] This is so due to (i) 'the identity of purposes of human rights protection, as well as the proximity of these branches [human rights and refugee law] in the conceptual, normative, hermeneutic and operational plans';[5] (ii) the need for an integral view of the protection of human beings as brought along by the Vienna Declaration of 1993;[6] (iii) the fact that every refugee is the consequence of a pattern of gross violation of international recognized human rights;[7] (iv) the fact that the 1951 Convention, by recognizing the protection of refugees, reinforces the idea that every person should be free of persecution and, thus, the idea of non-

---

[2] Hathaway, *Rights*, p. 91.

[3] For further details *cf.* Zimmermann/Mahler on Art. 1 A, para. 2, *passim.*

[4] Hathaway, *JRS* 4 (1991), p. 113.

[5] Piovesan, *Temas*, p. 94.

[6] *Ibid.*, pp. 94–95.

[7] *Ibid.*, pp. 95 and 102.

discrimination and equality present on the basis of the human rights regime; and (v) the fact that the 1951 Convention, in its preamble, recalls the Universal Declaration of Human Rights (UDHR), suggesting that they share a common basis in the enjoyment of fundamental freedoms without discrimination.[8] The alignment between refugee law and protection and human rights is a trend and a constant in the Americas, and is one of the most important lessons the region can teach the global system.

Such bond is relevant as, in a holistic approach to refugee law and protection, human rights have to be upheld in all phases of the lives of refugees given that, as human beings, they are entitled to all rights proclaimed in the UDHR. One can identify four relevant phases.[9]

The first phase relates to the period prior to the refuge in which the violation of human rights results in the seeking of asylum and in it the rights 1) of equality and non-discrimination; 2) to life, to liberty, and personal security; 3) of equality before the law; 4) not to be subjected to torture or to cruel, inhuman, or degrading treatment or punishment; 5) not to be subjected to arbitrary interference with his or her privacy, family, home, or correspondence; 6) of freedom of thought, conscience, and religion; and 7) freedom of opinion and expression, are extremely relevant.

The second phase relates to the flight of refugees in which the rights 1) not to be subjected to arbitrary arrest, detention, or exile; 2) to freedom of movement and to leave any country; 3) to seek and to enjoy in other countries asylum from persecution; 4) of recognition that the family is the natural and fundamental group unit of society and is entitled to protection by society and the State; 5) to life, to liberty, and personal security; and 6) not to be subjected to torture or to cruel, inhuman, or degrading treatment or punishment (including sexual abuses), can be said to be the most significant.

The third phase encompasses the period of refuge in which the rights 1) of equality and non-discrimination; 2) to life, to liberty, and personal security; 3) not to be subjected to arbitrary arrest, detention, or exile; 4) not to be subjected to torture or to cruel, inhuman, or degrading treatment or punishment; 5) of equality before the law in the determination of refugee status; 6) not to be subjected to arbitrary interference with his privacy, family, home, or correspondence; 7) to seek and to enjoy in other countries asylum from persecution; 8) to an adequate standard of living; 9) to education; 10) of non-discrimination as to race, religion, or country of origin; 11) to freedom to practice their religion and freedom as regards the religious education of their children; 12) to acquire property; 13) of protection of industrial and intellectual property; 14) to freedom of association; 15) of access to courts and to judicial assistance; 16) to work; 17) to education; 18) to freedom of movement; 19) to identity and travel documents; 20) to at least the same treatment as foreigners in general; 21) to the same treatment as nationals in terms of public assistance, labour legislation, social security, and taxes; 22) to administrative assistance; and 23) of *non-refoulement*, shall be respected.

---

[8] For further details *cf.* Alleweldt, Preamble 1951 Convention, *passim.*

[9] Piovesan, *Temas*, pp. 107 *et seq.*

It is interesting to note that while freedom of movement is listed as a right, the text of the 1951 Convention states that it is a right of refugees lawfully in the territory of a State, which, combined with mass influxes, is sometimes used as a justification for the detention of asylum seekers pending their refugee status determination (RSD). This practice exists nowadays in the Americas, mainly in the United States; which contrasts with the practice of other States—such as Brazil—in which asylum seekers (and refugees) have the freedom to move inside the territory as long as they notify the authorities vested with the responsibility of RSD and of protecting refugees.

Also, it is relevant to highlight the fact that, according to Art. 5 of the 1951 Convention,[10] other rights recognised for refugees are not to be limited by this document. This recognition can be used as another bridge between refugee law and protection and human rights and demonstrates that the goal is the most protective framework possible, with the 1951 Convention only guaranteeing minimum standards that can (and should) be completed by States.

The fourth phase of the lives of refugees in which human rights have to be present relates to the moment of durable solutions in which the rights 1) to return to one's country; 2) to nationality; 3) of non-discrimination; 4) of equality before the law; 5) of political participation; 6) which are indispensable for a persons' dignity and the free development of his or hers personality (*i.e.* economic, social, and cultural rights); 7) to work; 8) to an adequate standard of living; 9) to a social and international order in which human rights and freedoms can be fully realized, and the duties towards the community in regard to the respect of the rights of others and respect of law can be said to be the most relevant.

Furthermore, the 'problem of refugees has to be addressed not only from the angle of protection but also through the lenses of prevention and solution (durable and permanent)'.[11] In this sense the 1951 Convention can be said to have been early in adopting this integral view of the protection of the human being, combining refugee law with human rights since its drafting process.

The *travaux préparatoires* of the 1951 Convention counted with the participation of five American States: Brazil, Canada, Colombia, the United States, and Venezuela.[12] The participation of these States reflects the diversity of the American region both in terms of economic development and politics.

To analyse any aspect of social science in the context of the Americas as a region is challenging. This is so due to the fact that the region is extremely diverse. In terms of economy, one can see, in the region, two developed countries (the United States and Canada), several developing countries in different stages of development, and at least one country that is categorized as a "least developed country"—Haiti.[13] This diversity is even more complex if one adds the historical

---

[10] Art. 5 of the 1951 Convention: 'Nothing in this Convention shall be deemed to impair any rights and benefits granted by a Contracting State to refugees apart from this Convention'. For further details *cf.* Skordas on Art. 5, *passim.*

[11] Piovesan, *Temas*, p. 107 (translated from Portuguese).

[12] For further details *cf.* Einarsen, Drafting History, *passim.*

[13] *Cf.* UN-OHRLLS, Least Developed Countries: Country Profiles, available at <http://www.unohrlls.org/en/ldc/related/62>.

and political situation of the region. In this sense, the division is visible between the United States and Canada and their democratic history and respect for human rights on one side, and Latin America and its history of political uprisings on the other. It can be said that Latin America is:

> ... *a region marked by a high level of exclusion and social inequality, to which one adds the fact that the democracies are being consolidated. The region still lives with the reminiscence of the authoritarian and dictatorial regimes' legacy, with a cultural of violence and impunity, with a low density of the Rule of Law and with the precarious tradition of the respect of human rights in the domestic arena.*[14]

These dissimilarities are reflected in the protection of refugees and, therefore, pose a challenge for this chapter. In light of this, and in order to present the most comprehensive analysis of the regional developments in the Americas, both realities will be tackled and the distinguishable features of each scenario will be highlighted during the present examination.

As mentioned,[15] the diversity among American countries was present in the *travaux préparatoires* of the 1951 Convention. Even though the United States was part of the styling committee, Canada can be said to have been the most active participant from the region; as it (i) was the American country that presented more proposals to the drafting of the 1951 Convention;[16] (ii) was a part of the working group vested with the responsibility of drafting the definition of a refugee in Art. 1 of the 1951 Convention;[17] and (iii) voiced several comments during the discussions of the texts which were dominated by the European States. It is also relevant to mention that Canada expressed a humanitarian approach to the protection of refugees, being 'in favour of the widest possible definition',[18] given that: 'The purpose of the Convention was to protect refugees, not States.'[19].

This approach, however, was not shared by the other American countries, which preferred a narrow definition restricted by temporal and geographical limitations. While Colombia 'recalled that in Latin America the term "refugee" was applied only to European refugees'[20] and explained that it had 'not imagined that the Conference would attempt to solve the problem of Latin American refugees which, in fact, was non-existent',[21] a statement with which Venezuela concurred, the United States expressed its views that 'one constructive step should be taken at a time, and felt that a convention drafted to meet European requirements was the first step'.[22]

---

[14] Piovesan, *Direitos*, p. 85 (translated from Portuguese).

[15] *Cf. supra*, MN 16–17.

[16] The American States proposed amendments to Arts. 23, 25, and 26 of the 1951 Convention. Canada also requested the phrase 'public order' in Art. 27 of the 1951 Convention to be clarified so as to adjust its national practice of deportation to the international standards, *cf.* Conference of Plenipotentiaries, UN Doc. A/CONF.2/SR.14 (1951).

[17] Conference of Plenipotentiaries, UN Doc. A/CONF.2/105 (1951).

[18] Conference of Plenipotentiaries, UN Doc. A/CONF.2/SR.19 (1951), p. 6.

[19] Ibid.

[20] Conference of Plenipotentiaries, UN Doc. A/CONF.2/SR.21 (1951), p. 13.

[21] Ibid.

[22] Conference of Plenipotentiaries, UN Doc. A/CONF.2/SR.19 (1951), p. 22. In response to the apprehension that the limited definition would exclude millions of refugees from protection, the US

In the cases of Venezuela and Colombia it is also interesting to note that they were opposed to the idea of 'asylum being a duty incumbent upon States'[23] but defended the view that it should be considered rather 'a right to be claimed by refugees'[24]; insofar as 'the granting of asylum remained a matter for the discretion of individual States'.[25]

Even though the 1951 Convention followed this trend without expressly recognizing a right of asylum, it established in Art. 33 of the 1951 Convention the principle of *non-refoulement* as an obligation for States. This article prohibits States to 'expel or return ("refouler") a refugee in any manner whatsoever to the frontiers of territories where his life or freedom would be threatened on account of his race, religion, nationality, membership of a particular social group or political opinion'. This provision is deemed as the most important in the system created by the 1951 Convention;[26] and according to Art. 42 of the 1951 Convention it cannot be subjected to reservation.[27] It is said to be, nowadays, a norm of *jus cogens*[28] (*i.e.* a peremptory international norm) and appears in several documents relating directly or indirectly to refugee law,[29] such as the OAU Convention Governing the Specific Aspects of Refugee Problems in Africa (OAU Refugee Convention),[30] the Cartagena Declaration,[31] the American Convention on Human Rights: 'Pact of San José, Costa Rica' (ACHR),[32] and the Convention against Torture and Other Cruel, Inhuman or Degrading Treatment or Punishment (CAT).[33]

The principle of *non-refoulement* implies at least a duty to grant temporary refuge as a State cannot summarily expel a person on the frontier or summarily re-conduct

---

representative said that: 'It must be recognized, however, that so far as the exclusion of the so-called millions was concerned, nothing was known of where they were or of their condition. It was true that there were still millions of refugees on German territory, but they were taken care of by paragraph D of article 1, as were also the hundreds of thousands of refugees in Turkey, and the millions in India and Pakistan. Similarly, paragraph C of article 1 took care of the hundreds of thousands of Arab refugees from Palestine. So far as he could see, the situation with regard to refugees in the Far East was still obscure, and very little was known of those from continental China in particular. On the whole, therefore, it would be unrealistic for the Conference to attempt to legislate for refugees in the Far East.' Statement of Warren (US), Conference of Plenipotentiaries, UN Doc. A/CONF.2/SR.21 (1951), pp. 14–15.

[23] Conference of Plenipotentiaries, UN Doc. A/CONF.2/SR.13 (1951), p.12.

[24] Ibid.

[25] *Ibid.*, p. 14.

[26] For further details *cf.* Kälin/Caroni/Heim on Art. 33, para. 1, *passim.*

[27] For further details *cf.* Pellet on Art. 42/Art. VII MN 4, 22.

[28] *Cf. e.g.* Cartagena Declaration, Part. III, para. 5, which states: 'To reiterate the importance and meaning of the principle of *non-refoulement* (including the prohibition of rejection at the frontier) as a corner-stone of the international protection of refugees. This principle is imperative in regard to refugees and in the present state of international law should be acknowledged and observed as a rule of *jus cogens.'* *Cf.* also Kälin/Caroni/Heim on Art. 33, para. 1 MN 32.

[29] Lauterpacht/Bethlehem, in *Refugee Protection*, pp. 87, 90 *et seq.*

[30] Art. 2, para. 3 OAU Refugee Convention: 'No person shall be subjected by a Member State to measures such as rejection at the frontier, return or expulsion, which would compel him to return to or remain in a territory where his life, physical integrity or liberty would be threatened for the reasons set out in Art. I, paras. 1 and 2.'

[31] Cartagena Declaration, Part. III, para. 5, *cf. supra*, fn. 28.

[32] Art. 22, para. 8 ACHR: 'In no case may an alien be deported or returned to a country, regardless of whether or not it is his country of origin, if in that country his right to life or personal freedom is in danger of being violated because of his race, nationality, religion, social status, or political opinions.'

[33] Art. 3 CAT: 'No State Party shall expel, return (refouler) or extradite a person to another State where there are substantial grounds for believing that he would be in danger of being subjected to torture.'

a person to the frontier without any procedural investigation of his or her refugee status. It is in light of this that a customary norm of temporary protection is said to have been established.[34]

The general unwillingness of States—and in the case of Latin America especially Colombia—to accept the granting of asylum as an obligation of States[35] is even more significant in light of Art. 27 of the American Declaration of the Rights and Duties of Man that ascertains a right of asylum,[36] which was subsequently adopted by Art. 22, para. 7 ACHR.[37] Nevertheless the Latin American States were opposed to any kind of broader obligations towards refugees, which is also exemplified by their disapproval of the obligation in relation to the issuance of visas[38] and of the headings of the articles of the 1951 Convention being part of its normative aspect[39] and, therefore, binding on States.

These distinctive approaches of the American States during the *travaux préparatoires* of the 1951 Convention testify to the political scenarios that each country had: while Canada has since the inception of the universal refugee regime tried to be the most humane possible; the United States always dealt with refugees as a part of its international political agenda;[40] and the Latin American countries, living with restrictive internal regimes, were not willing to commit to high international standards of human rights protection, of which, as mentioned, refugee law is a part. The latter would dramatically change in future years with the consolidation of democracies in the region which led to a desire to improve respect for human rights, and, in turn, to the development of a regional broadening of the refugee concept of the 1951 Convention.

II. Ratification and Implementation

Once the 1951 Convention was finalized it became the keystone of refugee law, and, therefore, its ratification by States is extremely important. In the Americas, as of 10 October 2008, 30 States were part of the international system,[41] with 28 States

---

[34] Jubilut, *Direito*, p. 94.

[35] Conference of Plenipotentiaries, UN Doc. A/CONF.2/SR.13 (1951).

[36] Art. XXVII American Declaration of the Rights and Duties of Man: 'Every person has the right, in case of pursuit not resulting from ordinary crimes, to seek and receive asylum in foreign territory, in accordance with the laws of each country and with international agreements.' For further details *cf.* also Lambert on Art. 2 MN 25.

[37] Art. 22, para. 7 ACHR: 'Every person has the right to seek and be granted asylum in a foreign territory, in accordance with the legislation of the state and international conventions, in the event he is being pursued for political offenses or related common crimes.' It is interesting to note that, as will be seen below (MN 27–33), in Latin America the institutes of refuge and asylum coexist under the umbrella of the right of asylum. For a more comprehensive view of the differences between these two institutes *cf.* Jubilut, *JRS* 19 (2006), pp. 22, 28 *et seq.*; Jubilut, *Direito*, pp. 35 *et seq.*

[38] Conference of Plenipotentiaries, UN Doc. A/CONF.2/SR.18 (1951), pp. 7–16.

[39] Conference of Plenipotentiaries, UN Docs. A/CONF.2/SR.33 (1951) and A/CONF.2/SR.35 (1951).

[40] *Cf.* Campbell, 'United States' Refugee and Asylum Policy: The Story of a Closing Door', *passim*; Zucker/Zucker, *JRS* 2 (1989), p. 359. The same is said about another country regarded as a traditional country of asylum: Mexico. Mexico's asylum policy is perceived as 'never based exclusively on purely humanitarian purposes, but has always been heavily influenced by aspects of political affinity', *cf.* Wollny, *JRS* 13 (2000), p. 184.

[41] UNHCR, States Parties to the 1951 Convention Relating to the Status of Refugees and the 1967 Protocol, available at <http://www.unhcr.org/3b73b0d63.html>.

parties to the 1951 Convention[42] and two States only to the 1967 Protocol.[43, ***]

This is germane in the case of Latin America given that, in the region, the approval of the 1951 Convention meant the coexistence of the institutes of refuge and asylum. Both institutes aim to protect people in light of persecution, having, thus, a humanitarian aspect, and are encompassed in the right of asylum stipulated by the UDHR.

However, in Latin American practice, the institutes are applied in different circumstances and have important differences, which can be summarized as follows.[44]

The institute of asylum dates back to ancient times and is a discretionary act of the State, mainly used nowadays in Latin America, without legal limitations regarding its concession. It is limited to political persecution—which has to exist in fact—and can be granted inside the State of origin or residency of the person fleeing persecution (diplomatic asylum)[45] or in the territory of the granting State (territorial asylum). The decision to grant asylum is considered a constitutive act, meaning that it is the decision that makes the person asking for asylum an asylee.

On the other hand, the institute of refuge was established in the early decades of the twentieth century and is regulated by international norms, being supervised by the UNHCR.[46] It is not a discretionary act of States and has limitations regarding its application. It has a more comprehensive application based on a well-founded fear of persecution for reasons of race, religion, nationality, social group, or political opinion and can only be granted to people outside their State of origin, thus requiring alienage. The recognition of refugee status generates responsibilities regarding the protection of the refugee by the granting State and is considered a declaratory decision (*i.e.* it is the situation in the country of origin or residence and not the decision of the State which makes a person a refugee).

The fact that with the 1951 Convention refuge became a part of the normative humanitarian practice of Latin America alongside asylum (which is regulated both by treaties and by customary law) increases the possibility of apolitical and technical protection and expands the hypothesis in which people fleeing persecution can count on international protection, thus enhancing the protection of fundamental rights.

This coexistence, however, also has some negative aspects given that as 'there is some confusion about the roles of the two institutions (as for example always

---

[42] The American States parties to the 1951 Convention are: Antigua and Barbuda, Argentina, Bahamas, Belize, Bolivia, Brazil, Canada, Chile, Colombia, Costa Rica, Dominica, Dominican Republic, Ecuador, El Salvador, Guatemala, Haiti, Honduras, Jamaica, Mexico, Nicaragua, Panama, Paraguay, Peru, Saint Kitts and Nevis, Saint Vincent and Grenadines, Suriname, Trinidad and Tobago, and Uruguay, *cf.* UNHCR, States Parties to the 1951 Convention Relating to the Status of Refugees and the 1967 Protocol, available at <http://www.unhcr.org/3b73b0d63.html>.

[43] The American States parties only to the 1967 Protocol are: the US and Venezuela, *cf.* UNHCR, States Parties to the 1951 Convention Relating to the Status of Refugees and the 1967 Protocol, available at <http://www.unhcr.org/3b73b0d63.html>.

*** The data is still true as of April 2015, which is the most recent update of UNHCR on the matter.

[44] Jubilut, *JRS* 19 (2006), pp. 22, 29.

[45] For further details *cf.* Denza, Diplomatic Asylum, *passim.*

[46] For further details *cf.* also Zieck on Art. 35/Art. II, *passim.*

referring to refugees as political refugees, as the only cause of granting asylum is political persecution which is not the case for granting refuge) the adequate application of both can be put in jeopardy.'[47]

Despite this problem, the institutes of refuge and asylum coexist in Latin America on the basis of a more humane attitude on refugee law and protection in the region. A 'tradition of protection' founded in this comprehensive approach of the right of asylum is always cited in the developments and advancement of protection in the region, which were only possible with the ratification and implementation of the 1951 Convention.

Moreover, the ratification and implementation of the 1951 Convention in the region is relevant given that, as of April 2010, 21 States have created internal legislation that implements the 1951 Convention and the 1967 Protocol,[48], **** and 11 States have incorporated the right of asylum in their constitutions.[49] And as of November 2010, two other States (Mexico and the Dominican Republic) are on the process to granting the right of asylum constitutional standing. *****

Based on sheer numbers, the implementation of the 1951 Convention in the Americas can be said to have been successful; however, this argument is even more true if one realizes that most of the American States have created adequate procedures of RSD allowing the UNHCR not to have to recognize refugees within its mandate in almost all countries of the region, with the exception of Cuba and a few other countries in the Caribbean.[50]

The RSD procedures in the region are 'mainly done in 3 systems: 1) institutional collegiate commissions [generally named National Committee on Refugees (which have the acronym CONARE in Portuguese and Spanish)]—(majority of the countries); 2) general directions of migration (Costa Rica and Honduras); and 3) ad-hoc mechanisms (Mexico and Cayman Islands)'.[51]

All the national procedures have the 1951 Convention as a legal parameter and as a minimum standard of protection;[52] and in many cases the interpretation of the

---

[47] Jubilut, *JRS* 19 (2006), pp. 22, 30.

[48] UNHCR, Países con Legislación que Implementa la Convención de 1951 y su Protocolo de 1967 (2008), available at <http://www.acnur.org/biblioteca/pdf/2549.pdf>.

**** The most current data from UNHCR (of February 2014) lists 20 countries, as Ecuador has changed its national legislation.

[49] Murillo González, in *XXXV Curso de Derecho Internacional*, pp. 351 *et seq.*(The authors would like to thank Juan Carlos Murillo—UNHCHR regional legal officer for the Americas—for this text).

***** The most current data from UNHCR (of June 2011) lists 14 countries that have constitutional provisions on the right of asylum in the region.

[50] Ibid.

[51] *Ibid.* (translated from Spanish).

[52] In this regard it seems interesting to highlight the RSD procedure in Brazil, given that it was regarded as a model in South America and inspired similar procedures in the region: RSD procedure in Brazil begins with the asylum seeker's request for refuge to the competent authority. This authority is the Federal Police, which will formalise the request into a Declaration Term (*Termo de Declaração*). This document contains the civil qualification of the asylum seeker (name, nationality, name of parents, birth date) as well as the main reasons for which the asylum seeker left his or her country of origin and is asking for refugee status in Brazil. The date of the Declaration Term is deemed to be the date of the beginning of the procedures. . . . After having this document issued, the asylum seeker is instructed that he or she has to continue with the proceedings in order to be recognised as a refugee in Brazil. If the asylum seeker remains six months or more without responding to the requests of the proceeding or abandons it, the procedure is archived without having

provisions of this document by courts has been done in the most humane manner. Examples are 1) the case of exclusion clauses in Canada in which:

> ... *the Canadian courts have described [the serious reasons for considering that the person has committed a crime against peace, war crime or a crime against humanity and therefore is excluded from the system of refugee protection] the standard is more than mere suspicion, but less than the balance of probabilities, and it is for the Minister to show serious reasons for considering that the individual concerned has committed the crime or act in question . . .*[53]

and 2) of extraditions in Brazil in which the Supreme Court has ascertained the constitutionality of Art. 33 of the Brazilian Refugee Act, which prohibits the extradition of refugees.[54]

III. Domestic Legislation on Refugees

In general, with regard to its implementation, the minimum standards of protection established by the 1951 Convention are respected in the Americas and when violations occur they are topical rather than systemic.

There is always, however, room for improvement as for instance in the cases of the suppression of the stipulation of a maximum period for requesting refugee status, as established by the legislation of Peru and Colombia, or of the inclusion of a representative from civil society that works with refugees with voting rights in the institutional collegiate commissions in charge of RSD (as is already the case in Brazil).[55]

Moreover, even if not the rule, systemic violations have occurred. Two practices

---

its merits analysed. The step following the issuance of the Declaration Term is the completion of a more thorough standard questionnaire. . . . After the questionnaire is filled in, it is sent to CONARE and the asylum seeker is granted authorisation to have a provisory identification issued. This document is the Provisional Protocol (*Protocolo Provisório*). The asylum seeker, then, has to go through two interviews. The first interview is conducted by a lawyer from civil society. The interview is conducted individually and whenever possible in the language of the asylum seeker. When an interpreter is required, the interpreter is instructed about the confidentiality of the proceedings. The second interview is conducted by a representative of CONARE and follows the same rules as the first interview. As mentioned above, CONARE is a collective deliberative body. It has both governmental and non-governmental members and the UNHCR has "voice-no-vote" status. The government representatives come from the Ministry of Justice, the Ministry of Foreign Affairs, the Ministry of Health, the Ministry of Labour and Employment, the Ministry of Education and Sports, and the Federal Police. The representative of the civil society comes from an NGO that is involved in the assistance and protection of refugees. Nowadays this seat is occupied by Cáritas Arquidiocesana de São Paulo, with Cáritas Arquidiocesana do Rio de Janeiro being the alternate. . . . After the two interviews have taken place, there is a meeting by a Preliminary Analysis Group (*Grupo de Estudos Prévios*) to assess the merits of the case. . . . With the pre-analysis executed the cases go to the CONARE's plenary to be decided. In the plenary each member is entitled to one vote, and decisions are made by majority. If the decision is positive, the asylum seeker is recognised as a refugee in Brazil. If the decision is negative, there is the possibility of an appeal. This appeal is also an administrative procedure, which has to take place within fifteen days after the asylum seeker is notified of it, in order to be timely. The appeal is analysed by the Minister of Justice, who gives the final decision on RSD in Brazil. If he changes CONARE's decision, the person is recognised as a refugee; if he does not, the person is subject to the general foreigner's regimen and is not a refugee in Brazil', Jubilut/Apolinário, *Refuge* 25, No. 2, 2008. p. 31-32..

[53] Goodwin-Gill/McAdam, *Refugee*, p. 165.

[54] *Cf. e.g.* Supremo Tribunal Federal (Supreme Court, Brazil), Judgment of Extradition 1008 of 2007 (which involved the request by Colombia for the extradion of Oliverio Media), available at <http://www.stf.jus.br/portal/processo/verProcessoAndamento.asp?incidente=2324865>.

[55] Jubilut, *JRS* 19 (2006), pp. 22, 32–33.

in the United States are the main examples of said infringements. The first one relates to the norm of *non-refoulement*. Mainly in light of its internal legislation regarding Cubans and the flows of asylum seekers from the Caribbean, the United States has long adopted the practice of preventing boats carrying asylum seekers—most notoriously in the case of Haitians—from reaching its coast.[56] For some this can be regarded as an incorrect interpretation of the principle of *non-refoulement*. As instead of understanding the principle to mean that asylum seekers should not be returned *to* a place where they may face well-founded fear, they would be using the idea of being able to return asylum seekers *from* a place as they did not reach the United States. This interpretation is not in keeping with the text of the 1951 Convention given that the perspective of Art. 33 of the 1951 Convention in relation to the return is of the country of origin and not of the host country; and should, in light of the 'humanitarian objective of the Convention, . . . be constructed liberally in a manner that favours the widest possible scope of protection'.[57] Besides, Art. 33 of the 1951 Convention is understood to apply not only to recognized refugees but also to asylum seekers, as it implies a duty of a procedural analysis of the request of refuge in light of the fact that the granting of refuge is a declaratory and not a constitutive act.[58]

The second practice is more recent and relates to the 'war on terror' following the terrorist attacks of 11 September 2001. Combining the provisions of the 2001 US Patriot Act and the 2005 Real ID Act that prohibits 'material assistance to terrorism',[59] and applying them broadly, the United States has been excluding thousands of people from the possibility of being recognized as refugees.

The problem is that in some cases, mainly in the early state of this practice, the same circumstances that were the basis of the well-founded fear were the ones that were deemed to characterize material assistance. For instance, people who have been coerced into giving goods or services to terrorist groups; who, due to their professions, have provided medical care to persons who have 'engaged in terrorist activity'; or who even have paid bribes under coercion to 'terrorists' were excluded from the refugee regime. In some cases people who have had any kind of contact (voluntarily or involuntarily) were also included in the material assistance bar.

More recently, 'duress waivers', mainly in the case of Colombians, are in place, meaning that if the 'material support' was granted under duress, the exclusion from the refugee regime does not apply. This is surely a positive development, however, some cases—such as those involving minor children being compelled to join conflicts (child soldiers)—are not covered by the 'duress waivers' and, therefore, the people in these circumstances cannot have their refugee status recognized; which also does not seem to be in keeping with the humanitarian character of the

---

[56] Goodwin-Gill/McAdam, *Refugee*, p. 270.

[57] Shacknove, A., '*Non-refoulement*', lecture given at The University of Oxford and The George Washington University Joint Programme in International Human Rights Law (2002); *cf.* Lauterpacht/Bethlehem, in *Refugee Protection*, pp. 87, 132.

[58] Jubilut, *Direito*, pp. 42 *et seq.*

[59] For more information on the 'material assistance bar' in the refugee regime in the US see the information on the Refugee Council USA webpage, available at <http://www.rcusa.org>. On this particular topic the authors would like to thank Elizabeth Campbell for her assistance.

1951 Convention.

Despite these setbacks there are also improvements in the implementation of the 1951 Convention in the region, both in relation to refugees and to other persons of concern in the field of forced migration. In relation to the former, one can highlight the adoption of guidelines for protection in cases of gender-related persecution—as in the United States and Canada—or the inclusion of persecution based on gender or sex as an additional cause for recognition as a refugee—as in the cases of El Salvador, Nicaragua, Panama, Paraguay, Uruguay, and Venezuela.[60] This is relevant given that women and girls 'constitute 47 per cent of refugees and asylum-seekers, and half of all IDPs [internally displaced persons] and returnees (refugees)'[61] and that the recognition of gender-related persecution indicates the need for diverse forms of protection for the most vulnerable, realizing the transversal protection proposed by UNHCR in its tripartite axis (*i.e.* gender, age, and diversity).

In relation to 'other persons of concern in the field of forced migration' the main concern in the region is with internally displaced persons (IDPs), as Colombia has one of the world's highest rates (three million) of people in this situation.[62] In this regard it is significant that Colombia and Peru have established internal legislation on IDPs.[63]

Moreover, in light of the connection between refugee law and human rights law it is important to note that developments in the latter have also been made—as concerns human trafficking, civil registration, and indigenous people—which can benefit the protection of refugees.[64]

This is even more important considering that, in the region, the spectrum of refugee protection varies from developing countries that are among the largest receivers of refugees, to countries 'producing' refugees,[65] *i.e.* violating refugee and human rights law.

C. More Comprehensive Assessment of Refugee Status

I. The Cartagena Declaration

The violation of human rights is the foundation of the first regional approach to refugee law and protection in the Americas: the Cartagena Declaration.

---

[60] Murillo González, in XXXV Curso de Derecho Internacional, pp. 351 et seq.

[61] UNHCR, 2008 Global Trends, p. 2.

[62] *Ibid.*, p. 19.

[63] Murillo González, in *XXXV Curso de Derecho Internacional*, pp. 351 *et seq*. The internal legislation can be found at <http://www.acnur.org/biblioteca/pdf/2883.pdf> (Peru's legislation on internally displaced people) and <http://www.acnur.org/secciones/index.php?viewCat=1055> (for Colombia's rules on internally displaced people).

[64] Murillo González, in *XXXV Curso de Derecho Internacional*, pp. 351 et seq.

[65] Murillo González highlights 7 situations in the Americas in relation to refugee protection: (1) developed countries with complex systems of asylum which receive large numbers of refugees; (2) countries receiving large numbers of asylum seekers and refugees; (3) countries receiving small numbers of asylum seekers and refugees; (4) countries with grave situations of IDPs; (5) countries that are outside the international regime of refugee protection; (6) countries that are not part of the international instruments on refuge and/or that do not have mechanisms for RSD; and (7) countries with issues concerning statelessness. *Cf.* Murillo González, in *XXXV Curso de Derecho Internacional*, pp. 351 *et seq*.

In the early 1980s, Central America experienced gross violations of human rights and civil conflicts which led to a massive influx of refugees in the area. In light of this, an academic colloquium, with the presence of the UNHCR and with the support of the Colombian government, was held in Cartagena, with the purpose of re-evaluating the international protection of refugees in the region. As a result the Cartagena Declaration was adopted.

This document is regarded as 'one of the most encompassing approaches to the refugee question',[66] as it brings forth more comprehensive criteria for RSD as well as a new perspective on durable solutions[67] while reaffirming the relevance of the 1951 Convention[68] and the principle of *non-refoulement* even in mass influx situations, regarding it as *jus cogens*,[69] as mentioned.

The most notable advancement of the Cartagena Declaration is its more comprehensive criteria for RSD. It establishes in its third conclusion that:

> *The definition or concept of a refugee to be recommended for use in the region is one which, in addition to containing the elements of the 1951 Convention and the 1967 Protocol, includes among refugees persons who have fled their country because their lives, safety or freedom have been threatened by generalized violence, foreign aggression, internal conflicts, massive violation of human rights or other circumstances which have seriously disturbed public order.*

The recognition of massive violation of human rights or other circumstances which have seriously disturbed public order as criteria for RSD, alongside the traditional universal criterion, is highly relevant in the context of Latin America. This is so due to the fact that:

> . . . *human rights issues in the Americas have often concerned gross, as opposed to ordinary, violations of human rights. They have been much more to do with the forced disappearance, killing, torture and arbitrary detention of political opponents and terrorists than with particular issues concerning, for example, the right to a fair trial or freedom of expression . . . .*[70]

Moreover, while:

> *Latin American constitutions also contained long lists of protected rights and corresponding checks on government action . . . In actual fact, however, governments rarely tested the full measure of that inclination, since they committed the most flagrant human rights delinquencies secretly or at least behind the often thin veil of official denial.*[71]

Besides, the comprehensive approach of the Cartagena Declaration seems to recognize the above-mentioned intrinsic connection between human rights and refugee law and protection, and, therefore, to expand protection in a holistic manner in keeping with the most modern conceptions of the protection of human beings. In this sense, it can be said that by listing gross violation of human rights as

---

66 Goodwin-Gill/McAdam, *Refugee*, p. 38.
67 Hathaway, *Rights*, p. 119.
68 Ibid.
69 Goodwin-Gill/McAdam, *Refugee*, p. 212.
70 Harris, in Human Rights in Context, p. 874.
71 Farer, in Human Rights in Context, p. 877.

a possibility for refugee status, the Cartagena Declaration has inserted 'the matter in the conceptual universe of human rights',[72] which means that refugee law and protection—including the 1951 Convention—'must be interpreted in harmony with the Universal Declaration of Human Rights of 1948 and with all the most relevant international treaties on the protection of human rights'[73].

This more holistic approach is also reflected in the implementation of the rights of refugees, asylum seekers, and displaced persons in the region through the actions of the IACmHR and the IACtHR, which have a growing jurisprudence on the topic,[74] including decisions on *non-refoulement*, nationality, and the right to life. This participation of the Inter-American organs was provided for in the fifteenth conclusion of the Cartagena Declaration,[75] and builds on the integrated approach of the eighth conclusion[76] of this document.

The new criteria of the Cartagena Declaration have, thus, not only established a logical, objective, and legally sound way to expedite individual RSD while recognizing the effect the local situation has on individual fear of persecution,[77] but have also enhanced the inevitable connection between refugee law and the protection of human rights.

The concept of massive violation of human rights (or of gross and generalized violation of human rights as cited in some legislation in the region) has not been defined, but in practice, generally, it seems to apply to the context of civil strife or civil conflicts, dictatorships, or cases in which the national system cannot guarantee the life, security, and liberty of the person, which are cornerstones of the third conclusion of the Cartagena Declaration.

The Cartagena Declaration was clearly inspired by the OAU Refugee Convention, and is said to have brought along an expanded definition of the concept of 'refugees'. This statement, however, does not seem to be correct. Insofar

---

[72] Piovesan, *Temas*, pp. 110–111 (translated from Portuguese).

[73] *Ibid.*, p. 104 (translated from Portuguese). In this sense the provision of art. 48 of the Brazilian Refugee Act is relevant as it states that: 'The provisions of this Act shall be interpreted in harmony with the Universal Declaration of Human Rights of 1948, the Convention on the Status of Refugees of 1951, the Protocol on the Status of Refugees of 1967, and with every pertinent provision of international instruments on the protection of human rights with which the Brazilian government is committed' (translated from Portuguese).

[74] The IACtHR has, as of November 2007, judged 11 cases, has given 3 advisory opinions and determined provisional measures in 5 cases relating to refugees and asylum seekers, according to the information available at <http://www.acnur.org/biblioteca/pdf/2869.pdf>. The IACmHR has passed one recommendation, approved 24 reports, determined 14 provisional measures, and analysed 23 individual petitions on the topic, *cf.* IACmHR, Protección de Refugiados y Solicitantes de Asilo en el Sistema Interamericano de Derechos Humanos (2006), available at <http://www.acnur.org/biblioteca/pdf/2868.pdf>.

[75] Cartagena Declaration, Part III, para. 15: 'To promote greater use of the competent organisations of the inter-American system, in particular the Inter-American Commission on Human Rights, with a view to enhancing the international protection of *asilados* and refugees. Accordingly, for the performance of this task, the Colloquium considers that the close co-ordination and co-operation existing between the Commission and UNHCR should be strengthened.'

[76] Cartagena Declaration, Conclusion 8: 'To ensure that the countries of the region establish a minimum standard of treatment for refugees, on the basis of the provisions of the 1951 Convention and 1967 Protocol and of the American Convention on Human Rights, taking into consideration the conclusions of the UNHCR Executive Committee, particularly No. 22 on the Protection of Asylum Seekers in Situations of Large-Scale Influx.'

[77] O'Connor, in *Refugee Convention*, pp. 31, 36.

as the Cartagena Declaration changes the focus of analysis of the RSD from the individual well-founded fear of persecution to the objective situation of the country of origin,[78] it does not seem to establish an expanded definition given that it is not adding hypothesis to the international criteria but rather creating a new parameter of analysis. Therefore it seems more adequate to speak of more comprehensive criteria for RSD rather than of an expanded definition.

It is germane to highlight that for the countries that have adopted the Cartagena Declaration, the persons recognized under the more comprehensive criteria are recognized as refugees and not only as persons of international concern. The latter category may be the classification of these persons in States that are outside the region[79] or that have not adopted the document, but not for the ones that have embraced the 'spirit of Cartagena' and adopted the more comprehensive RSD.

Although not having binding character as a norm of international law, the Cartagena Declaration was recommended for adoption by all American States by the General Assembly of the Organization of American States (OAS)[80] and has enormously influenced the practice of refugee law and protection in the Americas—especially in Latin America—coating it with a more humanitarian and humane approach.

II. The Cartagena Declaration in Domestic Legislation

The 'spirit of Cartagena' has had three main effects on refugee law and protection in the Americas. First, as mentioned above, it has greatly influenced Latin American countries in their protection of refugees. This can be noted from the fact that 15 States[81] have incorporated in their domestic legislation the more comprehensive criteria of the Cartagena Declaration, having it co-exist with the traditional international criteria of RSD.

The majority of these States (Argentina, Bolivia, Chile, Colombia, Ecuador, El Salvador, Guatemala, Mexico, Nicaragua, Paraguay, and Peru) have adopted the same (or very similar) wording as that of the Cartagena Declaration,[82] *i.e.* recognizing as refugees 'persons who have fled their country because their lives, safety or freedom have been threatened by generalised violence, foreign aggression, internal conflicts, massive violation of human rights or other circumstances which have seriously disturbed public order'. This definition is the one proposed for a model law to the countries of MERCOSUL. However, four countries have opted to incorporate the 'spirit of Cartagena' but not its wording.

Belize has combined the wording of the Cartagena Declaration and that of the OAU Refugee Convention to clarify that the events giving rise to the need for

---

[78] It is interesting to note that the Cartagena Declaration does not adopt the possibility of problems in a region of the country as a basis for refuge as does the Convention of the African system. Jubilut, *Direito*, p. 105.

[79] O'Connor, in *Refugee Convention*, pp. 31, 35.

[80] Hathaway, *Rights*, p. 119.

[81] The States that have adopted the Cartagena Declaration in their national legislations are (as of April 2010): Argentina, Belize, Bolivia, Brazil, Chile, Colombia, Ecuador, El Salvador, Guatemala, Honduras, Mexico, Nicaragua, Paraguay, Peru, and Uruguay, *cf.* UNHCR, Países de América.

[82] For the texts of the national legislations incorporating the Cartagena Declaration *cf.* UNHCR, Definición Ampliada de Refugiados.

refuge may lie in the whole or parts of a country.[83] Honduras opted to be more specific in the determination of each situation, defining its understanding of the criteria listed in the Cartagena Declaration. Although mainly based in international documents (such as the Charter of the United Nations), these actions can be said to have limited the application of the Cartagena Declaration as one can argue that the situations not listed do not give rise to refugee claims.[84] Brazil, on the other hand, chose a more compact formula encompassing all the criteria of the Cartagena Declaration in the phrase 'gross and generalised violation of human rights'.[85] And, lastly, Uruguay went a step further and included terrorism in its more comprehensive criteria for refugee status.[86]

The second effect of the Cartagena Declaration can be found in the fact that it establishes periodic revision and evaluation mechanisms which create:

> . . . *debate forums among Latin American States and allow for the appearance of innovative regional solutions in regards to refugee protection, as for instance, the proposals of the Mexican Declaration and Plan of Action to Enhance Refugee Protection in Latin America, established in 2004 during the celebration of the 20th anniversary of the Cartagena Declaration, . . .*[87]

which will be analysed below.[88]

And as a third effect, the Cartagena Declaration permeated Latin America with a more humane and humanitarian attitude to refugee protection, enabling States to deepen their national systems in order to guarantee more than the minimum standards of the 1951 Convention.

III. New Developments in Expanding the Definition of Refugee Status

An example of the above-mentioned more humane and humanitarian view of refugee protection with which the Cartagena Declaration has imbued the Latin American States is the expansion of the traditional criteria of RSD in the region, which apply in several situations.

As mentioned above,[89] some States have included gender-based persecution in their RSD criteria, which is immensely germane as one recalls that the majority of

---

[83] Art. 4 (c) of the Belizean 1991 Refugee Act: 'owing to external aggression, occupation, foreign domination or events seriously disturbing public order in either part or the whole of his country of origin or nationality, he is compelled to leave his place of habitual residence in order to seek refuge in another place outside his country of origin or nationality'.

[84] Art. 42, para. 3 of the Honduran Migration and Foreigners Act: 'have fled their country because their life, security or liberty were at risk by any of the following reasons: a) gross, continuous and generalized violence, b) foreign aggression meant as the use of armed forced by a State against the sovereignty, territorial integrity or political independence of the country of origin, c) internal armed conflicts brought along by the armed forces of the country that one is fleeing from, and by armed forces or groups, d) massive, permanent and systematic violation of human rights' (translated from Spanish).

[85] Art. 1, para. 3 of the Brazilian 1997 Refugee Act.

[86] Art. 2 B of the Uruguayan 2006 Refugee Act: 'have fled their country because their life, security or liberty were at risk due to generalised violence, foreign aggression or occupation, terrorism, internal conflicts, gross violation of human rights or any other circumstance that seriously disturbed public order' (translated from Spanish).

[87] Jubilut, *Direito*, p. 105.

[88] *Infra*, MN 71–90.

[89] *Supra*, MN 44–45.

refugees in the world are females and that gender-based violations can occur 1) during the persecution; 2) while they are fleeing persecution; or 3) even after they have left their countries of origin and become female foreigners in situations of vulnerability.[90] Violence within the family (*i.e.* domestic violence) is also a gender-related problem, and Costa Rica, Ecuador, and Mexico have recognized victims of such violence as refugees.[91]

Another expansion of protection has occurred in Ecuador, where about 35,000 people will be protected as refugees under a programme of 'broader registry', which combines a geographical and a thematic approach.[92] Also in situations related with refuge, Brazil, Ecuador, and Panama have recognized victims of trafficking with a well-founded fear, as qualifying for refugee status.[93]

In relation to age, Argentina, Guatemala, Paraguay, Peru, and Uruguay have established in their national legislation, norms regarding refugee children.[94]

All of the above represent developments in expanding the definition of refugee status and are direct results of the Cartagena Declaration.

D. New Developments in Protecting Refugees

I. The Mexico Plan of Action (MPA)

In 2004, during the continuous process of re-evaluation and revision of the Cartagena Declaration, a new regional development in refugee law and protection appeared in Latin America—the MPA.

Having the Cartagena Declaration as its foundation and the Colombia refugee crisis[95] as its backdrop, the MPA appeared as a 'regional strategic and operational framework developed to address the complex humanitarian situation resulting from forced displacement in Latin America'.[96]

Prior to the adoption of the MPA by 20 States of the region,[97] preparatory conferences were held in which representatives of governments, the UNHCR, and civil society contributed ideas for the improvement of refugee protection in Latin America.

The MPA aims, on the one hand, to enhance protection and humanitarian assistance in the region and, on the other hand, to address the impact of large

---

[90] Carneiro, in *Refugiados*, pp. 55, 69–70.

[91] Murillo González, in *XXXV Curso de Derecho Internacional*, pp. 351 et seq.

[92] Ibid.

[93] Ibid.

[94] Ibid.

[95] It is estimated that in Ecuador there are 250,000 people who fled the Colombia crisis and in Venezuela another 200,000 people in the same situation, *cf. e.g.* Aiber/Eby, Colombian Refugees—Fact Sheet, available at <http://www.rcusa.org/uploads/pdfs/Colombian%20Refugees%20Backgrounder,%205-4-09.pdf>; UNHCR, ¿Qué es el Plan de Acción de México?, available at <http://www.acnur.org/pam>; UNHCR, Gobierno Ecuatoriano Manifiesta a los Refugiados Su Derecho al Acceso Gratuito a los Servicios de Salud Pública (2007), available at <http://www.acnur.org/index.php?id_pag=6806>; UNHCR, En Ecuador y Venezuela Hay 450.000 Colombianos Refugiados (2007), available at <http://www.acnur.org/index.php?id_pag=7023>.

[96] UNHCR, Mexico Plan of Action, p. 11.

[97] *Ibid.*, p. 15.

influxes of refugees.[98] In this sense, it can be said that the MPA considers both the needs of refugees and asylum seekers—and among them focuses on the most vulnerable groups, such as women, children, indigenous people, afro-descendants, and marginalised minorities[99]—and the needs of States, trying to combine them in the search for a better refugee regime in the region. This trend is one of the most relevant contributions of the MPA to refugee law and protection, as the balance of States' interests and the needs of refugees can build a more humane and effective system of protection.

In order to achieve this balance, the MPA is divided into two components: the protection component and the durable solutions component, which are discussed below.[100]

II. The Protection Component of the MPA

The protection component of the MPA has four main objectives: 1) strengthening the legal and operational framework for the protection of refugee and IDPs in the region; 2) strengthening the national commissions in charge of RSD; 3) strengthening the national and regional protection networks; and 4) improving the training and promotion of International Refugee Law (research and doctrinal development). To these four objectives a fifth was added in terms of achievement—the enhancement of legislation targeting the protection of the most vulnerable groups, especially in relation to age and gender.

Besides the mentioned developments in protection, such as the adoption of the Cartagena Declaration in national legislation and the expansion of the motives for recognizing refugee status, the protection component of the MPA was also successful in twinning-practices, and in highlighting best practices to be followed in the region.

In relation to the twinning-practices, they have occurred both with States within Latin America (especially with regard to the strengthening of the national commissions in charge of RSD as in the cases of Brazil assisting Paraguay) and outside the region (especially in relation to durable solutions, mainly resettlement). And in terms of best practices, the UNHCR stressed the relevance of a compendium of the Brazilian National Committee on Refugees which will 'aid in one of the MPA's core goals: decentralizing the refugee status determination process, to make it more regionally based'.[101]

In the five years since the adoption of the MPA, one can see that the protection of refugees and IDPs in the region has improved. The developments seem to arise from theory and then influence practice and may assist in the enhancement of refugee law and protection not only in the region but maybe universally.

III. The Durable Solutions Component of the MPA

The durable solutions component of the MPA builds on the traditional durable solutions of local integration and resettlement to adapt them to the regional

---

[98] Ibid.
[99] UNHCR, Mexico Plan of Action, p. 11
[100] *Infra*, MN 76–90.
[101] UNHCR, Mexico Plan of Action, p. 12.

context. This component is divided into three key areas: 1) borders of solidarity; 2) cities of solidarity; and 3) resettlement in solidarity.[102]

The borders of solidarity component derives from the massive influx of refugees and other persons in need of protection from Colombia to neighbouring countries and focuses on the need to strengthen protection in frontier areas. It can be said to be inspired by the sixth conclusion of the Cartagena Declaration[103] and it focuses on two different areas. On the one hand, it aims to enhance protection mechanisms at the borders by (i) training border officials, (ii) establishing offices and protection networks to guarantee access to adequate RSD procedures, and (iii) combating abuses (sexual and otherwise) that may take place in border areas.

On the other hand, the borders of solidarity initiative focus on the receiving communities in order to minimize the large and disproportionate impact that a mass influx of refugees may cause. In this sense, the initiative has established community projects of comprehensive assistance and humanitarian assistance at the borders. This is important as it is estimated that 25 to 30 per cent of the population in need live close to frontiers.[104] In this initiative, cooperation among States, the UNHCR, and other agencies has been the rule.

The cities of solidarity initiative focus on local integration of refugees in urban settings and acts in two main areas. On the one hand, it aspires to facilitate access to basic services demonstrating the same concern for assistance as the borders in solidarity initiative. And, on the other hand, it aims to forge alliances with governments (at the municipal and regional levels) to facilitate local integration. As of 2007, 25 cities of solidarity had signed agreements with the UNHCR in the framework of this initiative.[105]

In relation to local integration, an important component of the cities of solidarity initiative is the development of public policies that include or are specific to refugees. In this sense the establishment of forums to debate this development is important. In Brazil two such forums, in addition to the National Committee on Refugees that is vested with primary responsibility for RSD and public policies for the refugee population, have been established on local or regional levels: the State Committee for Refugees in the ambit of the States of São Paulo and of Rio de Janeiro, and the Paulista Committee for Immigrants and Refugees coordinated by the City of São Paulo Human Rights Commission.

The resettlement in solidarity initiative was proposed by the Brazilian government and was adopted as a part of the MPA. It aims to 'strategically resettle those in need of protection within the region'[106] and has proved to be an innovative

---

[102] This chapter uses the terminology 'resettlement in solidarity' as this seems to be a translation more in keeping with the original concept of *'reassentamento solidário'* than the generally used terminology of 'solidarity resettlement'.

[103] Cartagena Declaration, Part III, para. 6: 'To reiterate to countries of asylum that refugee camps and settlements located in frontier areas should be set up inland at a reasonable distance from the frontier with a view to improving the protection afforded to refugees, safeguarding their human rights and implementing projects aimed at their self-sufficiency and integration into the host society.'

[104] UNHCR, Mexico Plan of Action, p. 12.

[105] *Ibid.*, p. 13.

[106] Ibid.

approach to the durable solution of resettlement.

Before the MPA, Latin America had two emerging resettlement countries—Brazil and Chile—which were or would be involved in the implementation of traditional resettlement. With the adoption of the MPA the focus of resettlement in the region changed: it became more regionally focused although not closed to other possibilities (as the resettlement of Iraqi refugees from Jordan and Syria starting in 2007 has proved).

The idea was to provide for the resettlement of Colombian refugees within the region, thus assisting the refugees in need of protection and the States that were receiving large numbers of refugees from this humanitarian crisis—namely Ecuador and Costa Rica.

Since the adoption of the MPA, the resettlement in solidarity has achieved the resettlement of over 900 people. This was possible given that Brazil and Chile were joined by Argentina and, more recently, by Paraguay and Uruguay as resettlement countries, and that the civil society in the region has also joined this initiative. For example, it is estimated that in Brazil 80 new partners are now involved in resettlement activities.[107]

Apart from the above-mentioned improvements, one can say that one of the most relevant contributions of the durable solutions component of the MPA is the addition of the idea of solidarity in all of its actions. Besides enhancing the duty of solidarity as a principle of refugee law and protection in the region, this inclusion changes the traditional rhetoric on the subject insofar as, instead of the concept of burden-sharing, it adopts the idea of actions in solidarity.

This change allows for a more humane approach to refugee law and protection and enables actions to be taken in solidarity with States and with refugees, providing for a more comprehensive and humanitarian framework of action. This is a clear link between the MPA and the Cartagena Declaration and can be said to be the core of the regional developments in refugee law and protection in the Americas: a more comprehensive regional approach to refugee law and protection in which the ideas of solidarity and humanitarianism are present and aspire to be the cornerstone of the refugee regime.

E. Conclusions

Despite being an extremely diverse region with developed countries that rank among the largest receivers of refugees and still having refugee-producing countries, there have been significant regional developments in refugee law and protection in the Americas. Especially in Latin America, the adoptions of the Cartagena Declaration and the MPA were clear signals of improvement.

These documents purport to bring along a more humane and humanitarian approach to refugee law and protection aiming to establish a region in which solidarity and the willingness to respect human rights and human beings will be the goal, with a special concern towards specific vulnerability as in the cases of women and children.

---

[107] Nogueira/Marques, *FMR* 30 (2008), p. 57.

REFUGEE PROTECTION IN BRAZIL AND LATIN AMERICA

The region has been, since the early 1980s, in a continuous process of deepening its commitment to refugee law and protection and of finding regional solutions for the refugee question, inspired by the human rights approach and by the value of solidarity.

References

Campbell, E., United States' *Refugee and Asylum Policy: The Story of a Closing Door* (currently in print—manuscript on file with the authors)

Carneiro, W.P., 'A Declaração de Cartagena de 1984 e os Desafios da Proteção Internacional dos Refugiados, 20 Anos Depois', in *Refugiados* (da Silva, C.A.S./Rodrigues, V.M., eds., 2005), pp. 55–74

Farer, T., 'The Rise of the Inter-American Human Rights Regime: No Longer a Unicorn, Not Yet an Ox', in *International Human Rights in Context* (Steiner, H.J./Alston, P., eds., 2nd edn., 2000), pp. 877–881

Goodwin-Gill, G.S./McAdam, J., *The Refugee in International Law* (3rd edn., 2007)

Harris, D., 'Regional Protection of Human Rights: The Inter-American Achievement', in *International Human Rights in Context* (Steiner, H.J./Alston, P., eds., 2nd edn., 2000), pp. 874–877

Hathaway, J.C., *The Rights of Refugees under International Law* (2005)

——, 'Reconceiving Refugee Law as Human Rights Protection', *JRS* 4 (1991), p. 113–131

IACmHR, Protección de Refugiados y Solicitantes de Asilo en el Sistema Interamericano de Derechos Humanos (2006), available at <http://www.acnur.org/biblioteca/pdf/ 2868.pdf>

Jubilut, L.L., 'Refugee Law and Protection in Brazil: A Model in South America?', *JRS* 19 (2006), pp. 22–44

——, *O Direito Internacional dos Refugiados e sua Aplicação no Ordenamento Jurídico Brasileiro* (2007)

Jubilut, L.L./Apolinário, S.M.S., 'Refugee Status Determination in Brazil: A Tripartite Enterprise', *Refuge* 25, No. 2 (2010), pp.29-40.

Lauterpacht, E./Bethlehem, D., 'The Scope and Content of the Principle of Non-Refoulement: Opinion', in *Refugee Protection in International Law: UNHCR's Global Consultations on International Protection* (Feller, E./Türk, V./Nicholson, F., eds., 2003), pp. 87–177

Murillo González, J.C., 'La Protección Internacional de Refugiados en el Continente Americano: Nuevos Desarrollos', in *XXXV Curso de Derecho Internacional (Comité Jurídico Interamericano, Departamento de Derecho Internacional*, Secretaría de Asuntos Jurídicos, Secretaría General, eds., 2008), pp. 351 et seq.

Nogueira, M.B./Marques, C., 'Brazil: Ten Years of Refugee Protection', *FMR* 30 (2008), pp. 57–58

O'Connor, C.M., 'Regional Approaches to Forced Migration: Latin America', in *The Refugee Convention at Fifty: a View from Forced Migration Studies* (van Selm, J./Kamanga, K./Morrison, J./Nadig, A./Spoljar-Vrzina, S./van Willingen, L., eds., 2003), pp. 31–37

Piovesan, F., *Direitos Humanos e Justiça Internacional* (2006)

——, *Temas de Direitos Humanos* (2009)

Shacknove, A., 'Non-refoulement', lecture given at The University of Oxford and The George Washington University Joint Programme in International Human Rights Law (2002)

UNHCR, Mexico Declaration and Plan of Action to Strengthen the International Protection of Refugees in Latin America (2004), available at <http://www.acnur.org/biblioteca/ pdf/3453.pdf>

——, *Mexico Plan of Action: The Impact of Regional Solidarity* (2007)

——, Países de América Latina Que Han Incorporado la Definicion de Refugiado de la Declaración de Cartagena sobre los Refugiados en Su Legislación Nacional (2008), available at <http://www.acnur.org/biblioteca/pdf/2542.pdf>

——, States Parties to the 1951 Convention Relating to the Status of Refugees and the 1967 Protocol (2008), available at <http://www.unhcr.org/3b73b0d63.html>

——, *2008 Global Trends: Refugees, Asylum-Seekers, Returnees, Internally Displaced and Stateless Persons* (2009), available at <http://www.unhcr.org/4a375c426.html>

——, Definición Ampliada de Refugiados en América Latina: Incorporación de la Declaración de Cartagena sobre Refugiados en la Legislación de los Países de la Región (2009), available at <http://www.acnur.org/biblioteca/pdf/2541.pdf>

UN-OHRLLS, *Least Developed Countries: Country Profiles*, available at <http://www.unohrlls.org/en/ldc/related/62>

Wollny, H., 'Asylum policy in Mexico: A Survey', *JRS* 13 (2000), pp. 184–204

Zucker, N.L./Zucker, N.F., 'The Uneasy Troika in US Refugee Policy: Foreign Policy, Pressure Groups, and Resettlement Costs', *JRS* 2 (1989), pp. 359–372

Travaux Préparatoires

Conference of Plenipotentiaries, Text of Article 1 Proposed by the Drafting Group (Belgium, Canada, Holy See, United Kingdom), UN Doc. A/CONF.2/105 (1951)

Conference of Plenipotentiaries, 13th Meeting, UN Doc. A/CONF.2/SR.13 (1951)

Conference of Plenipotentiaries, 14th Meeting, UN Doc. A/CONF.2/SR.14 (1951)

Conference of Plenipotentiaries, 18th Meeting, UN Doc. A/CONF.2/SR.18 (1951)

Conference of Plenipotentiaries, 19th Meeting, UN Doc. A/CONF.2/SR.19 (1951)

Conference of Plenipotentiaries, 21st Meeting, UN Doc. A/CONF.2/SR.21 (1951)

Conference of Plenipotentiaries, 33rd Meeting, UN Doc. A/CONF.2/SR.33 (1951)

Conference of Plenipotentiaries, 35th Meeting, UN Doc. A/CONF.2/SR.35 (1951)

FORA AND PROGRAMMES FOR REFUGEES IN LATIN AMERICA (2014)

Liliana Lyra Jubilut[*]

Introduction

In a book concerning regional protection of asylum seekers, a contribution focusing on Latin America[1] could not be absent. This is due to the fact that (i) the region has been involved, since the 1980s[2], in the advancement of International Refugee Law and protection through collective efforts and agendas, and (ii) that said efforts have been praised[3] and the region came to be regarded as something of a model in the topic by the international community.[4]

The regional approach has proved to have reflexes in two different scenarios. First, it reflects on national practice and policies, as States seem to be inspired by the collective initiatives adopted by the region and try to include the developments brought along by them into the national legal systems, which may lead to improved protection. Second, it reflects on the region as a whole as collective standards and actions enhance international solidarity and cooperation and aim to balance the

---

[*] Liliana Lyra Jubilut, PhD and Masters in International Law (Universidade de São Paulo, Brazil) and LLM in International Legal Studies (NYU School of Law, New York), is Visiting Scholar at the Columbia Law School, Professor of the Post-graduate Program *Stricto Sensu* in Law at Universidade Católica de Santos, Brazil and has been working with refugee issues in Brazil for 14 years.

[1] For the purposes of this paper the expression 'Latin America' will be employed broadly to encompass all American countries located below Mexico, excluding States in the Caribbean even if they have a Latin-based language or a Latin-based historical background. The States in Latin America, thus, are the States of Central and South America combined; as defined by the United Nations Statistical Division (data available at <http://unstats.un.org/unsd/methods/m49/m49region.htm#americas>). In light of this the term Latin America in this paper refers to: Argentina, Belize, Bolivia, Brazil, Chile, Colombia, Costa Rica, Ecuador, El Salvador, Guatemala, Guyana, Honduras, Mexico, Nicaragua, Panama, Paraguay, Peru, Suriname, Uruguay, and Venezuela.

[2] With the Cartagena Declaration of 1984, Latin America can be said to have started its regional approach to refugee protection.

[3] The region has been said to use a 'creative, innovative and pragmatic approach' to refugee protection as well as to providing 'an example of how political will, regional and international solidarity, and shared responsibility are essential principles for offering protection and reaching durable solutions'. See UNHCR, *The Refugee Situation in Latin America: Protection and Solutions Based on the Pragmatic Approach of the Cartagena Declaration on Refugees of 1984 – Discussion Document* (2006) 18 Int'l. Refugee L. 255. It also has been said that 'Latin America has a generous, long-standing tradition of asylum and protection of refugees'. See P Lavanchi, 'The Mexico Declaration and Plan of Action: Reaffirming Latin America's Generous Tradition of Asylum and Innovative Solutions' (2006) 18 Int'l J. Refugee L. 450.

[4] As was the case of pronouncements by UNHCR staff during the International Meeting on Refugee and Stateless Persons Protection and Mixed Migratory Movements in the Americas that took place in Brasilia in November 2010.

interests and needs of States and of the refugee population, thus enabling a more humane approach to International Refugee Law and protection.[5]

In light of this, it is important to describe how Latin America has been creating regional approaches to the protection of asylum seekers and refugees, through the establishment of fora and programs, which is the aim of this contribution.

In order to present as comprehensive scenario as possible, this chapter will highlight the backdrop against which Latin America's regional approach is set and the main documents that have emerged from the region. It will also note the main national developments that originate from the regional approach to International Refugee Law, with the purpose of allowing for conclusions on whether or not the region can truly be seen as a model of protection of asylum seekers and refugees in a regional or even international perspective.

This contribution is thus divided into three main sections: first, there is an assessment of refugees' protection emerging from a regional approach. This is followed by a description of the right of asylum in Latin America. The last part focuses more extensively on refugees' protection in Latin America, highlighting three important regional documents on the matter: the Cartagena Declaration, the Mexico Declaration and Plan of Action and the Brasilia Declaration.

Refugees' Protection Through a Regional Approach

It can be said that regionalism lies at the foundation of refugee protection, given that the first initiatives on the topic 'were regional in the sense that they were directed at a perceived "European" problem'.[6] In this sense, the term seems to have a delimiting significance, even a negative one as it is limiting the scope of attention and of protection.

This negative connotation also appears when regionalism leads to protectionism or when it serves as an excuse to not develop international mechanism and documents on refuge protection, and hence may lead to the diminishing of the universal international standards. In all of these cases, it seems that the inadequacy of the concept arises from the imposition of limitations to refugee protection, though the adoption of excluding concepts and/or the adoption of collective practices that, in reality, limit and violate International Refugee Law.

Nowadays, however, when one speaks of regionalism it seems to have a different undertone, rather as a new approach to refugee protection that can enhance the international system by coexisting with it and tailoring initiatives and documents to a region's reality.[7]

Regionalism can be said to mean 'a collective or communal response within a

---

[5] LL Jubilut and WP Carneiro, 'Resettlement in Solidarity: a regional new approach towards a more humane durable solution' (2011) 30(3) *Refugee Survey Quarterly*.

[6] S Kneebone and F Rawlings-Sanaei (eds), *New Regionalism and Asylum Seekers: Challenges Ahead* (Berghahn Books, 2007), 4.

[7] On the different meanings of regionalism see for instance International Law Commission, 'Report of the work of the Study Group on the Fragmentation of International Law: Difficulties arising from the diversification and expansion of international law' UN Doc A/CN.4/L.682 (2006), paras 195–217, available at <http://daccess-dds-ny.un.org/doc/UNDOC/LTD/G06/610/77/PDF/ G0661077.pdf? Open Element> p

region to a global issue where the parties share a common purpose or destiny'.[8] It is in this sense that the UNHCR seems to have embraced regionalism as a way forward in the aspect of refugee protection with a view to strengthening it,[9] and has declared regional documents to be a part of International Refugee Law.[10]

This positive facet of regionalism seems to be the one in place when a region comes together in trying to enhance International Refugee Law and protection, through the adoption of new concepts, new documents and new initiatives that build upon the international system's minimum criteria to develop refugee protection. This seems to be the case of Latin America's attitude toward refugee protection since the 1980s[11] with the adoption of the Cartagena Declaration.

The adoption of a regional approach to Refugee Law and protection is not exclusive to Latin America. It seems, actually, to be the current trend in refugee protection.[12]

The regional approach to the protection of asylum seekers and refugees can be said to have started with the Organization of African Unity's Convention Governing the Specific Aspects of Refugee Problems in Africa[13] in 1969, which enlarged the definition of refugees,[14] tailoring it to the realities of the African continent, and has been producing results since them.[15] The regional approach to asylum differs from situation to situation, and 'sometimes, as in Central America and South East Asia, regional organizations have led the effort in close partnership with UNHCR. In other cases, such as Cambodia, Liberia or Rwanda, regional organizations may cooperate with U.N. peacekeeping missions that include UNHCR'.[16]

In reality, in an age of closed borders and mixed migratory fluxes, with many States – including major players of the international arena – not willing or not prepared to advance refugee protection in universal documents and efforts,[17]

---

[8] Kneebone and Rawlings-Sanaei, New Regionalism and Asylum Seekers: Challenges Ahead 2.

[9] UNHCR. Executive Committee of the High Commissioner's Program, *Note on International Protection*, UN Doc A/AC.96/930 (7 July 2000), para 39, available at <http://www.unhcr.org/cgi-bin/texis/ home/opendocPDFViewer.html?docid=3ae68d6c4&query=note%20on%20international%20protection>.

[10] Ibid. para 32: 'The international refugee protection regime is a dynamic body of universal and regional refugee law and standards […]'.

[11] It is interesting to note that regionalism in general has seen a revival and change in the 1980s. See J Mittelman, 'Rethinking the "New Regionalism" in the Context of Globalization' (1996) 2 *Global Governance* 189–213.

[12] In an issue dedicated to regional solutions in 1995 (issue 99), *Refugees Magazine* pointed to the fact that 'regional and comprehensive responses may be the only possible solution to the complexity and magnitude of today's refugee problems', available at http://www.unhcr.org/cgi-bin/texis/vtx/ search?page =search&docid=3b5423494&query=regionalism.

[13] Adopted by the Organization of African Unity on 10 September 1969, available at <http://www.africa-union.org/Official_documents/Treaties_%20Conventions_%20Protocols/ Refugee_Convention.pdf>.

[14] Art 1(2), which states that 'The term "refugee" shall also apply to every person who, owing to external aggression, occupation, foreign domination or events seriously disturbing public order in either part or the whole of his country of origin or nationality, is compelled to leave his place of habitual residence in order to seek refuge in another place outside his country of origin or nationality'.

[15] As will be seen throughout this book.

[16] BN Stein, 'Regional solutions' (1995) 99 *Refugees Magazine*.

[17] The Convention Plus initiative from UNHCR seems to be built upon this idea, proposing new approaches to International Refugee Law and protection but not sponsoring a new universal document or

regional developments appear sometimes to be the only viable way forward.[18] This type of regionalism, especially when paired with the continuous respect to and advancement of the international standards,[19] appears to have a positive outcome in general, which certainly seems to be the case of Latin America.

The Right of Asylum in Latin America

A regional approach has been in place in Latin America since the 1800s in relation to granting protection for people suffering or that may suffer persecution in the form of the right of asylum.[20] In fact the first regional normative on this right is said to have been the one in this region.[21]

The right of asylum began to be theorized by Hugo Grotius[22] and was first declared in a Constitution after the French Revolution in 1793.[23] In Latin America it first appeared in a regional document in 1889 with the Treaty of International Penal Law of Montevideo (*Tratado de Direito Penal de Montevideo*).[24] The Treaty dedicated its second title to the subject of asylum, and established in its articles 15 to 18 provisions to protect people who had committed non-political offenses who it regarded as political refugees.[25]

Even though the mixture of the concepts of asylum and refuge are not technically adequate, as will be explored below, the Treaty is an important instrument in highlighting a regional concern with people suffering or that may suffer persecution since the end of the 19th century, and can be said to have inaugurated the legislation on the right of asylum in the region.[26] Such a right has been stated contemporarily both in universal and regional documents, with the latter being more assertive than the former.

In the universal arena the right is stated in Article 14 of the Universal Declaration of Human Rights which establishes that:

---

even a reform of the existing legal norms.

[18] See for instance the conclusion of UNHCR that: 'The international system has been in a state of significant transformation since the end of the Cold War. There was hope that these changes would result in the strengthening of international law and multilateral approaches to address international problems. Developments have not, however, fully realized this hope'. See *Note on International Protection* above n 9, para 31.

[19] This seems to be the position of UNHCR. See for instance UNHCR. Executive Committee of the High Commissioner's Program, *Note on International Protection*, EC/62/SC/CRP.12 (31 May 2011), paras 2, 6, 8 and 80, available at <http://www.unhcr.org/cgi-bin/texis/vtx/home/opendocPDF Viewer.html?docid= 4de4f6fc9&query=note%20on%20international%20protection>.

[20] LL Jubilut, *O Direito Internacional dos Refugiados e sua aplicação no ordenamento jurídico brasileiro* (São Paulo: Método, 2007) 38.

[21] JH Fichel De Andrade, *Direito internacional dos refugiados – Evolução Histórica (1921-1952)* (Renovar, 1996) 18.

[22] E Reut-Nicolussi, 'Displaced Persons in International Law' (1948) 73 *Recueil des Cours de la Academie de Droit International* 27.

[23] Ibid.: 16.

[24] Available at <http://www.unhcr.org/refworld/type,MULTILATERALTREATY,AMERICAS, ,3ae6b3781c,0.html>.

[25] See especially Arts 16 and 17.

[26] It is important to note that the Treaty was adopted in the South American Congress on Private International Law in Montevideo on 23 January 1889; and although it is not a document for the whole of Latin America it served as the first document with a regional approach to people suffering or that may suffer persecution.

(1) Everyone has the right to seek and to enjoy in other countries asylum from persecution; (2) This right may not be invoked in the case of prosecutions genuinely arising from non-political crimes or from acts contrary to the purposes and principles of the United Nations.[27]

In the regional arena, the right of asylum appears both on (i) Article 27 of the American Declaration of the Rights and Duties of Man which states that: 'Every person has the right, in case of pursuit not resulting from ordinary crimes, to seek and receive asylum in foreign territory, in accordance with the laws of each country and with international agreements',[28] and on (ii) Article 22 (7) of the American Convention of Human Rights which establishes that 'Every person has the right to seek and be granted asylum in a foreign territory, in accordance with the legislation of the state and international conventions, in the event he is being pursued for political offenses or related common crimes'.[29]

From the wording of the provisions, one sees that the regional norm grants not only the right to seek asylum but also to be granted asylum in face of persecution, therefore reinforcing the protective framework of asylum in the Americas.

However, the broader wording of the universal provision can be said to expand the possibility of protection as it does not limit the persecution to cases of political offenses or related common crimes, as the American provision seems to do. In fact the universal norm does not qualify persecution in its general provision, thus enabling the formation of a larger protection network.

Besides being based on both regional and universal frameworks and of being in place since the end of the 19th century, the protection of people suffering or that may suffer persecution in Latin America has yet another relevant aspect to be noted: the right of asylum in the region is upheld through two distinct, yet complementary, institutes.

One the one hand, the region implements the right of asylum by means of the institution of asylum[30] which can take two different forms: territorial asylum – when the protection is requested in the territory of the granting States – and diplomatic asylum – when the protection is sought in representations of the granting State (for example Embassies).[31] On the other hand, the region upholds the basic premises of the right of asylum through its commitment to the institution of refuge. It is possible to highlight the major differences[32] between asylum and refuge in a schematic way, so as to make them clear but not detour from the focus of this contribution. In this sense while asylum: (i) exists since Ancient Times; (ii) is a sovereign and discretionary decision by the granting State; (iii) does not have legal standards to be met for concession; (iv) can only be granted in face of actual political persecution; (v) can be diplomatic – when granted inside the state of origin or residency of the person fleeing persecution – or territorial – when granted in the

---

[27] Available at <http://www.un.org/en/documents/udhr/index.shtml#a14>.

[28] Available at <http://www.cidh.oas.org/Basicos/English/Basic2.American%20Declaration.htm>.

[29] Available at <http://www.oas.org/juridico/english/treaties/b-32.html>.

[30] See Jubilut, *O Direito Internacional dos Refugiados e sua aplicação no ordenamento jurídico brasileiro* 37–8.

[31] Ibid, 38.

[32] See also LPTF Barreto, *Das diferenças entre os institutos jurídicos, asilos e refúgio*, available at <www.mj.gov.br/sns/artigo_refugiado.htm>.

territory of the granting State; (vi) the only obligation that stems from it is legal residency and (vii) only exists once the State decides to grant it, consequently being based on a constitutive decision by the granting state; the institute of refuge (i) appeared in the beginning of the twentieth century; (ii) has an international normative; (iii) has its implementation supervised by an international organ – since the 1950s the United Nations High Commissioner for Refugees (UNHCR); (iv) cannot be applied in certain cases (exclusion clauses); (v) applies to cases of well-founded fear of persecution based on race, religion, nationality, social group or political opinion; (vi) requires alienage to be applied (i.e. the person seeking to be recognized as a refugee has to be outside their state of origin or habitual residence; (vii) generates responsibilities to the granting State in relation to the refugee and (viii) is a right of the refugee to be recognized as such in the cases set down by the normative standards; being hence granted by a declaratory decision.[33]

Nonetheless, both institutes aim at protecting people from (existing or possible) persecution and have a humanitarian nature, being, consequently, complementary[**] forms of protection.[34]

Given that refuge has a deeper sense of normativity and hence assists many more people, it can be said to have been the preferred method in the region for advancing protection for people suffering or that may suffer persecution. In this sense, the commitment of the States in the Americas to the Convention Relating to the Status of Refugees of 1951 (1951 Convention)[35] and the Protocol Relating to the Status of Refugees of 1967 (67 Protocol) is paramount.

As of October 2013, 27 States[36] in the Americas and Caribbean were a part of the Convention,[37] and 2 States[38] were a part only of the 67 Protocol. This means that within Latin America, with the exception of Guyana,[39] all States in the region are committed to the universal documents on International Refugee Law, and,

---

[33] Liliana L. Jubilut, 'International Refugee Law and Protection in Brazil: a model in South America?' (2006) 19(1) *Journal of Refugee Studies*, 29.

[**] Complementary in the sense that the institutes can be deemed to complement each other, protecting diferente persons, and enlarging the humanitarian protection space.

[34] Ibid. at 29. See also Flavia Piovesan and Liliana L. Jubilut, 'Regional Developments: Americas', in Andreas Zimmermann (ed.), *Commentary on the 1951 Convention Relating to the Status of Refugees and its 1967 Protocol*, 2011 at 213.

[35] Available at http://www.unhcr.org/3b66c2aa10.html.

[36] Such States are: Antigua and Barbuda; Argentina; Bahamas; Belize; Bolivia; Brazil; Canada; Chile; Colombia; Costa Rica; Dominica; Dominican Republic; Ecuador; El Salvador; Guatemala; Haiti; Honduras; Jamaica; Mexico; Nicaragua; Panama; Paraguay; Peru; Saint Vincent and the Grenadines; Suriname; Trinidad and Tobago and Uruguay (cf. data available at http://treaties.un.org/pages/ ShowMTDSG Details.aspx?src=UNTSONLINE&tabid=2&mtdsg_no=V-5&chapter=5&lang=en#Participants, and, http://treaties.un.org/pages/ViewDetailsII.aspx?&src= UNTSONLINE&mtdsg_no=V~2&chapter=5&Temp=mtdsg2&lang=en. Access on October 23, 2013).

[37] Saint Kitts and Nevis is a part only to the 51 Convention (cf. data available at http://treaties.un.org/ pages/ShowMTDSGDetails.aspx?src=UNTSONLINE&tabid=2&mtdsg_no=V-5&chapter=5&lang=en#Participants. Access on October 23, 2013).

[38] Such States are the United States of America and Venezuela (cf. data available at http://treaties. un.org/pages/ViewDetailsII.aspx?&src=UNTSONLINE&mtdsg_no=V~2&chapter=5&Temp=mtdsg2&l ang=en. Access on October 23, 2013).

[39] It is important here to remember the definition of Latin America for this chapter (as seen in footnote 1 supra), which excludes States such as Cuba, which are also not a part of the international system of refugee protection.

therefore, have obligations in implementing refugees' protection and therefore protecting both refugees and asylum seekers.

The Asylum Seeker's Protection in Latin America

The regional commitment to refuge, however, goes farther than the adoption of the universal standards, given that, as in the case of the right of asylum, truly regional approaches have been developed.

In the 1980s the Latin American region was faced, on the one hand, with armed conflicts in Central America[40] which generated massive fluxes of refugees[41] and, on the other hand, with waves of re-democratization[42] that brought about renewed commitments to human rights. With this scenario as its background, a balance between the needs of States and of refugees in a response to the Central American refugee crisis was required.[43] As a response to this need, a mainly academic symposium that also congregated governments' representatives and members of civil society organizations was held in Cartagena de Indias in Colombia in 1984.[44] From this seminar emerged the Cartagena Declaration on Refugees (Cartagena Declaration) that changed, and continues to change, the regional approach to refugee protection in the region.[45]

The Cartagena Declaration

The Cartagena Declaration[46] was adopted on 22 November 1984 and contains four main parts.[47] The first part consists of the preamble divided into seven paragraphs. The second part makes reference to the Contadora Act on Peace and Co-operation in Central America, a document related to the Central America conflict of the 1980s and which aims at ending it and dealing with its consequences that include over 2 million refugees.[48] This reference highlights the links between the Cartagena Declaration and the context of political strife in the region and helps explain the reasoning behind its adoption.

The Colloquium on the International Protection of Refugees in Central

---

[40] R William I, *Transnational Conflicts: Central America, Social Changes and Globalization* (Verso, 2003).

[41] See for instance A Suhrke, 'A crisis diminished: refugees in the developing world' (1992–93) 48 *Int'l J.* 218. In this paper the author points to 2 to 3 million people displaced due to the conflicts in Central America.

[42] GA Lopez and M Stohl, *Liberalization and Redemocratization in Latin America* (Greenwood Press, 1987).

[43] See *The Refugee Situation in Latin America: Protection and Solutions Based on the Pragmatic Approach of the Cartagena Declaration on Refugees of 1984 –Discussion Document* above n 3, 263.

[44] The symposium was sponsored by UNHCR, the government of Colombia, the University of Cartagena de Indias and the Regional Center for Third World Studies, according to CO Miranda, 'Toward a Broader Definition of Refugee: 20th Century Development Trends' (1989–90) 20 *Cal. W. Int'l L.J.* 323.

[45] See, for instance, F Piovesan and LL Jubilut, 'Regional Developments: Americas' in A Zimmermann (ed.), *Commentary on the 1951 Convention Relating to the Status of Refugees and its 1967 Protocol* (Oxford University Press, 2011) and Jubilut and Carneiro, 'Resettlement in Solidarity: a regional new approach towards a more humane durable solution'.

[46] Cartagena Declaration on Refugees, 22 November 1984. Available at <www.unhcr.ch/refworld/refworld/legal/instrume/asylum/cart_eng.htm>. <http://www.unhcr.org/refworld/docid/3ae6b36ec.html> or at http://www.unhcr.org/basics/BASICS/45dc19084.pdf.

[47] In the version presented at http://www.asylumlaw.org/docs/international/CentralAmerica.PDF the Cartagena Declaration has only three parts.

[48] W Spindler, 'The Mexico Plan of Action: protecting refugees through international solidarity' (2005) 24 *Forced Migration Review* 24.

America, Mexico and Panama – Legal and Humanitarian Problems (*Colloquio sobre la Protección Internacional de los Refugiados en América Central, México y Panamá – Problemas Jurídicos y Humanitários*) from which the Cartagena Declaration stems 'acknowledges with appreciation the commitments with regard to refugees included in the Contadora Act [...] the basis of which the Colloquium fully shares').[49] After presenting its context, the Cartagena Declaration establishes 17 conclusions that form the core of the prescriptive provisions of the document, and which are followed in the subsequent parts by five recommendations and two paragraphs containing acknowledgments.

The main provisions of the Declaration are, thus, contained in its conclusions which bring important changes (and improvements) to International Refugee Law and protection in Latin America, leading to the Cartagena Declaration being regarded as 'one of the most encompassing approaches to the refugee question'.[50]

The first change brought about by the Declaration relates to establishing a regional commitment to refugees and asylum seekers and their protection in a region comprised mainly by democracies that are, as a result, willing to keep faith with their human rights obligations, as well as human rights' recognition and defense. This is important since, even if there had been previous regional efforts in Latin America, they were mainly devoted to the right of asylum broadly, as mentioned above, and were produced in the context of a region with dictatorships and/or military regimes. The Declaration of Cartagena was the first landmark of a new regional approach to refugees and allows for the topic to be developed within the context of States that are willing to advance the rule of law and human rights.[51]

In light of the above, the Cartagena Declaration endeavours to take into account the needs of refugees and proposes new initiatives that were tailored to the region's need; being, thus, a document with both a practical and an aspirational side.

The commitment to a regional approach to refugee law can be seen, for instance, in the call for 'systematic harmonization of national legislation on refugees' which appears in the First Conclusion of the Cartagena Declaration.

On the other hand, the commitment to human rights is highlighted in the second change brought along by the Cartagena Declaration: the establishment of a broader definition for the recognition of refugees.

The Declaration proposes, in its Third Conclusion, an enlargement of the universal definition by adding to it the possibility of including among refugees the asylum seekers,

> ... *who have fled their country because their lives, safety or freedom have been threatened by generalized violence, foreign aggression, internal conflicts, massive violation of human rights or other circumstances which have seriously disturbed public order.*

The Cartagena Declaration states that this new criterion is motivated by the Organization of African Unity Convention Governing the Specific Aspects of

---

[49] Cartagena Declaration on Refugees, above n 46. 1st paragraph of the preamble,
[50] GS Goodwin-Gill, *The Refugee in International Law* (2nd edn, Oxford University Press, 1996) 38.
[51] See Piovesan and Jubilut, 'Regional Developments: Americas' 218.

Refugee Problems in Africa[52] and also the reports of the InterAmerican Commission of Human Rights,[53] thus demonstrating that the region avails itself of the best practices on International Refugee Law and protection around the world.

It has been said that the Cartagena Declaration has established a new criterion of recognizing refugees, an expanded definition[54] or a more comprehensive criteria[55] but this seemingly

> *falls short of explaining the concept of Cartagena. In fact it is not simply an extension, as it does not introduce new criteria within the ranks of an individualized perspective. It builds the refugee definition upon the objective situation and the social and political environment of the country of origin as the main definition criterion. The recognition as a refugee, therefore, occurs regardless of the individual attributes of the person in need of protection (as religion, or ethnicity) as in the traditional universal criteria.*[56]

The possibility of recognizing people fleeing massive violation of human rights as refugees is an important advancement of International Refugee Law and protection in the region, and allows for the protection of people escaping from civil conflicts or strife, war and even dictatorships, given that all of these situations are in themselves or can lead to violations of human rights.

It is important to highlight that the regional definition of refugees is to be used alongside the universal criteria, as it does not mean to replace but complement it.

In this sense: 'The Cartagena Declaration declares that aside from the refugees recognized under the 1951 Convention there exists other persons that require international protection'.[57]

The Cartagena Declaration itself highlights the importance for States to accede and/or to respect the universal standards of International Refugee Law and protection[58] and recalls some of its most relevant provisions such as: (i) 'the peaceful, non-political and exclusively humanitarian nature' of granting refugee status;[59] (ii) the imperative nature of the *non-refoulement* principle, which is a cornerstone of International Refugee Law and protection and which it declares to be a rule of *jus cogens*;[60] and (iii) the fact that the 1951 Convention and the 1967 Protocol establish a minimum standard of treatment for refugees.[61]

The Cartagena Declaration was approved by the General Assembly of the Organization of American States in 1985, 'which resolved to urge member states

---

[52] See Cartagena Declaration above n 46, 3rd Conclusion.

[53] See Cartagena Declaration above n 46, 3rd Conclusion. See also *The Refugee Situation in Latin America: Protection and Solutions Based on the Pragmatic Approach of the Cartagena Declaration on Refugees of 1984 – Discussion Document*, (2006) above n 3, 264.

[54] Carlos Ortiz Miranda. Op. cit. supra at 44 at 324.

[55] J. C. Hathaway, *The Rights of Refugees under International Law*, 2005 at 67.

[56] Liliana L. Jubilut and Wellington P. Carneiro.
'Resettlement in Solidarity: a regional new approach towards a more humane durable solution'.supra at 5 at 67.

[57] See *The Refugee Situation in Latin America: Protection and Solutions Based on the Pragmatic Approach of the Cartagena Declaration on Refugees of 1984 – Discussion Document* above n 3, 262.

[58] See Cartagena Declaration above n 46, 1st and 2nd Conclusions.

[59] See Cartagena Declaration above n 46, 4th Conclusion.

[60] See Cartagena Declaration above n 46, 5th Conclusion.

[61] See Cartagena Declaration above n 46, 8th Conclusion.

to extend support and, insofar as possible, to implement the conclusions and recommendations to the Cartagena Declaration on Refugees'.[62]

Given that the Declaration was inspired by the InterAmerican Human Rights System, as already mentioned, and that this system has approved the Declaration, one can see that the topic of International Refugee Law and protection in Latin America is, on the one hand, being treated in a holistic manner and in a context of human rights,[63] consequently allowing for a more integral protection and that, on the other hand, it has different fora in which it is to be dealt with, which can enable debates with different actors and against different backgrounds.

The Cartagena Declaration's definition of refugees has been adopted by 15 Latin American States[64] in their national legislation, which is relevant in so far as the Declaration itself is a soft law instrument. Some States have kept the original wording of the Declaration and others have changed it[65] but maintaining the so-called 'spirit of Cartagena' that has come to mean an approach to International Refugee Law and protection that is (i) broader in scope, (ii) more closely related to human rights and (iii) more beneficial in terms of people being protected given the added criterion for refugee status.

This relation to human rights is also present in the sense that,

> ... [t]he Declaration includes the protection and treatment that should be offered to refugees during the entire cycle of forced displacement. In fact, it deals with a summary of good practices, based on the 1951 Convention relating to the Status of Refugees and its 1967 Protocol, which brings together the generous tradition of asylum in Latin America and is complemented by the integration of the norms and standards of human rights protection, in particular the American Convention on Human Rights, and international humanitarian law.[66]

Also, 'the Cartagena Declaration makes a pioneering reference as much for the economic, social and cultural rights of the asylum seekers and refugees as for the problem of the internally displaced persons'.[67]

This close link between Refugee Law and protection to human rights is important given that 'nowadays the prevailing view is that refugee law and protection are a part of international human rights law in its broader sense (i.e.

---

[62] Cf. data available at <http://www.hrea.org/index.php?doc_id=413>.

[63] See Piovesan and Jubilut, 'Regional Developments: Americas' 218 and seq.

[64] Such States are Argentina, Belize, Bolivia, Brazil, Chile, Colombia, Ecuador, El Salvador, Guatemala, Honduras, Mexico, Nicaragua, Paraguay, Peru and Uruguay (cf. data available at <http://www.acnur.org/t3/que-hace/proteccion/declaracion-de-cartagena-sobre-los-refugiados/paises-que-incorporan-cartagena-en-la-legislacion-nacional/?L=gulnlxwoshxdx> and on <http://www.acnur.org/t3/fileadmin/scripts/doc.php?file=biblioteca/pdf/2541>). (It is relevant to note that the data here is a combination of both sources as, for instance, Ecuador does not appear on the list present on the former but appears on the latter.) Accessed on October 23, 2013. In 2012 Ecuador has changed its legislation and is not currently using the criteria from the Cartagena Declaration, so only 14 States have now the Cartagena Declaration definition of refugees in their national legislation.

[65] Piovesan and Jubilut, 'Regional Developments: Americas' 219–20.

[66] See *The Refugee Situation in Latin America: Protection and Solutions Based on the Pragmatic Approach of the Cartagena Declaration on Refugees of 1984 – Discussion Document*, (2006) above n 3, 262.

[67] Ibid.: 263.

international law on the protection of human beings)'.[68] Besides this, refugees as human beings have to have their human rights respected in order for protection to be considered integral.[69]

Moreover, in relation to the Latin American context this link between human rights and International Refugee Law and protection shows a change in the politics of the region which have been marked by human rights abuse[70] in the past and seem nowadays to be more committed to international human rights and show, as a result, the protection of the rights stemming from human dignity; thus providing for a more holistic approach and protection of refugees.[71]

This more comprehensive attitude towards refugees has had some impact on national legislation, leading some Latin American countries to establish gender-based persecution or sexual violence as reasons for refugee status[72] and others to have specific provisions for refugee children in their national legislation.[73]

The third change produced by the Cartagena Declaration is the establishment of fora to debate International Refugee Law and protection with a view to continuing to improve it in the region. Such debates occur in periodical assessment meetings of the implementation of the Declaration, and from which new regional instruments have emerged.

The Regional Instrumental Consequences of the Cartagena Declaration

Since the adoption of the Cartagena Declaration, regular regional meetings, where debate fora were established, have been held. Generally the meetings that have had the most impact have occurred in commemoration and/or celebration of the most relevant anniversaries of the documents on International Refugee Law and protection. This was the case, for instance, of the San Jose Declaration on Refugees and Displaced Persons,[74] adopted in 1994, during the International

---

[68] See Piovesan and Jubilut, 'Regional Developments: Americas' 208.

[69] LL Jubilut and SMOS Apolinário, 'A necessidade de proteção internacional no âmbito da migração' (2010) 11(6)(1) *Revista Direito GV* 275 and seq.

[70] D Harris, 'Regional Protection of Human Rights: The Inter-American Achievement' in HJ Steiner and P Alston (eds), *International Human Rights in Context* (2nd edn, Oxford University Press, 2000) 874–77.

[71] See Piovesan and Jubilut, 'Regional Developments: Americas' 218.

[72] See for instance as in the cases of Guatemala that have listed gender-based persecution and sexual violence as criteria for refugee status in art. 11(d) of Acuerdo Gubernativo No 383 del 14 de Septiembre de 2001 – Reglamento para la protección y determinación del estatuto de refugiado en el territorio del Estado de Guatemala, available at <http://www.acnur.org/t3/fileadmin/scripts/doc.php?file= biblioteca/ pdf/1410>. And see of Honduras, in art. 42, 3, e of Decreto No 208 del 3 de marzo de 2003 – Ley de migración y extranjería, available at <http://www.acnur.org/t3/fileadmin/scripts/doc.php? file=biblioteca /pdf/2528>.

[73] JCM González, 'La Protección Internacional de Refugiados en el Continente Americano: Nuevos Desarrollos' 2008, in Comité Jurídico Interamericano, Departamento de Derecho Internacional, Secretaría de Asuntos Jurídicos, Secretaría General (eds) (2008) *XXXV Curso de Derecho Internacional* 358.

[74] See San José Declaration on Refugees and Displaced Persons, 7 December 1994, available at <http://www.unhcr.org/refworld/docid/4a54bc3fd.html>. There have been other regional documents adopted in the region. However they either had (i) a specific focus; or (ii) were developed by civil society and did not count with States' commitments; or (iii) are considered to be of lesser importance to the development of Refugee Law and protection in the region; or (iv) do not represent the most current perceptions on International Refugee Law. These documents are: Declaración de Quito, 2010 (a document from civil society); Declaración de Quito sobre migraciones, democracia, desarrollo y derechos humanos. Quito, Ecuador, 2002 (a document from civil society); Declaración de Río sobre la institución del refugio. Rio de Janeiro, Brasil, 2000 (a document by MERCOSUL, Bolivia and Chile); Declaración de Tlatelolco, México,

Colloquium in Commemoration of the 'Tenth Anniversary of the Cartagena Declaration on Refugees'. The San Jose Declaration[75] stressed the importance of the Cartagena Declaration and highlighted that

> *pursuant to the adoption of the Cartagena Declaration a significant process in the search for durable solutions has been initiated, whereby such solutions have been integrated within the framework of convergence between respect for human rights, peace-building and linkage with economic and social development.*[76]

In its conclusions, the San Jose Declaration mostly repeats and reinforces the provisions of the Cartagena Declaration, but states through an innovative proposition the 'complementary nature and convergence between the systems of protection to persons established in International Human Rights Law, International Humanitarian Law and International Refugee Law'.[77]

It also encourages 'governments to seek humanitarian solutions, within a coordinated framework'[78] which means that the San Jose Declaration not only continues with the idea of regional fora and the 'spirit of Cartagena' to tackle the issue of refugees but also sets the premises for further advancing International Refugee Law and protection in Latin America, which will be done in a profound way ten years later.

The Mexico Declaration and Plan of Action

A new significant regional program in dealing with refugee protection was achieved in the celebration of the Twentieth Anniversary of the Cartagena Declaration: the Mexico Declaration and Plan of Action (MPA).[79]

The MPA 'is a regional strategic and operational framework developed to address the complex humanitarian situation resulting from forced displacement in Latin America'[80] which was adopted in 2004[81] by 20 States,[82] including 17 States

---

1999 (a document from the Seminario de Tlatelolco de 1989 sobre Acciones Prácticas en el Derecho de los Refugiados en América Latina y el Caribe, that presents refuge and asylum as synonyms); and Declaración y compromiso del Primer Foro Regional 'Enfoque de género en el trabajo con las mujeres refugiadas, repatriadas y desplazadas' (FOREFEM), Guatemala, 1992. (Cf. data available at <http://www.acnur.org/t3/que-hace/proteccion/declaracion-de-cartagena-sobre-los-refugiados/antecedentes-juridicos-y-desarrollos-de-la-declaracion-de-cartagena-sobre-refugiados/ and http://www.cartamesoamericana.com/modules.php?name=News&file=article&sid=477> on the topic of the Declaration of Tlatelolco take on refuge and asylum).

[75] See San José Declaration above n74.
[76] Ibid. Part I, para 4.
[77] Ibid. 3rd Conclusion.
[78] Ibid. 6th Conclusion.
[79] ACNUR, Mexico Declaration and Plan of Action to Strengthen the International Protection of Refugees in Latin America, 16 November 2004, available at <http://www.acnur.org/ biblioteca/ pdf/3453.pdf>.
[80] UNHCR, *Mexico Plan of Action: The impact of regional solidarity* (1st edn 2007), 11.
[81] The MPA was adopted after meetings in San Jose, Brasilia, Cartagena and Bogota. See *The Refugee Situation in Latin America: Protection and Solutions Based on the Pragmatic Approach of the Cartagena Declaration on Refugees of 1984 – Discussion Document* above n 3, 252.
[82] The MPA was adopted by Argentina, Bolivia, Brazil, Chile, Colombia, Costa Rica, Cuba, Dominican Republic, Ecuador, El Salvador, Guatemala, Haiti, Honduras, Mexico, Nicaragua, Panama, Paraguay, Peru, Uruguay and Venezuela. Cf. data obtained with Juan Carlos Murillo González – UNHCR Regional Legal Officer for the Americas, who the author would like to thank for this contribution and at UNHCR, *Memoir*

from Latin America,[83] and has as its context not only the celebration of the Cartagena Declaration but also the Colombian refugee crisis.[84]

Once again, one sees that the region is compelled to deal with a significant refugee crisis – with numbers of refugees and internally displaced people sitting at over four million[85] – stemming from a conflict that has been in place for over 40 years[86] and choosing to do so in a regional framework.

More specifically, the MPA proposed a regional approach to the Colombian refugee crisis, building upon the 'spirit of Cartagena'. In this sense the MPA developed a two-pillar strategy. On the one hand, one finds the second chapter of the MPA which deals with the international protection of refugees, and, on the other hand, the third chapter of the MPA that deals with durable solutions.[87] Each chapter is being referred to as one component of the MPA – the protection component and the durable solutions component.[88]

This double focus can be justified by the fact that '[t]he primary aim in drafting the Mexico Plan of Action (MPA) was to move beyond empty rhetoric on the protection needs of refugees, internally displaced persons (IDPs), and others in Latin America. The fundamental goal was to produce concrete action [...]'.[89]

Focusing both on government and the civil society, the protection component aims to (i) strengthen research and doctrinal development and (ii) enhance training and institutional capacity-building.[90] It has obtained positive results, as the adoption or revision of national legislation on refugees in the region;[91, 92] and has fostered new forms of complementary protection.

Complementary protection has appeared in the region, for instance, through

---

of the Twentieth Anniversary of the Cartagena Declaration on Refugees (2005) 365–7, available at <http://www.acnur.org/biblioteca/pdf/3868.pdf?view=1>.

[83] Only Belize, Guyana and Suriname are not a part of the MPA. It is interesting to note though that (i) Belize was a Observer State at the event in which the MPA was adopted (see UNHCR above n 82, 367); (ii) that in a document assessing Latin America and the MPA, UNHCR has included these three States (see data available at:www.unhcr.org/455443b30.html); and that (iii) the Dominican Republic and Haiti that were Observer States during the adoption of the MPA later became parts of it (see UNHCR above n 82, 368).

[84] See *The Refugee Situation in Latin America: Protection and Solutions Based on the Pragmatic Approach of the Cartagena Declaration on Refugees of 1984 – Discussion Document* above n 3, 254.

[85] The numbers of displacement caused by the Colombia refugee crisis are not consensual, especially giving the disputed data on internally displaced persons in the country. The number used in this paper builds upon the numbers used by United Nations High Commissioner for Refugees (UNHCR), *Global Trends 2010* (2011), available at <http://www.unhcr.org/4dfa11499.html>.

[86] For more on the Colombian refugee crisis and on the background of the MPA see Jubilut and Carneiro (2011): 64 and seq. (64–6 on the Colombia refugee crisis, and 66–8 on the Cartagena Declaration as a background of the MPA). In 2010, the Colombian refugee crisis was the 6th major source of refugees in the world with 395,600 refugees and 3.6 million internally displaced persons. See UNHCR above n 85, 15.

[87] See *Mexico Declaration and Plan of Action to Strengthen the International Protection of Refugees in Latin America* above n 79.

[88] See, for instance, *Mexico Plan of Action: The impact of regional solidarity* above n 80.

[89] Ibid.: 5.

[90] See Mexico Declaration and Plan of Action to Strengthen the International Protection of Refugees in Latin America above n 79, chap 2.

[91] As in the cases of Argentina which adopted in 2006 the *Ley No 26.165 – Ley General de Reconocimiento y protección de refugiados*, available at <http://www.acnur.org/t3/fileadmin/scripts/ doc.php?file= biblioteca /pdf/4658>. And Mexico which adopted in 2011 the *Ley sobre Refugiados y Protección Complementaria*, available at <http://www.acnur.org/t3/fileadmin/scripts/doc.php? file=biblioteca/ pdf/8150>.

[92] See *Mexico Plan of Action: The impact of regional solidarity* above n 80, 16.

humanitarian visas, protection to victims of torture and new forms of legal residence, which have occurred in Mexico, Honduras, Panama and Costa Rica, Brazil and Argentina.[93]

The durable component presents three different programs: 1) borders of solidarity – focusing both on (i) security and access to secure areas at the borders and on (ii) the needs and structure of the receiving communities; 2) cities of solidarity – addressing local integration needs and self-reliance of refugees and 3) resettlement in solidarity – establishing a regional resettlement program for Colombian refugees.[94]

This component of the MPA has highlighted 'the importance of the diffusion of "best practices" in the region, allowing for a South-South cooperation, as well as the need of addressing two specific situations[95] with the aid of the international community'.[96]

Besides establishing specific programs, that can be evaluated through pragmatic tools and indexes,[97] the MPA enormously contributed to International Law and protection in Latin American by introducing, through a normative approach, the concept of solidarity into actions aimed at refugees. In this sense, the MPA brings about more humane and newer discourses in International Refugee Law in which one sees the use of the term responsibility-sharing *in lieu* of burden-sharing,[98],[99] which is relevant in so far as,

> ... *this change represents much more than a simple shift in semantics but rather a transformation of how refugee protection and refugees are perceived: not as a problem and a situation of sharing refugees but as a responsibility for protecting the victims of violations of human rights.*[100]

And thus, the MPA enables a more equitable balance between the needs of refugees and asylum seekers and the interests and needs of States.[101]

Based on this idea of solidarity, and despite being created as a regional instrument with a regional focus and allowing for the improvement of regional protection of refugees, the MPA has provided the basis for the protection of over 100 Palestinian refugees that have been resettled in Brazil and Chile,[102] in an

---

[93] Information obtained during presentations at International Meeting on Refugee and Stateless Persons Protection and Mixed Migratory Movements in the Americas, which took place in Brasilia in November 2010.

[94] See Mexico Declaration and Plan of Action to Strengthen the International Protection of Refugees in Latin America above n 79, chap 3. For more details on each program see *Mexico Plan of Action: The impact of regional solidarity* above n 80; Piovesan and Jubilut (2011): 223; Jubilut and Carneiro (2011).

[95] The Colombia refugee crisis has affected Ecuador and Costa Rica as receiving States, as a result the MPA focused on resettling refugees from these two countries to other countries in the region.

[96] González, 'La Protección Internacional de Refugiados en el Continente Americano: Nuevos Desarrollos' 363 (translation by the author).

[97] See for instance <http://www.pamacnur2010.com/>.

[98] See Jubilut and Carneiro, 'Resettlement in Solidarity: a regional new approach towards a more humane durable solution' 70.

[99] On burden-sharing see, for instance, PH Schuck, 'Refugee Burden-Sharing: A Modest Proposal' (1997) 22 *Yale J. Int'l L.* 243.

[100] See Jubilut and Carneiro, 'Resettlement in Solidarity: a regional new approach towards a more humane durable solution'70.

[101] Ibid. 84.

[102] Ibid. 83.

example of international solidarity.[103] In this regard, the MPA is a major advancement in Refugee Law and protection in Latin America with both theoretical and practical consequences that help to foster more protective standards for the whole refugee population in the region.

The Brasilia Declaration

The will to maintain the process of a continuing effort of regional approaches to International Refugee Law which started with the Cartagena Declaration and advanced with the MPA was demonstrated, once again, at the end of 2011, when 18 countries[104] adopted the Brasilia Declaration on the Protection of Refugees and Stateless Persons[105] in the Americas (Brasilia Declaration),[106] reaffirming their commitment to enhancing Refugee Law and protection in the region with a humane and humanitarian approach.

Differently from the MPA, the Brasilia Declaration was adopted not in the celebration of an anniversary of the Cartagena Declaration but rather in relation to the anniversaries of the Convention relating to Refugee Status of 1951, the Convention Relating to the Status of Stateless Persons of 1951[107] and the Convention on the Reduction of Statelessness of 1961,[108] which justified the focus not only on refugees but also on Stateless Persons.[109]

The Brasilia Declaration recalls and builds upon the mentioned regional documents, and tries to update them, mentioning the difficulties arising from mixed migration flows[110] and the need for the values of solidarity, respect, tolerance and multiculturalism to underscore the application of refuge.[111]

Besides this, the Brasilia Declaration is relevant as 'the number of persons affected by forced migration has not significantly decreased worldwide or in the Americas'[112] and that

---

[103] See *The Refugee Situation in Latin America: Protection and Solutions Based on the Pragmatic Approach of the Cartagena Declaration on Refugees of 1984 – Discussion Document* above n 3, 255.

[104] The Brasilia Declaration was signed by Argentina, Bolivia, Brazil, Chile, Colombia, Costa Rica, Cuba, Dominican Republic, Ecuador, El Salvador, Guatemala, Mexico, Nicaragua, Panama, Paraguay, Peru, Uruguay and Venezuela.

[105] See the Brasilia Declaration on the Protection of Refugees and Stateless Persons in the Americas (Brasilia Declaration), 11 November 2010, available at <http://www.unhcr.org/refworld/docid/4cdd44582.html>. It is relevant to note that Stateless Persons are comprised in the 'persons of concern' category of UNHCR ever since its creation. In the beginning referring only to refugees that were stateless and since 1974 to stateless persons more generally. See H Massey, *UNHCR and De Facto Statelessness. Legal and Protection Policy* (Research Series, 2010), I, available at <http://www.unhcr.org/ 4bc2ddeb9.pdf>.

[106] Available at <http://www.unhcr.org/4cdd3fac6.html>.

[107] Convention Relating to the Status of Stateless Persons, 28 September 1954, United Nations, Treaty Series, Vol. 360, 117, available at <http://www.unhcr.org/refworld/docid/3ae6b3840.html>.

[108] Convention on the Reduction of Statelessness, 30 August 1961, United Nations, Treaty Series, Vol. 989, 175, available at http://untreaty.un.org/ilc/texts/instruments/english/ conventions/ 6_1_1961.pdf.

[109] In relation to Stateless Persons it is interesting to note that besides from UNHCR's efforts to have States accede to the international documents on the matter, the American Convention on Human Rights establishes *ius solis* as a rule for nationality in order to avoid statelessness (Article 20(2)). The American Convention is, available at http://www.unhcr.org/refworld/docid/3ae6b36510.html.

[110] See Brasilia Declaration above n105, 3rd Resolution.

[111] Ibid. 8th Resolution.

[112] D Costa, 'Introductory note to the Brasilia Declaration on the Protection of Refugees and Stateless

the existing legal framework for the protection of refugees and stateless persons still contains significant gaps that need to be addressed. Some of the particular sections in the Brasilia Declaration reference themes that are not addressed in the existing regional instruments.[113]

In this sense, the Brasilia Declaration demonstrate that Latin America still wants to improve its commitment to International Refugee Law and protection through a regional approach, hence continuing with the region's tradition encompassed in the 'spirit of Cartagena'.

Conclusion

In light of all the above, one sees that Latin America has a tradition of having regional fora and programs in relation to refugees. Some of them have emerged from practical needs in the face of conflicts, but even so they have allowed for the continuing advancement of International Refugee Law and protection in the region in general.

The regional approach to International Refugee Law and protection however does not replace the universal standards, but rather serves as a way to encourage States to accede to these documents and to complement them with regional tailored programs and actions, therefore aiming to enhance the protection of refugees.

From the regional Latin American approach, improvements have been noted in national practice and legislation, as norms more in keeping with the international standards, complementary protection and a broader definition of refugees have emerged from the Cartagena Declaration, the San Jose Declaration, the MPA and the Brasilia Declaration.

In this sense, the existence of regional fora and programs in Latin America can be regarded as positive tools in ascertaining the rights of refugees and asylum seekers and guaranteeing protection; especially when they aim to have a practical approach and to balance the interests and needs of States with the needs of the refugee population.[114]

The regional efforts in Latin America on International Refugee Law and protection are, consequently, constructive examples that may lead to a more humane attitude towards refugees and asylum seekers and a better and more effective system of guaranteeing that the refugee population have integral protection, being in this sense a model in regionalism in International Refugee Law and protection.

Persons in the Americas' (2011) 50 *International Legal Materials* 357.

[113] Ibid. 358.

[114] See Jubilut and Carneiro 'Resettlement in Solidarity: a regional new approach towards a more humane durable solution' 5.

References

Barreto LPTF, *Das diferenças entre os institutos jurídicos, asilos e refúgio*. Available at <http://www.migrante.org.br/IMDH/ControlConteudo.aspx?area=001c1b0d-181f-450a-83fb-47915ce5f2eb>.

Costa D, 'Introductory note to the Brasilia Declaration on the Protection of Refugees and Stateless Persons in the Americas' (2011) 50 *International Legal Materials*.

Fischel de Andrade JH, *Direito internacional dos refugiados – Evolução Histórica (1921–1952)* (Renovar, 1996).

González JCM, 'La Protección Internacional de Refugiados en el Continente Americano: Nuevos Desarrollos'. In *XXXV Curso de Derecho Internacional* (Comité Jurídico Interamericano, Departamento de Derecho Internacional, Secretaría de Asuntos Jurídicos, Secretaría General, 2008).

González JCM, 'El derecho de asilo y la protección de refugiados en el continente americano'. In ACNUR. *La protección internacional de refugiados en las Américas*. (ACNUR; Oficina del Alto Comisariado de las Naciones Unidas para Derechos Humanos, 2011).

Goodwin-Gill GS and McAdam J, *The Refugee in International Law* (3rd edn, Oxford University Press, 2007).

Harris D, 'Regional Protection of Human Rights: The Inter-American Achievement' in HJ Steiner and P Alston (eds), *International Human Rights in Context* (2nd edn, Oxford University Press, 2000).

Hathaway JC, *The Rights of Refugees under International Law* (Cambridge University Press, 2005).

International Law Commission, *Report of the work of the Study Group on the Fragmentation of International Law: Difficulties arising from the diversification and expansion of international law*, UN. A/CN.4/L.682, 2006.

Jubilut LL, 'International Refugee Law and Protection in Brazil: a model in South America?' (2006) 19(1) *Journal of Refugee Studies*

Jubilut LL, *O Direito Internacional dos Refugiados e sua aplicação no ordenamento jurídico brasileiro* (Método, 2007).

Jubilut LL and Apolinário SMOS, 'A necessidade de proteção internacional no âmbito da migração' (2010) 11(6)(1) *Revista Direito GV*.

Jubilut LL and Apolinario SMOS, 'O Direito Internacional dos Refugiados e seu Contexto Atual na América Latina'. In Carlos F. Dominguez Avila and Renata de Melo Rosa (eds), *América Latina no Labirinto Global – Economia, Política e Segurança* (2nd edn, CRV, 2012).

Jubilut LL and Carneiro WP, 'Resettlement in Solidarity: a regional new approach towards a more humane durable solution' (2011) 30(3) *Refugee Survey Quarterly*.

Kneebone S and Rawlings-Sanaei F (eds), *New regionalism and asylum seekers: challenges ahead* (Berghahn Books, 2007).

Lavanchi P, 'The Mexico Declaration and Plan of Action: Reaffirming Latin America's Generous Tradition of Asylum and Innovative Solutions' (2006) 18 *Int'l J. Refugee L.*

Lopez GA and Stohl M, *Liberalization and Redemocratization in Latin America* (Greenwood Press, 1987).

Massey H, *UNHCR and De Facto Statelessness*. Legal and Protection Policy Research Series, 2010.

Miranda CO, 'Toward a Broader Definition of Refugee: 20th Century Development Trends' (1989–90) 20 *Cal. W. Int'l L.J.*

Mittelman J, 'Rethinking the "New Regionalism" in the Context of Globalization' (1996) 2 *Global Governance*.

Piovesan F and Jubilut LL, 'Regional Developments: Americas' in A Zimmermann (ed.), *Commentary on the 1951 Convention Relating to the Status of Refugees and its 1967 Protocol* (Oxford University Press, 2011).

Reut-Nicolussi E, 'Displaced Persons in International Law' (1948) 73 (II) *Recueil des Cours de la Academie de Droit International*.

Schuck PH, 'Refugee Burden-Sharing: A Modest Proposal' (1997) 22 *Yale J. Int'l L.*

Spindler W, 'The Mexico Plan of Action: protecting refugees through international solidarity' (November 2005) 24 *Forced Migration Review*.

Stein BN, 'Regional solutions – Package deals' (1995) 99 *Refugees Magazine.*

Suhrke A, 'A crisis diminished: refugees in the developing world' (1992–93) *48 International Journal.*

UNHCR. Executive Committee of the High Commissioner's Program, *Note on International Protection,* UN Doc A/AC.96/930, 2000.

UNHCR, Mexico Declaration and Plan of Action to Strengthen the International Protection of Refugees in Latin America, 2004.

UNHCR, *Memoir of the Twentieth Anniversary of the Cartagena Declaration on Refugees.* 1st edn, 2005.

UNHCR, 'The Refugee Situation in Latin America: Protection and Solutions Based on the Pragmatic Approach of the Cartagena Declaration on Refugees of 1984 – Discussion Document' (2006) 18 *Int'l J. Refugee L.*

UNHCR, *Mexico Plan of Action: The impact of regional solidarity.* 1st edn, 2007.

UNHCR, *Mexico Plan of Action: The impact of regional solidarity.* 1st edn, 2007.

UNHCR, Definición Ampliada de Refugiados en América Latina: Incorporación de la Declaración de Cartagena sobre Refugiados en la Legislación de los Países de la Región, 2009.

UNHCR. Executive Committee of the High Commissioner's Program, *Note on International Protection,* EC/62/SC/CRP.12 2011.

UNHCR, *Global Trends 2010,* 2011.

William RI, *Transnational Conflicts: Central America, Social Changes and Globalization* (Verso, 2003).

THE TRANSFORMATIVE POTENTIAL OF REFUGE: THE DEEPENING OF SOLIDARITY AND OF LIMITS TO SOVEREIGNTY AS A LEGACY OF THE CARTAGENA DECLARATION AND ITS REVIEW PROCESS (2014)[*]

Liliana Lyra Jubilut[**], Silvia Menicucci de Oliveira Selmi Apolinário[***] and João Carlos Jarochinski Silva[****]

1. Introduction

In 1993, the Report of the State of the World Population of the United Nations Population Fund[1] established that international migration would be the biggest problem of the transition from the 20th century to the 21st century[2].The forecast of the report has materialized as never before in political debates and social analysis the phenomenon of migration has received so much attention; either by the worldwide number of international migrants[3]; the various factors causing migration (international and non-international armed conflicts; religious, political, and social intolerance; gender issues; natural and human-made disasters; etc.), or by actions taken by countries to regulate these flows and their impacts[4].

This fact is accompanied by conditions that facilitate the mobility of people and information, as advancements in transportation and communication can attest. Although not a novelty in itself, such migration flows are significant and inserted in different contexts that may involve terrorism, national and international security,

---

[*] This text was translated from Portuguese to English by Lisa Stephane Sousa Barbosa. A final revision was performed by the authors.

[**] Liliana Lyra Jubilut has a PhD and Master's Degree in International Law from Universidade de São Paulo, has an LLM in International Legal Studies from NYU School of Law, was a Visiting Scholar at Columbia Law School and is a Researcher and Professor at Universidade Católica de Santos, where she coordinates the Research Group "Direitos Humanos e Vulnerabilidades". She has been working with refugee issues since 1999.

[***] Silvia M. O. S. Apolinário has a PhD and Master's Degree in International Law from Universidade de São Paulo, is the Executive Legal Manager at APEX-Brazil and a Member of the Research Group "Direitos Humanos e Vulnerabilidades". She has been working with refugee issues for 7 years.

[****] João Carlos Jarochinski Silva is a PhD candidate in Social Sciences with emphasis in International Relations at Pontifícia Universidade Católica de São Paulo, has a Master's Degree in International Law from Universidade Católica de Santos, is a Member of the Research Group "Direitos Humanos e Vulnerabilidades" and a Professor at Universidade Federal de Roraima.

[1] Since 1978, the United Nations Population Fund (UNFPA) publishes the Annual Report on the State of World Population. For more on the cited reference see: <www.unfpa.org.br/novo/ index.php/situacao-da-populacao-mundial>.

[2] BÓGUS, L. Esperança Além-Mar: Portugal no "Arquipélago Migratório" Brasileiro. In: MALHEIROS, J. (org.). *Imigração Brasileira em Portugal.* Lisboa: ACIDI, 2007.p. 39.

[3] The UN estimates the number of international migrants in the world at 232 million in 2014. See: <http://www.onu.org.br/mundo-tem-232-milhoes-de-migrantes-internacionais-calcula-onu/>.

[4] On a history of international migration, with emphasis on the particularities of the theme in the current world scenario, see JAROCHINSKI SILVA, J. C. As Migrações Internacionais e os seus impactos. In: JUBILUT, L. L. (Coord.). *Direito internacional atual.* Rio de Janeiro: Elsevier, 2014. p. 317-339.

economic and employment crises, among other factors, due to specific situations in each region of the world.

Obviously, in this respect, the so-called economic migrants are the most prominent in political and social discourses, since in numerical terms they are the most relevant[5]. However, after 20 years of the report, the migratory issue is not only linked to them. There are other categories of migrants that also present challenges to the international society at the beginning of the 21st century[6]. These other groups also need to have their particular condition debated so that they can count on with international protection and normative developments, either because of the specificity of their movements or because of the number of persons who fall into these categories.

Migration flows are guided by the logic of repulsion and attraction[7], because they are movements that necessarily have this double side. In this context, this paper will try to highlight the relevance of refugees, a specific group of migrants, as they have very particular factors of repulsion since their displacement is due to a well-founded fear of persecution, therefore, as a form of forced migration. Refugees were the subject of significant normative developments during the century, with a pioneering juridical approach, even becoming a reference in the protection of human beings, for recognizing the individual as a subject of International Law[8].

However, in spite of the numerous advancements made in refugee issues during the 20th century, new questions have arisen to demonstrate the need for further developments in this area. In this regard, Latin America has emerged as one of the most important *locus* of debate and policy-making, including proposals that broaden the definition of those covered by International Refugee Law.

The study of this normative development is essential at this moment. In some stances attempts to dismantle refugee protection are in place[9], with discourses that link the constraints to the States' autonomy brought by the 1951 Convention on the Status of Refugees (1951 Convention) and its Protocol of 1967[10] (1967 Protocol) as elements that are capable of imposing risks to the security of the

---

[5] By way of comparison, within the general number of migrants, the number of refugees would be 10.5 million people and that of forced migrants in general 45.2 million. According to the UNHCR *Global Trends 2012 – Displacement, the new 21st century challenge.* UNHCR: Geneva, 2013. p. 2-3. Available at: <http://www.unhcr.org/51bacb0f9.html>.

[6] An attempt to present different "categories" of migrants in order to improve their legal protection can be found at: JUBILUT, L .L.; APOLINÁRIO, S. M. O. S. A necessidade de proteção internacional no âmbito da migração. *Revista Direito GV*, 11, 6, 2010, p. 275 et seq.

[7] GLOVER, S.; GOTT C. et al. *Migration: an Economic and Social Analysis.* The Research, Development and Statistics Directorate, Occasional Paper n. 67, 2001.

[8] REIS, R. R. *Políticas de Imigração na França e nos Estados Unidos.* São Paulo: Hucitec, 2006. p. 17.

[9] See the famous speech presented at the inauguration of the Austrian Presidency of the European Union in 1998, which affirms the inaccuracy of the 1951 criteria for the current reality, suggesting a new approach that ceases to be based on an individual and subjective right, but that is based on the political offer from the States that receive the asylum.

[10] The 1951 Convention (Geneva) brought refugee protection to the international scene, and the 1967 Protocol (New York) expanded its scope of action by removing geographical and temporal limitations to the application of the refugee concept.

countries and, thus being at odds with national interests[11]. Moreover, there are cases of attempts to use refugee protection by other categories of immigrants, due to the more protective nature of refugee-related norms; which lead States to question the institute of refuge itself. The actions undertaken in Latin America, and in some of countries in this region, contrast with this scenario since they reinforce the protective and humanitarian nature of its norms.

In this sense, it is important to emphasize the particular logic that Latin America has been adopting regarding the protection and reception of refugees. This is the purpose of this text, especially in a commemorative year for the humanitarian practice of the region - on the occasion of the 30th Anniversary of the Cartagena Declaration.

To this end, the article will address the development of migration issues in Latin America, reinforcing the option of solidarity towards refugees adopted in the spirit of the Cartagena Declaration of 1984.

2. The International Construction of the Refuge Institute

Although the international juridical construction of refuge dates from the 20th century, the issue of refugees is not an innovation of this period. Since Ancient times references to the forced displacement of persons due to persecution and the granting of protection to them[12] have been made. Said protection was implemented through the institute of asylum, which had a religious connotation in Ancient Greece[13]. This connotation changed to something closer to the current idea of asylum in Rome due to its legal culture, which offers a clearer rule of granting asylum[14].

A reality of persecution of persons continued throughout the Middle Ages, mainly related to religious disputes. However, despite the longevity of this period, there were no new theoretical connotations of asylum. This situation only began to change with the advent of Modernity, in which the Protestant Reformation and the emergence and development of nation-States altered the interaction between individuals and States[15] and the issue of religious freedom, to the point in which Hugo Grotius, one of the founding fathers of International Law, was able to begin to theorize the institute[16].

After that, the theme became part of States' normative production, to the point of being present even in the debates of the French Revolution. However, until that

---

[11] REIS, R. R. Op. cit., p. 27.

[12] See on the subject ZOLBERG, A. The formation of new States as a refugee-generating process. *Annals of the American Academy of Politics and Social Science*, May 1983, p. 24-38; FISCHEL DE ANDRADE, J. H. *Direito Internacional dos Refugiados- Evolução Histórica (1921-1952)*. Rio de Janeiro: Renovar, 1996. p. 12-14; and JUBILUT, L. L. *O Direito Internacional dos Refugiados e sua Aplicação no Ordenamento Jurídico Brasileiro*. São Paulo: Método, 2007. p. 23-24.

[13] BARRETO, L. P. T. *Das diferenças entre os institutos jurídicos do asilo e do refúgio*. Available at: <www.migrante.org.br/textoseartigos.htm>

[14] JUBILUT, L. L. Op. cit., p. 37 et seq.

[15] On the link between the emergence of nation-states and the institute of refuge see, for example, ZOLBERG, A. Op. cit.; and HADDAD, E. *The refugee: a conceptual analysis- between sovereigns*. Cambridge: Cambridge University Press, 2008.

[16] FISCHEL DE ANDRADE, J. H. Op. cit., p. 14.

moment, protection was given through the idea of asylum, given that, even though being similar institutes and sharing a humanistic character[17], refuge had not yet been developed as a normative construction. In light of this it is necessary to highlight the main difference between the institutes of asylum and of refuge, i.e. how protection is implemented in each case. In asylum, this implementation is connected to the discretion of States, which might have the political will to grant protection or not. On the other hand, refuge is based on a right[18] and, therefore, removes the discretionary character of its recognition.

The discretionary aspect of its granting even turned asylum into a system restricted to individual cases with little efficacy in situations that involved many persons, for example, when persecution occurred to a large group of persons[19]. It was the case of the Russian Revolution of 1917, its consequent Civil War lasting until 1921, and the subsequent installation of Soviet Socialism, as well as of World War I. Such a context, led to the need to establishing a protective institute based on legal norms, which removed the discretion of granting protection by the State: the refuge.

However, this initial systematization remained limited to the context of the Russian reality at the time or of other specific social groups, such as Armenians, Assyrians, Assyrians- Chaldeans, Turks and Montenegrins[20], failing to provide adequate protection to all the victims of the enormous atrocities committed during the 20s and 30s of the 20th century in Europe; a time of rise and consolidation of Nazi-fascist regimes. Due to this lack of more comprehensive protection during the early 20th century, many people remained at the mercy of States with persecution agendas of groups and individuals, such as Hitler's Germany[21].

After the colossal violence of World War II, and as a direct consequence of the displacements caused by it, International Refugee Law began to develop intensely, sponsored by the newly established international organization for peace, the United Nations, which set the protection of human beings and his/her dignity as its immediate priorities[22].

Only after the risks of a fragile protection and a feeble system of solution of

---

[17] RAMOS, A. C. Asilo e Refúgio: semelhanças, diferenças e perspectivas. In: RAMOS, A. C.; RODRIGUES, G.; ALMEIDA, G.A. (orgs.). *60 anos de ACNUR - Perspectivas de futuro.* São Paulo: CLA, 2011. Available at: <http://www.acnur.org/t3/fileadmin/scripts/doc.php?file=t3/fileadmin/Documentos/portugues/Public acoes/2011/60_anos_de_ACNUR_-_Perspectivas_de_futuro>

[18] On this sense see, for exemple, JUBILUT, L. L. A Judicialização do Refúgio. In: RAMOS, A. C.; RODRIGUES, G.; ALMEIDA, G.A. (orgs.). Op. cit., p. 173-174.

[19] See, for instance, JUBILUT, L. L. O Direito Internacional dos Refugiados e sua Aplicação no Ordenamento Jurídico Brasileiro. Op. cit., p. 37 et seq. (especially p. 38); and JUBILUT, L. L. A Judicialização do Refúgio. Op. cit. (especially p. 168)

[20] FISCHEL DE ANDRADE, J. H. Op. cit., p. 75 et seq.

[21] It is important to note, however, the attempted at protection brought by the creation of the High Commissioner for Jewish Refugees from Germany established in 1936, and which, two years later, extended its jurisdiction also to Jews from Austria. See, for example, FISCHEL DE ANDRADE, J. H. Op. cit.; Id. Breve reconstituição histórica da tradição que culminou na proteção internacional dos refugiados. In: ARAÚJO, Nádia de; ALMEIDA, Guilherme Assis de. (Coord.) *O Direito Internacional dos Refugiados: uma perspectiva brasileira.* 2. ed. Rio de Janeiro: Renovar, 2001, p. 127; and JUBILUT, L. L. O Direito Internacional dos Refugiados e sua Aplicação no Ordenamento Jurídico Brasileiro. Op. cit., p. 77.

[22] As can be seen, for example, in the preamble of its constitutional treaty (the United Nations Charter).

controversies, such as that of the 20s and 30s of the 20th century, were evident to the entire international society that there was room for the development of a protective logic capable of prioritizing human beings to the detriment of States' interests. For the first time, there were conditions for reducing and limiting the sovereign actions of States, in favor of a logic of solidarity and of protection of human beings.

With this historical reality as a context, International Refugee Law was designed with a normative framework, which was (and still is) capable of reaching and protecting persons in several different situations and locations. It is not without reason that some authors posit that the advancement brought along by the issue of refugees was the element capable of inserting human beings in the category of subjects of International Law[23], a feat that would be unthinkable in the period before the Second World War[24].

The consolidation of refuge is testified by the creation of a supervisory body for this right, the United Nations High Commissioner for Refugees (UNHCR)[25], and by the adoption of the 1951 Convention.

According to the 1951 Convention a person is recognized as a refugee if s/he has a well-founded fear of being persecuted for reasons of race, religion, nationality, political opinion or membership of a social group and is outside his/her country of origin[26]. For this recognition, in addition to the above conditions, it is necessary that the individual does not fall into the cessation clauses[27] (that is, s/he needs international protection) and is not included in the exclusion clauses[28] (i.e., s/he deserves international protection) also established by the 1951 Convention.

Another important aspect of the conventional norm is the persistence of reservations or limitations; the first, a temporal limitation since it restricts recognition of refugee status to events establishing the well-founded fear of persecution that occurred before January 1, 1951[29] and, the second, a geographical limitation that allowed protection to apply exclusively to events in Europe[30]. These limitations, that might be considered odd nowadays, should not serve to disqualify the advancement brought by in 1951, under the risk of incurring in anachronism given the fact that the implementation of International Refugee Law had a proper role in the international scenario in limiting sovereign acts of States[31], sovereignty being until then the absolute defining element of relations between and among countries[32].

---

[23] REIS, R.R. Op. cit.

[24] For more details on the history of the institute of refuge see FISCHEL DE ANDRADE, J. H. Op. cit., and JUBILUT, L.L. O Direito Internacional dos Refugiados e sua Aplicação no Ordenamento Jurídico Brasileiro. Op. cit., p. 73 et seq.

[25] 1951 Convention - 6th preambular paragraph.

[26] 1951 Convention - Article 1°, A, 2.

[27] 1951 Convention - Article 1°, C.

[28] 1951 Convention - Article 1°, F.

[29] 1951 Convention - Article 1°, A, 2.

[30] 1951 Convention - Article 1°, B, a.

[31] Some authors even include the institute of refuge as the first action in this direction. See, for example, REIS, R. R. Op. cit.

[32] On the subject of sovereignty and its modifications, see JUBILUT, L. L. concept of sovereignty:

The transformative power of refuge as a limitation of state sovereignty and as a protective stance of human beings as subjects of International law, has as its broader legal basis article 14[33] of the Universal Declaration of Human Rights, on the right of asylum, in the sense of a right to be protected against persecution (whether through the institute of asylum or the institute of refuge).

Another relevant aspect of the 1951 Convention can further exemplify this link of refuge with human rights, in that it entitles refugees to civil and political rights, as well as with economic, social and cultural rights, imposing, as mentioned, limitations to sovereign acts of countries.

Such limitation of States' sovereignty had as its apex in the 1951 Convention the establishment of the principle of *non-refoulement*[34] - the basic rule of all of International Refugee Law.

Non-refoulement represents an expressive manner of diminishing States' sovereignty in relation to the individual, as it provides guarantees in prohibiting States from expelling or repelling, i.e. impeding States to "expel or return (*"refouler"*) a refugee in any manner whatsoever to the frontiers of territories where his life or freedom would be threatened on account of his race, religion, nationality, membership of a particular social group or political opinion"[35], thus affecting one of the most consensual rights of States, which is to regulate who can enter and remain in its territory[36].

In practice, the principle represents a protection so that the request for refugee status is properly analyzed, given that it establishes a duty to the States that are parties to the 1951 Convention, thus ascertaining at least a temporary protection[37]. Because of this obligation and the correlated protection of refugees, there are authors who consider *non-refoulement* as *jus cogens*[38] thus being possible to be applied even to States that are not part of the 1951 Convention, showing the full impact of this document.

Such guarantees were broadened in terms of which persons can benefit from them from 1967 onwards, given that the temporal and geographical limitations were allowed to cease to exist, consolidating a development, by the 1967 Protocol, that can from then on be considered universal[39].

Once *non-refoulement* has become universal, one must bear in mind that this principle is not only aimed at preventing devolution but also at ensuring all the

---

modifications and responsibility. In: FRANCO FILHO, M. T.; MIALHE, J. L.; JOB, U. S. (Org.). *Epitácio Pessoa e a Codificação do Direito Internacional.* Porto Alegre: Sérgio Antonio Fabris Editor, 2013. p. 247-270.

[33] Article 14 (1) "Everyone has the right to seek and to enjoy in other countries asylum from persecution".

[34] 1951 Convention - Article 33.

[35] Ibid.

[36] BAGANHA, M. I. A cada sul o seu norte: dinâmicas migratórias em Portugal. In: SANTOS. B. de S. (Org.). *Globalização: fatalidade ou Utopia?* 2. ed. São Paulo: Cortez, 2005

[37] JUBILUT, L. L. O Direito Internacional dos Refugiados e sua Aplicação no Ordenamento Jurídico Brasileiro. Op. cit., p. 93-94.

[38] See, for example, the 5th Conclusion of the Cartagena Declaration. See also, from a doctrinal perspective, Zimmermann, A. (Ed.) *Commentary on the 1951 Convention on the Status of Refugees and its 1967 Protocol.* Oxford: Oxford University Press, 2011, especially the specific comments on article 33 of the 1951 Convention.

[39] 1967 Protocol - Article 1°, § 2°.

rights set out in the 1951 Convention, even for those who are still having their requests for refuge analysed, i.e. asylum seekers.

In this regard, when the 1951 Convention establishes a series of rights to refugees, rather than only restraining States' actions to prevent the entry of refugees, the document demands the establishment of policies for the integration of these individuals, that is, measures capable of implementing at the national level the rights granted to refugees by it[40]. And, by applying the implicit logic in *non-refoulement*, such measures must be adopted from the moment a request for recognition of refugee status is placed[41].

States, therefore, need to play an effective role in recognizing the rights of refugee from the time of the request for recognition of refugee status, given that it is at the national level that said recognition occurs[42], in addition to respecting the rights; given that, as highlighted by the 1951 Convention itself, the document lays down minimum standards of protection[43], requiring States' actions, but preserving their essential characteristic of having to be guaranteed by States. Moreover, the international protection of refugees does not prevent States from deepening the provision of further guarantees and rights to them[44].

In the quest to ascertaining full protection it is necessary for States to advance in improving their migration policies. The migratory policies of States in general, including the policy for refugees, has a dual logic of action. One is related to border control, in which the connection to International Refugee Law is evident, i.e. in controlling the entry of foreigners, as it prevents refugees from being able to enter and remain in a given territory. However, International Law of Refugees does not set aside the other logic present in migration policies, which is integration.

The 1951 Convention and its 1967 Protocol, albeit establishing minimum provisions, end up having a greater efficacy and, therefore, presence, in the actions related to the control of entry of persons, being *non-refoulement* a visible expression of this. However, limiting refugee protection to this aspect does not assist in achieving the solidarity-driven aim to confer a high degree of protection to this vulnerable group, which is the goal of the 1951 Convention and its 1967 Protocol,

---

[40] According to Foucher, "[s]e o cruzamento ilegal de uma fronteira é passível de perseguições, o refugiado político pode fazê-lo sem autorização e encontrar abrigo atrás de uma linha protetora" ("even if an illegal crossing of a border is subject to persecution, the political refugee can do so without authorization and find shelter behind a protective line"- free translation). FOUCHER, Michel. *Obsessão por Fronteiras*. São Paulo: Radical Livros, 2009, p. 23.

This protective line represents the direct interference of the 1951 Convention and its 1967 Protocol in the sovereignty of States, especially when the right enshrined therein, expressed in non-refoulement, is now considered a standard of jus cogens. Given that, for the application of non-refoulement, it is necessary to use elements brought by the 1951 Convention, mainly by means of elements aimed at securing refugee rights outside of their State of origin, this results in the fact of the principle of flexibility of sovereignty directly interfering with the rights granted to refugees.

[41] Refugee Status Determination (RSD)

[42] MURILLO GONZALES, J. C. El derecho de asilo y la protección de refugiados en el continente americano. In: ACNUR. *La protección internacional de refugiados en las Américas*. Quito, 2011

[43] 1951 Convention - Article 5°.

[44] This is apparent from the reading Article 5 of the 1951 Convention, which provides that "Nothing in this Convention shall be deemed to impair any rights and benefits granted by a Contracting State to refugees apart from this Convention".

to the point of allowing for constrains to the sovereign logic of States[45].

Unfortunately, in spite of what is expressed in International Refugee Law, and that represents a break of the sovereign logic of border control, there is, in practice, no significant impediment for States to continue with relevant distinctions between nationals and foreigners. In light of this, one of the challenges of international refugee protection is its implementation. This problem requires constant efforts to develop International Refugee Law. While these efforts have not produced significant results at the global level, regional advancements have occurred, especially in Latin America since the 1980s.

3. The contemporary construction of a refugee regime in the American context

3.1. The Cartagena Declaration

After the creation and universal expansion of International Refugee Law in 1967, Latin America became a refugee-producing area[46], due to political instability, which is a relevant historical element for the countries of the region.

In the 1980s, the context of political instability and the existence of dictatorships had not yet changed, especially in Central America, where there were gross and generalized human rights violations, leading to the emergence of an enormous influx of refugees, estimated at approximately two million people[47]. With this latent reality, the need to think of a coordinated solution to this issue was perceived, and from this came the idea of a regional declaration that would encompass the events that were occurring in the region[48].

It is worth noting that this type of initiative in America, notably in Latin America, in the sense of producing regional norms was not a novelty, given that, at various other times and related to a variety of subjects, this region assumed a leading role in the creation of International Law rules with regional scope and effectiveness[49]. The novelty resided, then, on the topic of the initiative.

The result of this effort was the Cartagena Declaration, adopted in 1984 and stemming from an academic symposium held in Colombia, which included participants from civil society, governments, UNHCR and the academy. This document is divided into four parts: the first contains the preamble; the second

---

[45] According to Reis, "A convenção de Genebra e o Protocolo de Nova York representam um constrangimento para a autonomia decisória do Estado, no que diz respeito ao controle de suas fronteiras, e por isso, não se inserem na lógica do direito internacional tradicional, [...], que garante a soberania nacional no controle dos movimentos" ("The Geneva Convention and the New York Protocol represent a constraint to the autonomy of State's decision-making in regards of the control of its borders, and therefore do not fit into the logic of traditional international law.], Which guarantees national sovereignty in the control of movements"- free translation). REIS, RR Op. cit., p. 27.

[46] JUBILUT, L.L.; CARNEIRO, W. P. C. Resettlement in Solidarity: a regional new approach towards a more humane durable solution. *Refugee Survey Quarterly*, v. 30, n. 3, 2011. p. 67.

[47] SPINDLER, W. The Mexico Plan of Action: protecting refugees through international solidarity. *Forced Migration Review*, 24, November 2005, p. 24.

[48] The context of inspiration for the Cartagena Declaration is expressly mentioned in the Third Conclusion of the Declaration.

[49] For example, through the asylum system in the region, as well as the PanAmerican Conferences and with the development of the Inter-American human rights system, in the Americas as a whole.

contextualizes regional protection vis-a-vis international protection, referring to the Contadora Act for Peace and Cooperation in Central America and to actions to implement and improve international security based on universal standards in the region; the third brings the conclusions of the document; and the fourth, posits recommendations.

Undoubtedly, the most significant part of the Cartagena Declaration is the one related to the Conclusions, amounting to 17, as they bring the main novelties of the document, in so far as they intend to make advances in the protection of refugees in the region, even imposing changes, where necessary, in the traditional patterns of International Refugee Law[50]. It is worth noting that this innovative position does not jeopardize the previously granted protection, given that the 1951 Convention itself does not prevent progress towards the deepening of the safety of and guarantees for refugees[51].

In this sense, the most prominent element in the Cartagena Declaration was the inclusion of a new hypothesis for the recognition of refugee status, based on the idea of gross and generalized violation of human rights[52].

Such insertion offers a greater possibility of recognition of refugee status and, consequently of protection, and stems directly from the existing crisis context in Central America. In this respect, it bears a resemblance to the African perspectives of refugee protection that sought to mirror the realities of that continent[53]; being the Convention on the Specific Aspects of the Refugee Problem in Africa (1969), adopted within the framework of the Organization of African Unity (nowadays African Union), an inspiring source of the Cartagena Declaration, since it included the protection as refugees of those forced to leave their countries not only for reasons of persecution but also due to: external aggression, occupation, foreign domination and others serious events that disturb the public order.

In the same sense, the text of the Cartagena Declaration changes the focus of analysis in the recognition of refugee status[54], as, instead of basing itself exclusively on the individual well-founded fear of the asylum seeker, it also focuses the objective analysis of the places of origin, so as to verify whether there is gross and generalized violation of human rights in that context[55]; a scenario in which any person who is not covered by the exclusion clauses should be protected.

Obviously, the objective situation of a location has always been taken into account for refugee status recognition, however, traditionally it is related to the

---

[50] As, for example, Conclusions 3 and 15 of the Cartagena Declaration.

[51] 1951 Convention - Article 5°.

[52] Cartagena Declaration - Conclusion 3: "[...] the definition or concept of refugee recommended for use in the region is what, in addition to containing the elements of the 1951 Convention and the 1967 Protocol, also considers as refugees the People who have fled their countries because their life, security or freedom have been threatened by widespread violence, foreign aggression, internal strife, massive violation of human rights or other circumstances that have seriously disturbed public order. "

[53] ACNUR. Persons covered by the OAU Convention Governing the Specific Aspects of Refugee Problems in Africa and by the Cartagena Declaration on Refugees (Submitted by the African Group and the Latin American Group). EC/1992/SCP/CRP.6. International Protection (SCIP), 6 April 1992. Available at: <http://www.unhcr.org/3ae68cd214.html>.

[54] JUBILUT, L.L.; CARNEIRO, W. P. C. Op. cit., p. 67.

[55] Ibid.

proving of the possibility of this reality establishing a well-founded fear of individual persecution[56], while in the Cartagena Declaration, by the creation of a new standard of analysis, this fact becomes in itself the very motive of recognizing refugee status.

There is, however, no definition of what constitutes a scenario of "gross and generalized violation of human rights", but this criterion has been applied for refugee status recognition for people fleeing war or civil strives, dictatorships or that situations in which the institutions of the countries of origin or residence do not guarantee the freedom, security or life of the individual, hypothesis that are mentioned in the 3rd conclusion of the 1984 Cartagena Declaration.

It is important to note that the Cartagena Declaration by broadening the possibilities of recognition of refugee protection does not seek to exclude the refugee status recognition criteria universally recognized by the 1951 Convention, but rather aims to extend and complement this protection, so much so that it emphasizes that the regional definition must be used in conjunction with the 1951 Convention and its 1967 Protocol[57]. In addition, the Cartagena Declaration reaffirms in its conclusions important international elements of refugee protection, such as "peaceful, non-political and exclusively humanitarian nature of grant of asylum or recognition of refugee status "[58]; the principle of *non-refoulement* (including the prohibition of rejection at borders) as the basis for refugee protection and being, therefore, imperative, i.e. a *jus cogens* principle[59]; and the fact that refuge is an institute of complementary nature, as States bear the primary responsibility for the protection of the human rights, a concept that aims to reducing the need for the use of the institute of refuge [60] and, in cases where it applies, require States to guarantee the rights of refugees.

3.2. The solidarity character and States' sovereignty limitation in the Cartagena Declaration

The encouraging and innovative nature of the Cartagena Declaration, capable of establishing the so-called "spirit of Cartagena", is easily perceived, as the complementary innovation results in the need for States that wish to be bound by the regional system to follow the international standards for refugee status recognition by adhering to the documents in this matter, through the incorporation of these in their national legislation, and to also implement greater possibilities for the recognition of refugee status.

---

[56] JUBILUT, L.L.; APOLINÁRIO, S. M. O. S. O Direito Internacional dos Refugiados e seu Contexto Atual na América Latina. In: ROSA, R. M.; DOMÍNGUEZ AVILA, C. F. (Org.). *América Latina no Labirinto Global - Economia, Política e Segurança*. Brasília: CRV, 2012. p. 363.

[57] In the preamble to the Cartagena Declaration one finds the following wording: "in consideration of the necessary coordination and harmonization between universal, regional and national efforts". Moreover, in its 2nd Conclusion, the Declaration advocates adherence to the 1951 Convention and the 1967 Protocol, and in its 3rd conclusion expressly points out that the definition it establishes is in addition to the universal criteria for refugee status recognition.

[58] Cartagena Declaration - Conclusion 4.

[59] Cartagena Declaration - Conclusion 5.

[60] This statement follows from part of what is stated in Conclusion 9 of the Cartagena Declaration, which has as its central object internally displaced persons.

Undoubtedly, by expanding the system of refugee protection, the Cartagena Declaration is encouraging States to develop legislative advancements that benefit, in addition to their nationals, refugees, since there is a logic of expansion of rights that cannot be limited by a perspective of excluding non-nationals. This is one of the main consequences of the Cartagena Declaration that prioritizes humanitarian elements and facilitates the recognition of rights since such actions reinforce the need to broaden a logic so that it is not only guided by elements of national interest[61].

Such logic is capable of introducing a view that cooperation between States is the best way to deal with migration issues, fostering actions of effective integration while pursuing durable solutions[62] - i.e., in the case of refugees, local integration, repatriation, and resettlement[63].

It is interesting to note that this positive valorization of cooperation was not due to a binding legal instrument since as the Cartagena Declaration is a declaration, it does not formally have this capacity or nature. Furthermore, even though the adoption of the Cartagena Declaration is encouraged and recommended by the Organization of American States[64], adhering to it is still at the discretion of the States, and in that sense, the figures are very significant, given that there are already 15 countries[65] that incorporated, in whole or with some modifications, the document[66].

4. The Cartagena Declaration as a catalyst for a humanitarian space in Latin America

4.1. The "spirit of Cartagena" and complementary protection

One notes, thus, since the adoption of the Cartagena Declaration the undertaking of actions that together can be understood as the formation of a humanitarian space in Latin America. On the one hand, there is commitment to the universal and regional definitions of refugee status[67], and on the other, the

---

[61] Such a trend is defended by Rosita Milesi and Flavia Carlet when they affirm that the "revisão da noção tradicional de soberania absoluta do Estado acabou por cristalizar ainda mais a ideia de que o ser humano deve ter direitos protegidos na esfera internacional na condição de sujeito de direito. E é sob estas perspectivas que os direitos humanos devem ser enfocados, essencialmente os dos migrantes e refugiados" ("revision of the traditional notion of absolute sovereignty of the State has further crystallized the idea that the human being should have protected rights in the international sphere as subject of rights. And it is from these perspectives that human rights must be focused, essentially those of migrants and refugees"- free translation). MILESI, R.; CARLET, F. Refugiados e Políticas Públicas In: SILVA, C.A.S. (org.). *Direitos Humanos e Refugiados*. Dourados (MS): Editora UFGD, 2012, p. 84.

[62] HATHAWAY, J.C. *The Rights of Refugees under International Law*, 2005. p. 119.

[63] JUBILUT, L.L. O Direito Internacional dos Refugiados e sua Aplicação no Ordenamento Jurídico Brasileiro. Op. cit., p. 154 et seq.

[64] HATHAWAY, J. C. Op cit., p. 119.

[65] Argentina, Belize, Bolivia, Brazil, Chile, Colombia, Ecuador, El Salvador, Guatemala, Honduras, Mexico, Nicaragua, Paraguay, Peru and Uruguay (according to the combination of data available in October 2013 at: <www.acnur.org/t3/que-hace/proteccion/declaracion-de-cartagena-sobre-los-refugiados/paises-que-incorporan-cartagena-en-la-legislacion-nacional/?L=gulnlxwoshxdx> and <www.acnur.org/t3/fileadmin/scripts/doc.php?file=biblioteca/pdf/2541>). (It is important to note that recently Ecuador has removed the Declaration from its internal legal order)

[66] PIOVESAN, F.; JUBILUT, L. L. The 1951 Convention and the Americas: Regional Developments. In: ZIMMERMANN, A. (Org.) Op. cit., p. 219-220.

[67] In the Americas, almost all States are parties to the 1951 Convention and its Protocol, with the

pursuit of actions that lead to complementary protection - for forced and humanitarian migrants who do not qualify as refugees[68], as well as the quest of integral protection[69], especially with a view to integration.

Nevertheless, despite these improvements, the reality of refugees, due to their particular situations is, as a rule, overly precarious, requiring States to continue to advance in these topics[70]. In this sense, first steps have started to being taken in several Latin American countries, a fact that is not replicated in other regions of the world[71], and that, once again, indicate the encouragement of the Cartagena Declaration for the creation of a humanitarian space in the region.

These advancements are a reflection of the so-called "spirit of Cartagena," in an explicit reference to the Declaration that 30 years ago established a primarily humanistic approach to refugees[72]. Said spirit implies the adoption of a logic of sovereignty that is not based exclusively on national interests, but rather on the construction of a more just and humane society through the protection of all individuals, regardless of their nationality; combining States' interests and individuals' needs (in this case, especially refugees)[73].

If, as seen, limitations to sovereignty were universally ensured from the development of *non-refoulement*, advancements in aspects of solidarity are still minimum at the international level. However, in the Latin American regional context, starting with the Cartagena Declaration, the new logic towards refugees began to integrate solidarity as one of its fundamental cornerstones.

The Cartagena Declaration does not want to become a document that is stagnant in a specific context, as it knows that this may weaken its objective of guaranteeing adequate protection to refugees if/when new factors arise. In this regard, it is important to note that the establishment of periodic review and evaluation mechanisms, which function as "forums for discussion among Latin American States and provide for the emergence of innovative regional solutions for the protection of refugees"[74], is fundamental in a social context characterized by varied and multiple changes that affect migratory dynamics and, consequently, the recognition of refugee status, thus, allowing these rights to be expanded or to be pivoted so as to attend to those who really need protection.

In this sense, this text turns now to the analysis of the results of these discussion

---

exceptions of Cuba and Guyana who are not signatories to any of the documents and the United States and Venezuela who are only part to the 1967 Protocol.

[68] Such as the granting of humanitarian entry visas and residency permits due to humanitarian reasons.

[69] On the subject of integral protection see JUBILUT, L. L.; APOLINÁRIO, S. M. O. S. A população refugiada no Brasil: em busca da proteção integral. *Universitas - Relações Internacionais*, 6, 2, 2008, p. 9-38.

[70] Such statement does not mean that protection of other migratory groups should not be advanced. However, the extremely precarious nature of refugees, justifying special protection, cannot be denied.

[71] In Europe, for example, a wave of xenophobia, linked to the economic crisis, affects refugees. See BECK, U. *A Europa Alemã – de Maquiavel a "Merkievel": Estratégias de Poder na Crise do Euro*. Lisboa: Edições 70, 2013. p. 31.

[72] CARNEIRO, W. P. A Declaração de Cartagena de 1984 e os Desafios da Proteção Internacional dos Refugiados, 20 Anos Depois. In: SILVA, C.A.S. (org.). *Op. cit.*

[73] JUBILUT, L.L.; CARNEIRO, W. P. C. Op. cit., p. 73.

[74] JUBILUT, L. L. O Direito Internacional dos Refugiados e sua Aplicação no Ordenamento Jurídico Brasileiro. Op. cit., p. 105. (free translation)

forums to evaluate the progress that the Cartagena Declaration has brought along and can still bring to the Latin American context.

4.2 The progress made by the periodic review process of the Cartagena Declaration[75]

After the Cartagena Declaration and based on it, a periodic review process was established – with meetings every 10 years -, with the intention of following the construction of a regime for refugees in the American context, based on solidarity and on the limitations of sovereignty established in 1984.

The first meeting of this process took place in San José, Costa Rica, ten years after the Cartagena Declaration, in 1994, and resulted in the Declaration on Refugees and Displaced Persons[76] (Declaration of San José).

As its title demonstrates, the concern of the San José Declaration with the issue of forced and humanitarian migration, as well as with refugees, is observed, since it encompasses another group of forced migrants in need of protection at that historical moment: Internally Displaced Persons (IDPs)[77]. The San José Declaration brought two unique articles on IDPs, articles 17 and 18, which first reinforce the need to establish basic standards of protection for these persons in any situation or circumstance, and secondly, highlight the Latin American effort in the study and resolution of the problems related to this theme.

It should be noted that this concern on the part of the agents of the Cartagena review process, stems from the continuance of situations of persecution, as well as from the closing of borders, which jeopardize the crossing of these migrants to another State. However, within the perspective of solidarity established by the Cartagena Declaration, the Declaration of San José provision on IDPs allowed for limitations to sovereignty and imposed commitments to the States, bringing, thus, numerous benefits to how the issue was treated.

In addition to this innovation, this meeting reaffirmed the principles established by the Cartagena Declaration[78], a fundamental step in consolidating the commitments made in the regional document, and that reinforces that the Cartagena Declaration is the basis for the protection advancements. The work in

---

[75] The theme of the review process of the Cartagena Declaration was addressed by the authors Liliana Lyra Jubilut and Silvia Menicucci de Oliveira Selmi Apolinário in JUBILUT, L. L.; APOLINÁRIO, S. M. O. S. O Direito Internacional dos Refugiados e seu Contexto Atual na América Latina. Op. cit., p. 353-369.

[76] Available at: <www.acnur.org/t3/portugues/recursos/documentos/?tx_danpdocumentdirs_pi2%5Bdownload%5D=yes&tx_danpdocumentdirs_pi2%5Bmode%5D=1&tx_danpdocumentdirs_pi2%5Bsort%5D=doctitle:0&tx_danpdocumentdirs_pi2%5Bdownloadtyp%5D=stream&tx_danpdocumentdirs_pi2%5Buid%5D=262>.

[77] According to the Guiding Principles on Internally Displaced Persons of 1999, internally displaced persons are "internally displaced persons are persons or groups of persons who have been forced or obliged to flee or to leave their homes or places of habitual residence, in particular as a result of or in order to avoid the effects of armed conflict, situations of generalized violence, violations of human rights or natural or human-made disasters, and who have not crossed an internationally recognized State border". Available at: <http://www.unhcr.org/protection/idps/43ce1cff2/guiding-principles-internal-displacement.html>.
According to UNHCR, internally displaced persons differ from refugees as they have not crossed international borders and legally remain under the protection of their national States, even if they are displaced due to similar reasons as refugees and might be on the move to the actions of said State. According to: <http://www.acnur.org/t3/portugues/quem-ajudamos/deslocados-internos/> (free translation).

[78] San José Declaration - 2nd Conclusion.

San José enhanced the search for coordinated regional solutions for the protection of refugees.

In 2004, the 20th anniversary of the Cartagena Declaration had preparatory meetings in different Latin American cities before the main meeting was held in Mexico[79].

At these preparatory meetings, two of which took place in Colombia, the focus was on the refugee crisis in Colombia, where, due to the internal conflict that existed for more than 60 years, there were approximately 3.5 million people forced to flee[80].

From the main meeting resulted the Mexico Declaration and Plan of Action (MPA)[81] that was adopted by 20 countries[82] to face the complex humanitarian situation of IDPs and refugees in Latin America. As its name indicates, this plan sought to enable concrete actions, through discussions of good practices, with the objective of improving the protection system established in Cartagena and developed in San José[83].

One of the most impressive contributions was the divisions proposed by the MPA to improve actions. As there was a twin objective - to improve humanitarian protection and assistance and to respond to the impact of refugee flows[84], there was a perception that the division of actions would be more efficient. Thus, a group was established to draw up the protection component, and another group was vested with developments for durable solutions[85].

In the protection component, the actions proposed by the MPA have developed around the goals of strengthening legal frameworks, which include, for example, national incorporation of International Refugee Law and the betterment of the commissions vested with the processes of refugee status determination and refugee protection[86]. Also, attention was paid to the need to improve technical knowledge of and to disseminate knowledge on International Refugee Law[87].

Besides, there was also concern about vulnerable groups among refugees and IDPs, which resulted in the adoption of UNHCR's age-gender-diversity strategy[88].

---

[79] The preparatory meetings were held in Brasilia, Brazil; São José, Costa Rica; Cartagena de Indias and Bogotá, Colombia, according to the last preambular paragraph of the Mexico Declaration and Plan of Action. Available at: <http://www.acnur.org/t3/fileadmin/Documentos/portugues/ BD_Legal/ Instrumentos_ Internacionais/Declaracao_e_Plano_de_Acao_do_Mexico.pdf?view=1 >.

[80] See: <http://www.acnur.org/t3/pam/informacion-general>.

[81] Avaliable at: <http://www.acnur.org/t3/fileadmin/Documentos/portugues/BD_Legal/ Instrumentos_Internacionais/Declaracao_e_Plano_de_Acao_do_Mexico.pdf?view=1>

[82] The countries are: Argentina, Bolivia, Brazil, Chile, Colombia, Costa Rica, Cuba, Ecuador, El Salvador, Guatemala, Haiti, Honduras, Mexico, Nicaragua, Panama, Paraguay, Peru, Dominican Republic, Uruguay and Venezuela. See: JUBILUT, L.L.; APOLINÁRIO, S. M. O. S. O Direito Internacional dos Refugiados e seu Contexto Atual na América Latina. Op. cit. p. 365.

[83] ACNUR. Plan de Acción de México: El impacto de la solidariedad regional. Op. cit.

[84] Ibid.

[85] The protective component appears in chapter 2 of MPA and the Durable Solutions component in Chapter 3.

[86] MPA- Chapter 2°

[87] Ibid.

[88] UNHCR adopted a "diversity-age-gender" perspective to guide its actions from 2004 onwards. On this, see, for instance, <http://www.unhcr.org/cgi-bin/texis/vtx/home/opendocPDFViewer. html?docid=

In the durable solutions component, the MPA intended to transform the logic of these actions and directly introduced the idea of solidarity into the coordinated regional efforts. These measures resulted in the proposals of (i) borders of solidarity[89]; (ii) cities of solidarity[90]; and (iii) resettlement in solidary [91].

These proposals have a strong integrative character, thus innovating in relation to what is being developed in the rest of the world.

The proposed actions meant that the legal commitments start to be delineated with greater adequacy to reality, as there are specific contents for adequate protection and provisions related to the host population, given that the relationship of refugees and displaced persons is not only to government agencies, but also requires interaction with local populations based on non-discrimination, mutual respect and combating xenophobia.

In this regard, the ideas brought about by the durable solutions component innovate as they allow host authorities to adopt protective measures that go beyond only entry and stay, to attain integral protection, with an emphasis on integration. This is the mentioned "spirit of Cartagena" by which actions are established through an ideal of solidarity[92]; changing the old rhetoric that sees refugees as "burden-sharing"[93]; developing a framework in which the protection of these persons is a duty from the point of view of the international protection of refugees[94]; changing a conception of sovereignty that is only linked to the protection of national groups[95]; and moving towards something that is developed in favor of the full protection of humanity[96].

4c206b449&query=gender AND age>.

[89] The solidarity frontiers component takes into consideration the fact that between 25 and 30% of the population in need of protection is at border regions, and, therefore, aims to improving protection in these areas. Such protection is provided through actions aimed at official procedures, including RSD, and officers. See UNHCR. Op. cit., p. 12.

[90] The solidarity cities focus on local integration, highlighting actions that allow for access to basic services and partnerships with municipal and regional organs. See Ibid, p. 13.

[91] Resettlement in solidarity proposes that the region engage in resettlement actions focused on the Colombian refugee crisis and creates a regional approach to resettlement. Ibid, p. 13

[92] PIOVESAN, F.; JUBILUT, L. L. Op. cit., p. 224.

[93] The idea of burden-sharing is present at 4th preambular paragraph of the 51 Convention that states that "the grant of asylum the may place unduly heavy burdens on certain countries".

[94] JUBILUT, L. L.; CARNEIRO, W. P. Op. cit., p. 69 et seq.

[95] According to Carneiro, in addressing the amendments provided by the Cartagena Declaration that directly affect the concept of sovereignty, "[u]m elemento importantíssimo da Declaração de Cartagena foi que, há vinte anos, durante a Guerra Fria, teve a coragem de começar a enfraquecer a mediatização da soberania nacional para a proteção da pessoa humana. [...] Com este passo, a Declaração de Cartagena afirma no contexto dos deslocamentos forçados que a razão de humanidade deve prevalecer sobre a razão de estado, já que o conceito de soberania inclui o dever de proteger a população" ("[a] very important element of the Cartagena Declaration was that, twenty years ago, during the Cold War, it had the courage to begin to weaken the mediatization of national sovereignty for the protection of human beings. [...] With this step, the Cartagena Declaration affirms in the context of forced displacements that the reason of humanity must prevail over the reason of state, since the concept of sovereignty includes the duty to protect the population"- free translation) CARNEIRO, W. P. Op. cit., p. 21.

[96] In this sense, Habermas points out that: "Cada repatriamento de um requerente de asilo por trás das portas fechadas de um aeroporto, cada navio naufragado com refugiados da pobreza na rota do Mediterrâneo entre a Líbia e a ilha de Lampedusa, cada tiro na fronteira mexicana, constitui mais uma questão inquietante dirigida aos cidadãos do Ocidente. A primeira declaração dos direitos humanos estabeleceu um padrão que pode inspirar os refugiados, aqueles que caíram na miséria, os excluídos, ofendidos e humilhados, e dar-lhes

The MPA also innovated by seeking joint solutions that can balance the needs of refugees and host States[97]. The distinction between border control actions and integration actions begins to be set aside so as to enable the creation of a single movement in the sense of protecting refugees and displaced persons.

After the MPA, a last regional meeting to date took place in Brasília in 2011. This meeting was not held in the framework of the Cartagena Declaration, but rather was held within the framework of the anniversary celebrations of the 1951 Convention and of the Conventions on the Status of Stateless Persons of 1951 and the Reduction of the Cases of Statelessness of 1961, and resulted in the adoption of the Brasilia Declaration[98].

The Brasilia Declaration[99] maintained the spirit of the previous declarations of the review process of the Cartagena Declaration and sought to strengthen the commitment to the protection of refugees, IDPs and stateless persons, based on humane, humanitarian and solidarity criteria, reinforcing the importance of previous regional documents[100]. In addition to this reinforcement, States' obligations towards refugees and stateless persons have advanced, as, for instance, in discussing the issue of mixed migration flows[101]. References to the promotion of the "values of solidarity, respect, tolerance and multiculturalism"[102] in the application of law and in the protection of refugees and to "the right of every person to seek and receive refuge"[103] were also present in the Brasilia Declaration. The latter demonstrates a connection with the Inter-American Human Rights system[104], that can lead to improvements in the national level.

Besides the limitations to States' sovereignty, highlighting the right to refuge is relevant in a context in which the number of people affected by forced migration has not diminished (neither in the world nor in the Americas[105]).

---

consciência de que o seu sofrimento não possui o caráter de um destino natural. A positivação do primeiro direito humano criou a *obrigação jurídica* de concretização dos conteúdos morais superiores, enterrados na memória da humanidade"" ("Each repatriation of an asylum seeker behind the closed doors of an airport, each shipwreck with refugees from poverty on the Mediterranean route between Libya and the island of Lampedusa, every shot on the Mexican border, is another disturbing question addressed to the citizens of the West. The first declaration of human rights has set a standard that can inspire refugees, those who have fallen into misery, the excluded, offended and humiliated, and make them aware that their suffering does not have the character of a natural destiny. The positivation of the first human right created the juridical obligation to materialize the higher moral contents buried in the memory of humanity"- free translation). HABERMAS, J. *Um Ensaio sobre a Constituição da Europa.* Lisboa: Edições 70, 2012, p. 51.

[97] Ibid and PIOVESAN, F.; JUBILUT, L.L. Op. cit.

[98] Available at: <http://www.acnur.org/t3/fileadmin/Documentos/portugues/ BDL/ Declaracao _de_Brasilia_sobre_a_Protecao_de_Refugiados_e_Apatridas_no_Continente_Americano.pdf?view=1>

[99] The Brasília Declaration was adopted by 18 countries: Argentina, Bolivia, Brazil, Chile, Colombia, Costa Rica, Cuba, Ecuador, El Salvador, Guatemala, Mexico, Nicaragua, Panama, Paraguay, Peru, Dominican Republic, Uruguay and Venezuela.

[100] See JUBILUT, L.L.; APOLINÁRIO, S. M. O. S. O Direito Internacional dos Refugiados e seu Contexto Atual na América Latina. Op. cit., p. 368.

[101] Ibid. See, also, Brasilia Declaration – 3rd Resolution.

[102] See Brasilia Declaration – 8th Resolution.

[103] Brasilia Declaration - 4th preambular paragraph

[104] Especially due to Article 27 of the American Declaration of the Rights and Duties of Man and Article 22 of the American Convention on Human Rights.

[105] COSTA, D. Introductory note to the Brasilia Declaration on the Protection of Refugees and Stateless Persons in the Americas, *International Legal Materials*, 50, 2011, p. 357.

Due to these elements, one can state that, even though the Brasilia Declaration does not follow the regional tradition in relation to the dates of the adoption of the Cartagena Declaration for the creation of new documents on refugees' protection, it follows the tradition of previous events and documents in order to improve the protection of refugees and other vulnerable groups, such as stateless persons, increasing the commitment by States to International Refugee Law and establishing regional coordinated solutions in the topics it tackles[106].

In 2014 a new round of debates on the challenges to be faced at the regional level about refugees, IDPs and stateless persons, known as Cartagena+30, within the framework of the 30th anniversary of the Cartagena Declaration will occur. The main event will take place in Brazil - in Brasília - at the end of the year.

In order for the gaps in protection in the region to be suppressed, there are several demands that need to be debated, such as the emblematic case of forced migration resulting from climate change[107].

Mixed migration flows[108] that have occurred in the region should also be on the agenda of Cartagena+30.

These trends should be accompanied by the search for improvement of existing protective instruments, seeking mechanisms to enforce rights effectively, actually integrate refugees, and take care of the protection of specific groups - in particular, gender and sexual orientation (LGBT), similar to that previously developed for women and children[109].

It is believed that Cartagena+30 could be "a unique opportunity to present Latin America as a relevant humanitarian actor"[110] and it is hoped that the region can continue to contribute "to the development of the international agenda through a renewed commitment to the protection and pursuit of durable solutions for

---

[106] See JUBILUT, L.L.; APOLINÁRIO, S. M. O. S. O Direito Internacional dos Refugiados e seu Contexto Atual na América Latina. Op. cit., p. 365-366.

[107] About this theme, see RAMOS, E. P. *Refugiados Ambientais: em busca de reconhecimento pelo Direito Internacional.* Tese de Doutorado apresentada à Faculdade de Direito da USP, 2011. Available at: <http://www.acnur.org/t3/fileadmin/scripts/doc.php?file=t3/fileadmin/Documentos/ portugues/ eventos/Refugiados_Ambientais>.

[108] About this topic see JAROCHINSKI SILVA, J. C. Uma análise sobre os fluxos migratórios mistos. In: RAMOS, A. C.; RODRIGUES, G.; ALMEIDA, G.A. (orgs.). Op. cit. p. 201-220.

[109] UNHCR suggests that "Poderia se centrar em torno de áreas como a qualidade dos sistemas de refúgio e da determinação da condição de refugiado; a proteção nos fluxos migratórios mistos; a apatridia; as necessidades de proteção daquelas pessoas que fogem do crime organizado transnacional e de outras formas de violência; as preocupações de segurança nacional dos Estados e suas obrigações humanitárias/direitos humanos; as iniciativas inovadoras para soluções completas, inclusive a utilização de soluções migratórias, e o deslocamento causado por desastres naturais " ("It could focus around areas such as the quality of the systems of refuge and refugee status determination; protection on mixed migratory flows; statelessness; the protection needs of people fleeing transnational organized crime and other forms of violence; the national security concerns of States and their humanitarian/human rights obligations; innovative initiatives for comprehensive solutions, including the use of migratory solutions, and displacement caused by natural disasters"- free translation). ACNUR. *Nota Conceitual – Comemoração do 30° Aniversário da Declaração de Cartagena.* Abril de 2013.

[110] See the testimony of Marta Juarez for CARTAGENA + 30 = MAIS EXPECTATIVAS, publicada em 23 de março de 2014 em O estrangeiro. Available at: <http://oestrangeiro.org/2014/03/23/cartagena-30-mais-expectativas/>. (free translation)

refugees, internally displaced persons and stateless persons"[111].

It is hoped that progress will be achieved, maintaining the trend towards a solidarity-based stance of stakeholders, which has been premised on a logic of State action based on the protection of human rights and dignity, and which has been bearing fruits in the region.

5. Conclusion

There is a trend towards strengthening the refugee protection system at the regional level in Latin America, capable of encompassing other persons with vulnerability. This strengthening is achieved through the adoption of declarations seeking to expand internationally recognized rights, such as those provided by the 1951 Convention and its 1967 Protocol.

The Cartagena Declaration inaugurated a system based on solidarity and States' commitments, expressed in a process of permanent construction, through its review process.

This option for periodic meetings is interesting, especially considering the developing characteristics in refugee issues, the possibility of exchanging good practices for vulnerable groups, and the new challenges for the protection of forced migrants from a humanitarian perspective. Beyond the norms of treaties and declarations, a concern for their effectiveness through public policies and actions, many of which require the adoption of national legislation, is weaved, giving life to and implementing, in various forms, the commitments assumed by the States of the region.

Furthermore, the option of strengthening the institute of refuge regarding the right of recognition of refugee status is reinforced. This fact emphasizes the idea of a self-limitation of sovereignty, since its adopters opt for an international obligation in a humanitarian and humanitarian perspective on the subject of refuge, implementing "higher moral contents"[112].

Obviously, some challenges remain, but the progress made at the regional level, shared by several countries, deserves to be positively valued, as besides enhancing the search for coordinated and cooperative solutions, they increase the protection of those in need, keeping the spirit of the 1951 Convention alive, as it had already posited the need for complementary protection.

The option by Latin America that begun in 1984 with the Cartagena Declaration should serve as a reference, given that it makes a clear choice (and one that seems appropriate) for solidarity and cooperation to resolve the issue of refugees and of those who are in similar conditions of vulnerability. Besides, it highlights the deepening of solidarity and of limitation to state sovereignty as a legacy of the Cartagena Declaration and its review process, thus serving as an example of the transformative potential of refuge.

---

[111] Ibid.
[112] HABERMAS, J. Op. cit.

REFUGEE PROTECTION IN BRAZIL AND LATIN AMERICA

References

ACNUR. *Nota Conceitual – Comemoração do 30° Aniversário da Declaração de Cartagena.* Abril de 2013.
_____. *Plan de Acción de México: El impacto de la solidariedad regional.* San José, C.R.: EDITORAMA, 2007.

_____. Persons covered by the OAU Convention Governing the Specific Aspects of Refugee Problems in Africa and by the Cartagena Declaration on Refugees (Submitted by the African Group and the Latin American Group). EC/1992/SCP/CRP.6. International Protection (SCIP), 6 April 1992.

BAGANHA, M. I. A cada sul o seu norte: dinâmicas migratórias em Portugal. In: SANTOS. B. de S. (Org.). *Globalização: fatalidade ou Utopia?.* 2. ed. São Paulo: Cortez, 2005.

BECK, U. *A Europa Alemã – de Maquiavel a "Merkievel": Estratégias de Poder na Crise do Euro.* Lisboa: Edições 70, 2013.

BÓGUS, L. Esperança Além-Mar: Portugal no "Arquipélago Migratório" Brasileiro. In: MALHEIROS, J. (org.). *Imigração Brasileira em Portugal.* Lisboa: ACIDI, 2007.

CARNEIRO, W. P. A Declaração de Cartagena de 1984 e os Desafios da Proteção Internacional dos Refugiados, 20 Anos Depois. In: SILVA, C.A.S. (org.). *Direitos Humanos e Refugiados.* Dourados (MS): Editora UFGD, 2012.

COSTA, D. Introductory note to the Brasilia Declaration on the Protection of Refugees and Stateless Persons in the Americas. *International Legal Materials,* 50, 2011.

FISCHEL DE ANDRADE, J. H. Breve reconstituição histórica da tradição que culminou na proteção internacional dos refugiados. In: ARAÚJO, Nádia de; ALMEIDA, Guilherme Assis de. (Coord.) *O Direito Internacional dos Refugiados: uma perspectiva brasileira.* 2. ed. Rio de Janeiro: Renovar, 2001. p. 99-125.

_____. *Direito Internacional dos Refugiados- Evolução Histórica (1921-1952).* Rio de Janeiro: Renovar, 1996.

FOUCHER, Michel. *Obsessão por Fronteiras.* São Paulo: Radical Livros, 2009.

GLOVER, S.; GOTT C. et al. *Migration: an Economic and Social Analysis.* The Research, Development and Statistics Directorate, Occasional Paper n. 67, 2001.

HABERMAS, J. *Um Ensaio sobre a Constituição da Europa.* Lisboa: Edições 70, 2012.

HADDAD, E. *The refugee: a conceptual analysis- Between sovereigns.* Cambridge: Cambridge University Press, 2008.

JAROCHINSKI SILVA, J. C. As Migrações Internacionais e os seus Impactos. In: JUBILUT, L. L. (Coord.). *Direito internacional atual.* Rio de Janeiro: Elsevier, 2014. p. 317-339.

_____. Uma análise sobre os fluxos migratórios mistos. In: RAMOS, A. C.; RODRIGUES, G.; ALMEIDA, G.A. (orgs.). *60 anos de ACNUR - Perspectivas de futuro.* São Paulo: CLA, 2011. p. 201-220.

JUBILUT, L. L. A Judicialização do Refúgio. In: RAMOS, A. C.; RODRIGUES, G.; ALMEIDA, G.A. (orgs.). *60 anos de ACNUR - Perspectivas de futuro.* São Paulo: CLA, 2011. p. 163-178.

_____. JUBILUT, L. L. O conceito de soberania: modificações e responsabilidade. In: FRANCO FILHO, M. T.; MIALHE, J. L.; JOB, U. S. (Org.). *Epitácio Pessoa e a Codificação do Direito Internacional.* Porto Alegre: Sérgio Antonio Fabris Editor, 2013. p. 247-270.

_____. *O Direito Internacional dos Refugiados e sua Aplicação no Ordenamento Jurídico Brasileiro.* São Paulo: Método, 2007.

JUBILUT, L.L.; APOLINÁRIO, S. M. O. S. O Direito Internacional dos Refugiados e seu Contexto Atual na América Latina. In: ROSA, R. M.; DOMÍNGUEZ AVILA, C. F. (Org.). *América Latina no Labirinto Global - Economia, Política e Segurança.* Brasília: CRV, 2012. p. 353-369.

_____. A necessidade de proteção internacional no âmbito da migração. *Revista Direito GV,* 11, 6, 2010.

_____. A população refugiada no Brasil: em busca da proteção integral. *Universitas - Relações Internacionais,* 6, 2, 2008, p. 9-38.

MURILLO GONZALES, J. C. El derecho de asilo y la protección de refugiados en el continente americano. In: ACNUR. *La protección internacional de refugiados en las Américas.* Quito, 2011.

MILESI, R.; CARLET, F. Refugiados e Políticas Públicas In: SILVA, C.A.S. (org.). *Direitos Humanos e Refugiados*. Dourados (MS): Editora UFGD, 2012.

RAMOS, A. C. Asilo e Refúgio: semelhanças, diferenças e perspectivas. In: RAMOS, A. C.; RODRIGUES, G.; ALMEIDA, G.A. (orgs.). *60 anos de ACNUR - Perspectivas de futuro*. São Paulo: CLA, 2011.

PIOVESAN, F.; JUBILUT, L.L. The 1951 Convention and the Americas: Regional Developments. In: ZIMMERMANN, A. (Org.) *Commentary on the 1951 Convention Relating to the Status of Refugees and its 1967 Protocol*. Oxford: Oxford University Press, 2011. p. 205-224.

RAMOS, E. P. *Refugiados Ambientais: em busca de reconhecimento pelo Direito Internacional*. Tese de Doutorado apresentada à Faculdade de Direito da USP, 2011.

REIS, R. R. *Políticas de Imigração na França e nos Estados Unidos*. São Paulo: Hucitec, 2006.

UNHCR. *Global Trends 2012 – Displacement, the new 21st century challenge*. Genebra: UNHCR, 2012.

ZOLBERG, A. The formation of new States as a refugee-generating process. *Annals of the American Academy of Politics and Social Science*, May 1983, p. 24-38.

THE CHALLENGES OF PROTECTION OF REFUGEES AND FORCED MIGRANTS IN THE FRAMEWORK OF CARTAGENA+30 (2014)[*]

Liliana Lyra Jubilut[**] and André de Lima Madureira[***]

Introduction

Forced migration is a phenomenon that affects an increasingly larger number of persons. Although there are no consolidated and systematized numerical data, it is estimated that there are 51.2 million persons displaced due to violence and/or persecution,[1] and it is known that the estimate of the United Nations University of 50 million persons displaced by environmental reasons in 2010[2] has been confirmed.[3] However, in spite of these figures, there is a lack of established legal regimes to ensure full protection for most of these persons.

In addition, the increase in the numbers of unprotected persons may lead to heightened pressures on existing regimes, such as in International Refugee Law; making protection more difficult or, in some cases, allowing for only a more vulnerable protection scheme than the one that should be legally granted. These challenges need, nowadays, to be considered as a context for any analytical exercise and legal protective advancement.

It is in this scenario that, in 2014, the Cartagena+30 process occurs; following up on the revision processes of the 1984 Cartagena Declaration on Refugees in Latin America and proposing a protection agenda for the next 10 years for the region.

---

[*] This text was translated from Portuguese to English by Victor Augusto Mendes, and revised by Rosilandy C. C. Lapa. A final revision was performed by the authors.

[**] Liliana Lyra Jubilut is a Professor and Researcher at the Universidade Católica de Santos, Brazil.

[***] André de Lima Madureira is Master's degree candidate in International Law at Universidade Católica de Santos, Brazil.

[1] UNHCR. *Global Trends 2013*, p. 2.

[2] UNU-EHS. The Ranks of "Environmental refugees" swell worldwide, calls grow for better definition, recognition, support. *World day for disaster reduction* (press release).

[3] This fact is demonstrated, for example, by the Red Cross data that in 2008 there were already 51.1 million internally displaced persons, i.e. the UN estimative had already been exceeded even without counting international displacement. See: International Federation of The Red Cross and Red Crescent. *World Disasters Report*, 2012. Estimates for 2050 range from 25 million to 1 billion environmental displaced persons, with the most widely used figure being 200 million. See: LACZKO, Frank; AGHAZARM, Christine (eds.). *Migration, Environment and Climate Change: Assessing the Evidence.*

In this sense, and intending to contribute to this process, this article describes the main challenges for the protection of refugees and forced migrants, pointing out pathways for protection advancements for the framework of Cartagena+30.

1. Current challenges for refugees and forced migrants

As seen, there is a significant number of persons in forced migration situations who are in need of international protection. However, it appears that, in practice, the only currently existing protection regime is International Refugee Law.[4] This means that either protection comes through the recognition of the applicant as a refugee, or it depends exclusively on the political will of each State.

Since International Refugee Law is the only form of mandatory protection in the current scenario, it must be verified whether it allows for the protection of all forced migrants. And, in this sense, one finds that there are challenges both regarding the limits of the refugee definition itself and in relation to the new migratory flows.

1.1 Limits of the international refugee definition

International Refugee Law, which emerged during the 20th century, is a branch of the international regime for the protection of human beings and aims to design and implement protective mechanisms for persons displaced by a well-founded fear of persecution[5] and, thus, to implement the right of asylum.[6] It was due to World War I and the Russian Revolution that the international community started to take an interest in the issue of refugees,[7] since the institute of asylum, which allowed for protection until then began to not be enough to protect such persons,[8] especially due to its discretionary nature.

Throughout the first half of the 20th century[9] some entities were created and a few historical treaties were adopted to systematize and internationalize the institute of refuge,[10] but it was with (i) the end of World War II, (ii) the creation of the United Nations Organization (UN) and, most essentially, (iii) the creation of the United Nations High Commissioner for Refugees (UNHCR),[11] that the international protection of refugees was fostered, particularly with the drafting of the Convention Relating to the Status of Refugees of 1951 (1951 Convention), which universally conceptualized the institute of refuge, even though being based

---

[4] See, for instance, JUBILUT, Liliana L.; APOLINÁRIO, Silvia Menicucci O. S. A necessidade de proteção internacional no âmbito da migração. *Revista Direito GV*, v. 6, n. 1, 2010, p. 275- 294.

[5] See: JUBILUT, Liliana Lyra. *O Direito Internacional dos Refugiados e sua aplicação no ordenamento jurídico brasileiro*. São Paulo: Método, 2007.

[6] Ibid., p. 36.

[7] According to Eric Hobsbawm, World War I and the Russian Revolution generated between 4 and 5 million refugees, while World War II amounted to 40.5 million, decolonization of India 15 million, and the Korean War motivated displacement of 5 million people. See: HOBSBAWM, Eric. *Era dos Extremos - o breve século XX:* 1914-1991, p. 57 and 58.

[8] JUBILUT, op. cit., p. 38 and 44.

[9] For a historical summary of International Refugee Law right after World War II, see: FISCHEL DE ANDRADE, José Henrique *Direito Internacional dos Refugiados - Evolução Histórica (1921-1952)*. Rio de Janeiro: Renovar, 1996.

[10] See: JUBILUT, op. cit., p. 49 et seq.

[11] UN. General meeting. Resolution 428 (V), 1950.

on its own historical context.

From the universal definition, a refugee is an individual who has a well-founded fear of being persecuted for reasons of race, religion, nationality, political opinion or membership in a particular social group, that is outside of his/her country of origin or of residence (extraterritoriality),[12] and who needs international protection (i.e. is not covered by the cessation clauses also defined by the 51 Convention[13] and also does not have any other form of international protection at his/her disposal),[14] and is deserving of international protection (i.e., is not included in the exclusion clauses laid down by the 1951 Convention[15]).

The 1951 Convention also contains a temporal limitation – since it establishes that, to be a refugee, the well-founded fear must have occurred owing to events that took place before 1 January 1951[16] - and a geographical limitation – the system will only apply to persons who have experienced well-founded fear in Europe,[17] a condition to which the signatory states could accede or not.[18]

It is important to mention that such limitations were removed 16 years later by the international community due to the establishment of the Protocol relating to the Status of Refugees in 1967 (1967 Protoco.[19] In light of this refugee protection has indeed become universal, and people with a well-founded fear of being persecuted can henceforth rely on the protection of the international society through the institute of refuge without temporal or geographical limitations.

However, one notes that the concept delineated in the beginning of the second half of the last century is limited in view of the current challenges of refugee protection. The main limits are three.

The first aspect to be considered is the lack of a legal definition for one of the key elements of the refugee concept: the term "persecution".[20]

Although UNHCR sets out in its Handbook on Procedures and Criteria for Determining Refugee Status under the 1951 Convention and the 1967 Protocol relating to the Status of Refugees, of 1979, that persecution is any threat to life or liberty, and that it should be verified by objective and subjective criteria,[21] it is found that (i) such definition is very broad and thus difficult to implement, and that (ii) the definition comes from a non-legally binding instrument. Therefore, one can see that there is no legal definition for a fundamental element of the refugee concept.

The second limitation derives from the fact that the traditional concept of refugee, which categorically lists five grounds of persecution that must be present so as to give reason to the well-founded fear of being persecuted, do not consider some current situations of forced displacement. Examples are (i) the absence of

---

[12] 1951 Convention, article 1, A, 2
[13] The cessation clauses are found at article 1, C of the 1951 Convention.
[14] Article 1, D and E of the 1951 Convention.
[15] Article 1, F of the 1951 Convention.
[16] Article 1, B, 1, b of the 1951 Convention.
[17] Article 1, B, 1, a of the 1951 Convention.
[18] Article 1, B, 2 of the 1951 Convention.
[19] Article 1, 2 of the 1967 Protocol
[20] See: JUBILUT, op. cit., p. 45-46
[21] Ibid.

economic, social and cultural rights for the purposes of determining refugee status,[22] which would benefit persons persecuted due to their profession or activities, for instance; and (ii) gender-related issues - both gender-based violence and gender identity - as grounds of persecution, which limits the protection of women and LGBTI+ persons.

The third limit, however, derives from the lack of a greater integration between the refugee definition and other human rights. In this regard, one observes that there are mentions to the convergence between the two branches of International Law,[23] but, in practice, the refugee definition is such that interactions are hardly considered. An example of this fact can be seen in the possible convergence with environmental issues, considering that the right to a healthy environment is a human right.[24]

In fact, there have been updates to the concept brought by the 1951 Convention and the 1967 Protocol, but always at the regional level. In 1969 the Organization of African Unity (nowadays African Union) began a debate on the extension of the refugee definition in the context of the intensification of civil conflicts due to the decolonization processes that the African continent was experiencing. In 1984 this debate took place in Latin America. Considering the increase of refugees in the region due to the outbreak of various dictatorial regimes, an International Conference in Colombia culminated in the adoption of the Declaration of Cartagena[25] and the consequent expansion of the concept of refugee, which now has the "gross and generalized violation of human rights" as one of its central elements.

Such innovations do not alter the international concept of refugee, which, on the one hand, generates discrepancies in the recognition and application of International Refugee Law, but, on the other hand, allows for the extension of protection, even if only regionally. Leaving aside the question of the universal homogeneity of International Refugee Law - which is in itself a problem to be analyzed - and focusing on regional developments, it is necessary to verify whether these, especially the ones in Latin America as this is the object of this article, are enough for the protection of forced migrants in current migratory flows.

1.2. New flows of forced migrants

It is well known that migration is an ancient phenomenon that has been present throughout the history of mankind. Initially endowed with greater freedom, it has started to see limits imposed to it since the appearance of nation-States, which are

---

[22] JUBILUT, Liliana Lyra; APOLINÁRIO, Silvia Menicucci de O. S. O Direito Internacional dos Refugiados e seu Contexto Atual na América Latina. In ROSA, Renata de Melo; DOMÍNGUEZ AVILA, Carlos Federico (orgs.). *América Latina no Labirinto Global - Economia, Política e Segurança*. Brasília: CRV, 2012, p. 359.

[23] 1951 Convention, 1st preambular paragraph.

[24] See., for example, the Stockholm Declaration on the Human Environment and, in the American context, the Protocol of San Salvador (Article 11). Available at: <http: //www. direitoshumanos. usp. / Environment-declaration-of-stockholm-on-environment-human.html> and <http://www.cidh.oas. org/ Basics/Portugues/e.Protocolo_de_San_Salvador.htm>.

[25] The Cartagena Declaration and the extension of the concept of refugee will be studied in more detail in the third section of this article.

territorially delimited and endowed with sovereignty over the entry of and movement of persons within their territories.[26]

On the other hand, and understanding migration from an attraction and repulsion logic,[27] one can note, in recent times, an increasing number of factors of repulsion of persons and, thus, an increase in the number of forced migrants on the move.

The combination of these two factors builds a scenario in which regular migration is limited, while the number of forcibly displaced persons grows, resulting in a difficult equation to solve. This is aggravated by the legal gaps for protecting such persons, since, as mentioned, the only form of mandatory protection for forced migrants is found in International Refugee Law, which has limited categories of inclusion.

Among forced migrants that need to be highlighted as "new flows"[28] are Internally Displaced Persons (IDPs), environmentally displaced persons and persons in need of humanitarian protection, such as victims of human trafficking.

IDPs have joined the international agenda in the 1990s. Defined as "persons or groups of persons who have been forced or obliged to flee or to leave their homes or places of habitual residence, in particular as a result of or to avoid the effects of armed conflict, situations of generalized violence, violations of human rights or natural or human-made disasters, and who have not crossed an internationally recognized State border"[29]; IDPs are protected by the Guiding Principles on Internal Displacement,[30] which, however, is a provision of soft law, i.e. with lesser legal force.

Environmental displaced persons, defined as "persons who have been forced to leave their natural habitat, temporarily or permanently, because of a certain environmental disruption (natural or human-induced), which threatened their existence or seriously affect their quality of life",[31] are increasingly present in light of climate change and environmental disasters,[32] often caused by human action, and are not protected by the institute of refuge.

Also not legally protected by the refugee regime are the victims of trafficking, who are increasingly relying on domestic and international protection standards, but often find it difficult to secure ways to remain in a country other than their own

---

[26] JAROCHINSKI SILVA, João Carlos. Uma análise sobre os fluxos migratórios mistos. In RAMOS, André Carvalho; RODRIGUES, Gilberto; ALMEIDA, Guilherme Assis (orgs.). *60 Anos de ACNUR: perspectivas de futuro.* São Paulo: CLA Cultural, 2011, p. 201.

[27] GLOVER, Stephen; GOTT, Ceri et al. *Migration: an Economic and Social Analysis.* The Research, Development and Statistics Directorate.

[28] It is important to note that stateless persons are a group of human beings who also need international protection and who, in general, are protected by UNHCR' actions. But since its origin is remote, its inclusion in the group of "new flows" was not made.

[29] See the annex of the Representative of the UN Secretary-General on Internally Displaced Persons (E / CN.4 / 1998/53 / Add.2 of 11.02.1998).

[30] See: E / CN.4 / 1998/53 / Add.2 of 11.02.1998. Available at: <http://www.ohchr.org/ Documents / Issues / IDPersons / GPPortuguese.pdf>.

[31] EL-HINNAWI, Essam. *Environmental Refugees.* (free translation)

[32] On this subject see RAMOS, Erika Pires. *Refugiados Ambientais: em busca de reconhecimento pelo Direito Internacional.* Tese de Doutorado apresentada à Faculdade de Direito da USP, 2011.

or that of origin of the trafficking.

Treated separately (in each group) or collectively (all groups combined), there is a significant proportion of forced migrants who do not have mandatory international protection. This poses a challenge to their protection and the protection of refugees in the current international scenario.

2. The need for solution strategies

The challenge of protection of forced migrants not protected by International Refugee Law impacts not only their own protection but also that of refugees and asylum seekers. As the only mandatory form of protection in the event of forced migration, the institute of refuge has started to be used in situations where, due to its conceptual limits, it should not be possible to apply it.

In this context, there is a reduction of protection, mainly due to the increase in the number of asylum requests and the maintenance of the existing protection structures, which is further aggravated by mixed migration flows, where persons with various and different protection needs migrate in the same flows.[33]

In this regard, new solutions must be advanced so as to ensure that all refugees and forced migrants are able to enjoy the protection they need.

The lack of political will for the establishment of responsibility-sharing mechanisms for forced migrants[34] is one of the main reasons for the lack of progress in building new forms of protection that meet the protection challenges of forced migrants. In light of this, and, while not representing universal advances, "[a]n alternative route that could allow for new developments is a focus on regionalism".[35]

In this sense, Latin America has been placed at the world's forefront, especially due to the protection advancements in the context of the Cartagena Declaration and its revision processes.

3. The Cartagena Declaration as a process of possible construction of protection[36]

3.1. The 1984 Cartagena Declaration

The emergence of various dictatorial regimes in Latin America in the early 1970s was central to the emergence of large numbers of refugees in the region, since such regimes systematically disregarded mechanisms and instruments for the protection of human rights.

Thus, due to the political instability of these contexts and gross and generalized human rights violations, which lingered in the early 1980s mainly in Central

---

[33] On mixed flows see JAROCHINSKI SILVA, Op. cit., p. 201-220.

[34] JUBILUT, Liliana Lyra; RAMOS, Érika Pires. Regionalism: a strategy for dealing with crisis migration, *Forced Migration Review*, 45, p. 66.

[35] Ibid.

[36] Cf., JUBILUT, APOLINÁRIO, O Direito Internacional ..., Op. cit .; and JUBILUT, Liliana Lyra; APOLINÁRIO, Silvia Menicucci de O. S.; JAROCHINSKI SILVA, João Carlos. O Potencial Transformador do Refúgio: aprofundamento da solidariedade e da limitação à soberania como legado da Declaração de Cartagena e de seus processos revisionais. In RAMINA, Larissa; FRIEDRICH, Tatyana Scheila. (coords.). *Coleção Direito Internacional Multifacetado – Direitos Humanos, Guerra e Paz.* Curitiba: Juruá, 2014, p. 173-198.

America, there was a flow of refugees estimated at around two million individuals.[37] Therefore, there was the need to seek a common and coordinated response to such regional flow. As a result, an academic conference was held in the city of Cartagena das Índias, Colombia, in 1984.[38]

In order to rethink the international protection of refugees and find solutions to the humanitarian challenges faced by those persons in Central America, the academic symposium, which had the support of the Colombian government and UNHCR, drafted a document called the Cartagena Declaration.[39]

Adopted in November of 1984, the Cartagena Declaration is divided into four parts: preamble, contextualization of regional protection (with reference to the Contadora Act on Peace and Co-operation in Central America and to actions for the implementation and improvement of international protection arising from universal standards in the region), conclusions and recommendations.

When examining the text of the Cartagena Declaration, one may infer that the conclusions are the most relevant sections of the document. In total, the Declaration presents 17 conclusions, which aim to impose advancements on the protection of refugees in the region, including by modifying universal standards when necessary.

In light of this, it is essential to stress the 3rd conclusion,[40] which presents the most significant change brought by the document. Indeed, the inclusion of gross and generalized violation of human rights as a ground for recognition of refugee status was the most important modification established by the Cartagena Declaration. This inclusion has increased the chances of a person being recognized as a refugee, having been influenced by the context of crisis in Central America. Thus, it is possible to conclude that the document is directly related to the historical period experienced by the region at the time of its elaboration.

Regarding the gross and generalized violation of human rights element, it is important to highlight a few aspects.

First, there is no legal definition delimiting the contours of the expression "gross and generalized violation of human rights". In practice, its application can be seen in cases of civil wars, dictatorships, or in cases where countries are unable to guarantee the freedom, the safety or the life of the individual.[41]

Secondly, the regional definition should be considered in conjunction with the international criteria brought by the 1951 Convention and the 1967 Protocol. The 3rd Conclusion expressly indicates that the gross and generalized violation of

---

[37] SPINDLER, William. The Mexico Plan of Action: protecting refugees through international solidarity, *Forced Migration Review*, 24, p. 64.

[38] Cf. JUBILUT, APOLINÁRIO, O Direito Internacional..., Op. cit., p. 366.

[39] Ibid.

[40] Cartagena Declaration - 3rd Conclusion: "... the definition or concept of refugee recommended for use in the region is what, besides containing the elements of the 1951 Convention and the 1967 Protocol, also consider As refugees, persons who have fled their countries because their life, security or freedom have been threatened by widespread violence, foreign aggression, internal strife, massive violation of human rights or other circumstances that have seriously disturbed public order" [43] Cf. JUBILUT, APOLINÁRIO, O Direito Internacional Op. cit., p. 367.

[41] Cf. JUBILUT, APOLINÁRIO, O Direito Internacional ... Op. cit., p. 367.

human rights criterion is an addition to the elements in the universal definition of refuge.[42]

Thirdly, the new standard of analysis that the regional definition brings by ascertaining gross and generalized violation of human rights as a situation that allows for refugee status needs to be considered. The examination of an asylum claim is no longer based solely on the individual well-founded fear of being persecuted, but also on the objective situation of the country of origin in order to check if there is a context of gross and generalized human rights violations.[43]

The objective situation of the country of origin is also relevant when examining the individual fear of persecution. In other words, when examining the individual fear of persecution for reasons of race, nationality, religion, political opinion and/or membership of a certain social group, the objective reality of the country of origin is also analyzed to give credibility to the declarations of the asylum seeker. However, in the case of the gross and generalized violation of human rights, the examination of the objective situation of the country of origin is in itself an element which characterizes the refugee status. Thus, any individual from that country should be recognized as a refugee, provided that s/he does not fit the exclusion clauses. Hence, we have a new pattern of analysis which is based solely on the objective situation of the country of origin.[44]

The Cartagena Declaration, in addition to extending the traditional concept of refugee, also demonstrates the regional commitment to respecting human rights. Since its adoption, the region presents not only a relevant story about the institute of asylum,[45] but also begins to seek coordinated responses at the regional level for refugees. Therefore, it is important to note the emergence of a new perspective regarding durable solutions.[46] Those solutions consist of local integration, repatriation and resettlement.[47]

From all the above, one can see that, even though the Cartagena Declaration is not a binding document, it is considered a relevant landmark in the protection of refugees since it "established important precedents and a guide to the principles and criteria that should guide the international protection of refugees in our [Latin America] continent"[48] and "extended its concern for the situation of people facing forced displacement situations in Latin America in addition to the specific situation of refugees".[49]

---

[42] Cartagena Declaration - Conclusion 3: "... the definition or concept of refugee recommended for use in the region is what, in addition to containing the elements of the 1951 Convention and the 1967 Protocol [...] ".

[43] JUBILUT, APOLINÁRIO, JAROCHINSKI, Op. cit., p. 184-185.

[44] Ibid.

[45] See, for example, the Montevideo Criminal Law Treaty of 1889; The 1928 Convention on Asylum; Convention on Political Asylum, 1933; Convention on Political Asylum, 1939; Declaration of the Rights and Duties of Man on Territorial Asylum, 1948, and the 1954 Convention on Diplomatic Asylum.

[46] HATHAWAY, James. *The Rights of Refugees under International Law*, p. 119.

[47] JUBILUT, Op. cit., p. 154 et seq.

[48] DEMANT, Eva. 30 años de la Declaración de Cartagena sobre Refugiados. Avances y desafíos de la protección de refugiados en Latinoamérica. *Agenda Internacional*, XX, n. 31, 2013, p. 131-140, p. 131 (free translation).

[49] Ibid., p. 132 (free translation).

Notwithstanding its adoption being recommended by the Organization of American States (OAS), the Cartagena Declaration has its application subjected to the free decision of the States. However, the numbers are relevant, considering that currently 15 countries[50] have already incorporated the document entirely or with modifications.[51]

3.2. Reflections on the Cartagena Declaration: Advancements and Review Process

3.2.1. Progress from the Cartagena Declaration

Since 1984, the Cartagena Declaration directly influences the protection of refugees and other forced migrants in Latin America by establishing a more humane and humanitarian approach. In fact, the document promotes a humanistic view of the protection of refugees and other forced migrants in the region, considering that it sets not only commitments to international and regional criteria for determining refugee status[52] but also promotes the search for actions leading to both complementary protection (for humanitarian displaced persons and forced migrants who do not fit the definition of refugee) and integral protection,[53] especially in relation to local integration. Thus, the innovative and encouraging character of the Declaration, which establishes the so-called "spirit of Cartagena", can be perceived.

Indeed, the drafting and adoption of the Cartagena Declaration has fostered a series of changes and expansions of protection in national legislations of the countries of the region, which are in keeping with the required perspectives to adequately respond to the current major challenges in forced migration. The States of Latin American, in addition to offering protection to refugees, have also guaranteed protection to the rights of IDPs[54] and victims of international trafficking. Colombia and Peru have included in their domestic systems rules

---

[50] Argentina, Belize, Bolivia, Brazil, Chile, Colombia, Ecuador, El Salvador, Guatemala, Honduras, Mexico, Nicaragua, Paraguay, Peru and Uruguay (see the combination of information available as of October 2013 at: http://www.acnur.org/ /t3/fileadmin/scripts/ doc.php? file=biblioteca/pdf/2541>). Ecuador recently withdrew the Declaration from its internal order (See JUBILUT, Liliana L. Fora and Programs for Refugees in Latin America, p. 245-266).

[51] For the description and analysis of the modifications, see PIOVESAN, Flávia; JUBILUT, Liliana Lyra. The 1951 Convention and the Americas: Regional Developments. In ZIMMERMANN, Andreas (org.). *Commentary on the 1951 Convention Relating to the Status of Refugees and its 1967 Protocol.* Oxford: Oxford University Press, 2011, p. 219-220.

[52] Most American States are party to the 1951 Convention and its 1967 Protocol. However, Cuba and Guyana are not signatories to any of the documents and the United States and Venezuela are only parties to the 1967 Protocol. According to the data available at: <http://treaties. Un.org/ pages/View DetailsII.aspx?&src=UNTSONLINE&mtdsg_no=V~2&chapter=5&Temp=mt dsg2 & lang = en>

[53] About integral protection see JUBILUT, Liliana Lyra; APOLINÁRIO, Silvia Menicucci de O. S. A população refugiada no Brasil: em busca da proteção integral. *Universitas - Relações Internacionais,* v. 6, n. 2, 2008, p. 9-38.

[54] According to UNHCR, internally displaced persons "are internally displaced persons, but are often wrongly called refugees. Unlike refugees, internally displaced persons did not cross an international border to find security but remained in their home country, even if they fled for reasons similar to refugees (armed conflict, widespread violence, human rights violations), internally displaced persons remain legally under the protection of their own government, although this government may be the cause of the flight". Available at: <http://www.acnur.org/t3/portugues/quem-ajudamos/deslocados-internos/>.

relating to the protection of IDPs;[55] and Brazil, Ecuador and Panama, in turn, recognize as refugees those who are victims of international trafficking.

In addition, the establishment of new policies ranging from the granting of humanitarian visas and new means of legal residence to the protection of victims of torture[56] can be seen in the region.

It is also important to stress that the influence of the Cartagena Declaration on the protection of refugees and other forced migrants in the region goes beyond the legislative and practical measures already implemented. The Cartagena Declaration does not present itself as a statical action, given that the discussions pertaining to the protection of human rights must be continuous in order to respect current and future social changes. By providing periodic review mechanisms that act as "debate forums between the States of Latin America and provide the appearance of regional innovative solutions with regard to the protection of refugees",[57] the Cartagena Declaration shows an understanding of the social construction of human rights, and assures that future challenges to the protection of these rights will be debated and responded to in due course.

With regard to this review process, it is important to highlight the San Jose Declaration on Refugees and Internally Displaced Persons of 1994, the Mexico Declaration and Plan of Action of 2004 and, albeit indirectly, the Brasilia Declaration of 2010[58].[59]

3.2.2. The Review Process

The Cartagena Declaration sets the practice of periodic meetings (every 10 years) in order to keep the protection of forced migrants and the debate on the subject up to date. Such meetings are called the review process of the Cartagena Declaration.

A direct linkage between the debates for the advancement of protection with the real regional context, so that the latter directly reflects in the agenda to be proposed by the former has been perceived as a characteristic of the review process.

Thus, if the Cartagena Declaration was inserted in the context of the conflicts that occurred in Central America in the 1980s, its first revision was focused on the

---

[55] The texts of the legislation are available at: <http://www.acnur.org/biblioteca/pdf/2883.pdf> and <http://www.acnur.org/secciones/index.php?viewCat= 1055>.

[56] Such policies occurred in Mexico, Honduras, Panama, Costa Rica, Brazil, and Argentina. This information was obtained during the International Meeting on the Protection of Refugees, Stateless Persons and Mixed Migratory Movements in the Americas, which took place in Brasilia in November 2010. All these practices have been called Complementary Humanitarian Protection, and should apply to cases not inserted in the protection of refuge. On the subject see, for example, DICKER, Nicole. MANSFIELD, Joanna. *Filling the protection gap: current trends in complementary protection in Canada, Mexico and Australia.* UNHCR, 2012.

[57] JUBILUT, Op. cit., p. 105. (free translation)

[58] As will be seen in item 3.2.2. The Brasilia Declaration does not derive from an event commemorating the anniversary of the Cartagena Declaration and is not technically part of the review process of this document. It is in this sense that it was mentioned in the summary of this text that there have already been two revisionary meetings and that the official meeting of Cartagena+30 will be the third.

[59] Available at: <http://www.acnur.org/t3/english/recursos/documentos/?tx_danpdocument dirs_pi2% 5Bdownload% 5D = yes & tx_danpdocumentdirs_pi2% 5Bmode% 5D = 1 & tx_danpdocumentdirs_pi2% 5Bsort% 5D = doctitle: 0 & tx_danpdocumentdirs_pi2 % 5Bdownloadtyp% 5D = stream & tx_danpdocumentdirs_pi2% 5Buid% 5D = 262>.

Central American peace agreements and on the treatment of migrants by the repatriation (or return) of the displaced due to these conflicts.

Against this background, in 1994, the first review meeting of the Cartagena Declaration took place in the city of San José, Costa Rica, and the result was the adoption of the San José Declaration on Refugees and Displaced Persons. As the title of the San José Declaration indicates, the document dealt not only with the protection of refugees, but also the protection of IDPs, bringing two exclusive articles on this issue. Article 17 establishes the need for basic standards for the protection of these individuals to be created, while Article 18 emphasizes the Latin American effort to finding solutions to the reality faced by these persons.

After 10 years of the San José Declaration, in 2004, during the commemorative meeting of the 20th anniversary of the Cartagena Declaration, held in Mexico City, the Mexico Declaration and Plan of Action (MPA)[60] was adopted, in order to combat the problems faced by IDPs and refugees in Latin America.

Before the main meeting held on 15 and 16 November of that year, a series of preparatory meetings were held in different cities.[61] In these meetings, the debate on the refugee crisis in Colombia was central, given that there were about 3.5 million forcibly displaced persons due to the internal conflict that has lasted for more than 60 years.[62]

The MPA was adopted by 20 countries[63] and has two objectives.[64] On the one hand, it seeks to improve protection and humanitarian assistance in the region and, on the other, it responds to the large flows of refugees. Thus, the MPA is divided into two components, that of protection and that of durable solutions.

The MPA protection component has, at first, four objectives: 1) strengthening the legal and operational framework for the protection of refugees and IDPs in the region; 2) strengthening of national commissions charged with determining refugee status; 3) strengthening of national and regional networks of protection and 4) training on and promotion of International Refugee Law (research and doctrinal development).[65] Secondly, a fifth objective has been set, namely to improve legislation for the most vulnerable groups, particularly with regards to age and gender, in view of UNHCR's strategy on the cross-cutting line of " gender- age-diversity-".[66]

---

[60] Available at: <http://www.acnur.org/t3/fileadmin/Documentos/portugues/BD_Legal/Instrumentos_Internacionais / Declaracao_e_Plano_de_Acao_do_Mexico.pdf view = 1?>.

[61] The preparatory meetings were held in Brasília, Brazil; São José, Costa Rica; Cartagena de Índias and Bogotá, Colombia, according to the last preambular paragraph of the Mexico Declaration and Plan of Action. Available at: <http://www.acnur.org/t3/fileadmin/Documentos/portugues/ BD_Legal/ International Instruments / Declaracao_e_Plano_de_Acao_do_Mexico.pdf? View = 1>.

[62] See: <http://www.acnur.org/t3/pam/informacion-general>.

[63] Argentina, Bolivia, Brazil, Chile, Colombia, Costa Rica, Cuba, Ecuador, El Salvador, Guatemala, Haiti, Honduras, Mexico, Nicaragua, Panama, Paraguay, Peru, the Dominican Republic, Uruguay and Venezuela. See: JUBILUT, APOLINÁRIO, O Direito Internacional ..., Op. cit., p. 365.

[64] ACNUR. *Plan de Acción de México: El impacto de la solidaridad regional*, 2007, p. 11.

[65] Ibid., p. 16 et seq.

[66] The perspective of a cross-cutting axis "diversity-age-gender" was adopted by UNHCR in 2004 as a guideline to its actions. See, for example, <http://www.unhcr.org/cgi-bin/texis/ vtx / home / opendocPDFViewer.html? Docid = 4c206b449 & query = gender AND age>.

Through the component of durable solutions the MPA innovates and seeks to modify the logic of application of these actions, introducing the idea of solidarity into coordinated activities in the region. Such activities would be borders of solidarity,[67] cities of solidarity[68] and resettlement in solidarity[69].

These actions, based on the abovementioned "spirit of Cartagena", begin to actually look for adequate forms of protection and local integration. There is a concern to extend the protection of refugees beyond the activities of governmental bodies, while not neglecting the important interaction that must exist between foreigners and the local population, in particular to combat xenophobia and promote mutual respect. Thus, these actions demonstrate an ideal of solidarity[70]; modifying the traditional understanding that sees refugees as "burden sharing"[71]; innovating to demonstrate that it is possible to balance the needs of refugees and host States[72]; and further reinforcing the duty of protecting these people from the standpoint of International Refugee Law[73].

After the MPA, but outside of the framework of the review process of the Cartagena Declaration, the Brasilia Declaration on Protection of Refugees and Stateless Persons in the American Continent[74] [was adopted in 2010. The meeting, which resulted in the Brasilia Declaration, was among the celebrations of the 1951 Convention, the 1951 Convention relating to the Status of Stateless Persons and for the 1961 Convention for the Reduction of Statelessness, and not within the framework of the anniversary of the Cartagena Declaration; however, given that the Brasilia Declaration continued the regional advancements for the protection of forced migrants, the same is inserted here.

The Brasilia Declaration, which was adopted by 18 countries,[75] not only recommended the implementation of the MPA as a regional framework to meeting the new challenges of protecting in the region, such as statelessness and mixed migration flows, but also made reference to the promotion of "values of solidarity, respect, tolerance and multiculturalism"[76] in the application of Law and protection of refugees.

It is also important to point out that the Brasilia Declaration reaffirmed the

---

[67] This action aims to improve the situation at the borders, since between 25% and 30% of the population in need of protection is in border regions. This protection is provided by combating abuses that may be committed, by qualifying border agents, and by establishing appropriate service networks for procedures for refugee status determination (see UNHCR, p. 12).

[68] This action seeks to facilitate the local integration of refugees through access to basic services and the establishment of partnerships with municipal and regional public bodies (Ibid., p.13).

[69] It is proposed that resettlement actions begin to take a regional approach, especially in view of the Colombian refugee crisis (ibid., p.13).

[70] PIOVESAN, JUBILUT, Op. cit., p. 224.

[71] As a "burden". The 1951 Convention uses that word in its preambular paragraph 4 to recognize that the protection of large numbers of refugees may result in undue burdens for certain countries.

[72] PIOVESAN, JUBILUT, Op. cit.

[73] JUBILUT, Liliana Lyra; CARNEIRO, Wellington. Resettlement in Solidarity: a regional approach to a more humane durable solution, *Refugee Survey Quarterly*, v. 30, n. 3, 2011, p. 63-86.

[74] Available at: <http://www.acnur.org/t3/fileadmin/Documentos /portugues/ BDL/ Declaracao _de_ Brasilia_sobre_a_Protecao_de_Refugiados_e_Apatridas_no_Continente_Americano.pdf? View = 1>.

[75] They are: Argentina, Bolivia, Brazil, Chile, Colombia, Costa Rica, Cuba, Ecuador, El Salvador, Guatemala, Mexico, Nicaragua, Panama, Paraguay, Peru, Dominican Republic, Uruguay and Venezuela.

[76] See Brasilia Declaration, 8th Resolution.

"right of every person to seek and receive asylum"[77], demonstrating a connection with the Inter-American Human Rights system[78], a connection that will lead to actual improvements in national protection systems.

It is thus possible to infer that the Brasilia Declaration respects the tradition of previous documents and presents an evolution in the protection of refugees and other vulnerable groups, further committing States to International Refugee Law and creating coordinated solutions at the regional level in its provisions.[79]

3.3. Cartagena+30[80]

3.3.1 Cartagena+30 – the construction process

In 2014, considering the 30th anniversary of the 1984 Cartagena Declaration, a new periodic meeting will be held on December 2 and 3, in the city of Brasília, Brazil.[81]

Named "Cartagena+30", the event reserves a new round of debates on the current protection challenges of forced migrants in the region[82], especially in relation to refugees, IDPs, stateless persons, displaced persons due to humanitarian issues and so-called mixed flows, and aims to "adopt a new Declaration and Plan of Action to address the new challenges in the international protection of refugees in Latin America and the Caribbean over the next decade"[83].

Throughout 2014, 4 meetings were held in Latin America[84] so that all the realities of the region were presented and debated before the final meeting in early December. Counting on 4 main thematic axes (international protection; differentiated approach of age, gender and diversity; durable solutions; and statelessness), these four previous meetings resulted in several conclusions and recommendations.[85]

The first meeting, which was held in Argentina, presented, among other proposals, the evaluation of the establishment of protection mechanisms in migratory or refuge legislation to respond to displacements caused by climate

---

[77] See Brasilia Declaration, 4th preambular paragraph.

[78] Pursuant to Article 27 of the American Declaration of the Rights and Duties of Man and Article 22 of the American Convention on Human Rights.

[79] Cf. JUBILUT, APOLINÁRIO, O Direito Internacional ..., Op. cit., p. 365-366.

[80] Much of the information reported in this item was obtained at the International Colloquium Commemorating the 30th Anniversary of the Cartagena Declaration on Refugees conducted by the Universidade Católica de Santos on October 30 and 31, of 2014, in the city of São Paulo, Brazil.

[81] The realization of the event was agreed at the first meeting of the National Commission of Refugees and Member States and Associate Members of the MERCOSUR bloc (see ACNUR. Nota conceitual. Comemoração do 30° Aniversário da Declaração de Cartagena. Abril de 2013, p.2).

[82] Consolidated information on Cartagena+30 and its entire preparatory process can be found at: <http://www.acnur.org/cartagena30/pt-br>

[83] ACNUR. Nota conceitual. Op. cit., p. 2. (free translation)

[84] They were: 1st Meeting - Buenos Aires, March 18 and 19 (MERCOSUR region); 2nd Meeting - Quito, June 9 and 10 (Andean region); 3rd Meeting - Managua, July 10 and 11 (Mesoamerica); 4th Meeting - Georgetown, 10 and 11 September (Caribbean). Cf. data obtained at: <http: // www. Acnur. org/cartagena30/en/noticias-2/>.

[85] According to lecture given on October 31, 2014 by Virginius José Lianza da Franca, at the International Colloquium Commemorating the 30th Anniversary of the Cartagena Declaration on Refugees, held by the Universidade Católica de Santos.

change and environmental disasters[86].[87]

This meeting in Buenos Aires also determined that the protection of women and unaccompanied children should be strengthened under the "age-gender-diversity" approach. Also, it discussed the issue of extra-continental and labor resettlement.[88]

In turn, the meeting in Ecuador reaffirmed the need to adopt public policies to effectively combat the problems faced by migrants, including policies involving two or more countries[89], such as the current one between Colombia and Ecuador.[90]

The meeting held in Nicaragua has addressed the problem of forced displacement caused by organized crime.[91] An issue related to the countries of the Northern Triangle of Central America (Honduras, Guatemala and El Salvador), this type of forced migration must be addressed with a focus on human rights, shared responsibility and solidarity, and should be recognized as a motive capable of determining refugee status.[92]

The meeting in Managua also discussed the development of protection for displaced children[93] through the creation of a comprehensive regional mechanism to address the needs of these forced migrants.[94]

Finally, the meeting held in the Cayman Islands presented proposals aimed at the protection at sea, with the training of captains of ships on how to rescue and protect stranded persons.[95] As countries in the Caribbean region do not have adequate refugee status determination frameworks, the proposals aim to focus on the development of resettlement.[96] This is the first time that the Caribbean

---

[86] Ibid.

[87] According to lecture given Lecture given on October 31, 2014 by Andrés Ramirez at the International Colloquium Commemorating the 30th Anniversary of the Cartagena Declaration on Refugees, held by Universidade Católica de Santos.

[88] According to lecture given on October 31, 2014 by Virginius José Lianza da Franca, at the International Colloquium Commemorating the 30th Anniversary of the Cartagena Declaration on Refugees, held by the Universidade Católica de Santos

[89] Ibid.

[90] Available at: <http://www.refworld.org/cgi-bin/texis/vtx/rwmain?page=search &docid= 4ffeaa1 02 & skip = 0 & query = migration & coi = ECU>.

[91] According to lectures given on October 31, 2014 by Virginius José Lianza da Franca and Andrés Ramirez, at the International Colloquium Commemorating the 30th Anniversary of the Cartagena Declaration on Refugees, held by the Universidade Católica de Santos.

[92] According to lecture given on October 31, 2014 by Virginius José Lianza da Franca, at the International Colloquium Commemorating the 30th Anniversary of the Cartagena Declaration on Refugees, held by the Universidade Católica de Santos.

[93] According to lecture given on October 31, 2014 by Andrés Ramirez, at the International Colloquium Commemorating the 30th Anniversary of the Cartagena Declaration on Refugees, held by the Universidade Católica de Santos.

[94] According to lecture given on October 31, 2014 by Virginius José Lianza da Franca, at the International Colloquium Commemorating the 30th Anniversary of the Cartagena Declaration on Refugees, held by the Universidade Católica de Santos.

[95] According to lecture given Lecture given on October 31, 2014 by Andrés Ramirez at the International Colloquium Commemorating the 30th Anniversary of the Cartagena Declaration on Refugees, held by Universidade Católica de Santos.

[96] According to lecture given on October 31, 2014 by Virginius José Lianza da Franca, at the International Colloquium Commemorating the 30th Anniversary of the Cartagena Declaration on Refugees, held by the Universidade Católica de Santos.

countries have joined the review process of the Cartagena Declaration.[97]

Also, as an innovative landmark, it should be pointed out that Cartagena+30 is the review process so far with the greatest participation of civil society in the discussions[98] [100], which has been facilitated by the Norwegian Refugee Council (NRC).[99]

Among the proposals made by civil society bodies, it is worth emphasizing the creation of mechanisms for direct participation so that refugees and other forced migrants can monitor the services and policies of the host countries; as well as the need for a greater exchange of good practices on mixed migration flows; the implementation of actions to combat racism and xenophobia; and the recognition that local integration must rely on the direct participation of domestic communities.[100] It is also important to highlight the participation of the Academia, which resulted in the Declaration on the Comprehensive Protection of Forced Migrants and the Construction of an Effective Humanitarian Space in Latin America and the Caribbean, adopted in October 2014.[101]

All the official proposals presented and discussed at the meetings that took place during 2014 are being negotiated in the Group of Latin American and Caribbean Countries in Geneva (GRULAC)[102], in Switzerland, which is being chaired by Paraguay and Brazil and also counts with the participation of three academy specialists, Rosário Green (Mexico), Antônio Cançado Trindade (Brazil) and Diego García Sayán (Peru).[103]

3.3.2. Cartagena+30 - Expectations

With the final meeting of the review process being held for the first time the Southern Cone, Cartagena+30 is expected to be "a unique opportunity to promote Latin America as a relevant humanitarian actor"[104] and that the region can keep "contributing to the development of the international agenda, through a renewed commitment to the protection and to the seeking of durable solutions for refugees, internally displaced persons and stateless persons".[105]

---

[97] See: <http://www.acnur.org/t3/portugues/noticias/noticia/acnur-e-paises-do-caribe-debate ramprotecao-a-refugiados-e-apatridas>.

[98] Ibid.

[99] Available at: <http://www.acnur.org/t3/fileadmin/Documentos/Proteccion/ Cartagena30/ Carta gena30_Boletim_Fev_2014.pdf? View = 1>.

[100] According to lecture given on October 31, 2014 by Virginius José Lianza da Franca, at the International Colloquium Commemorating the 30th Anniversary of the Cartagena Declaration on Refugees, held by the Universidade Católica de Santos.

[101] More information on the Declaration, also known as the Declaration of the Academy, can be found at: <http://www.unisantos.br/portal/noticias/catedra-sergio-vieira-de-mello-lanca-declaracao-sobre-protecao-integral-a-migrantes-forcados>.

[102] According to lecture given on October 31, 2014 by Andrés Ramirez, at the International Colloquium Commemorating the 30th Anniversary of the Cartagena Declaration on Refugees, held by the Universidade Católica de Santos.

[103] See <http://www.acnur.org/t3/fileadmin/Documentos/Proteccion/Cartagena30/ Cartagena30 _Bulletin_Fev_2014.pdf? View = 1>.

[104] According to the testimony of Marta Juarez for CARTAGENA + 30 = MORE EXPECTATIONS, published on March 23, 2014 in O Estrangeiro. Available at: <http: // oestrangeiro.Org / 2014/03/23 / cartagena-30-plus-expectations. (free translation)

[105] Ibid. (free translation)

There are high expectations that the Brazil Declaration and Plan of Action will be adopted by an even greater number of countries than the other regional documents that preceded it (for example the MPA), reaffirming the Latin American commitment to high standards of protection for refugees, stateless persons and forcibly displaced persons[106] and allowing "Latin American and Caribbean governments to adopt a new strategic framework, based on measurable results, to foster and strengthen the protection and durable solutions for refugees, stateless persons, IDPs and other vulnerable groups who seek security and respect for human rights in the region".[107]

However, given the information available so far, and in view of (i) the expected objectives of Cartagena+30 and (ii) the various challenges presented in this text, it seems that caution is needed and it is prudent to minimize expectations.

This is so due to the fact that large part of the existing challenges is related to conceptual issues for the expansion or creation of mandatory forms of protection for forced migrants in the region, in which there seems to be no consensus or commitment on the part of the States.

The option that is being outlined in Cartagena+30 agreements in terms of protection is to consolidate alternative forms of protection, still linked to the discretion of States, regarding forced migrants that do not fit into the definitions of International Refugee Law; that is, a step forward in "complementary humanitarian protection".[108] If, on the one hand, this situation is commendable, since it demonstrates a greater openness of Latin American States to forced migrants than is found in other parts of the world, on the other hand, it does not seem to be able to solve the great concern of this text, i.e.: how to ensure that both refugees and forced migrants have mandatory forms of legal protection.

It seems that, only with this premise in mind, will the Brazil Declaration and Plan of Action be able to respond adequately to the challenges of international protection of refugees, stateless persons and other forced migrants in Latin America and the Caribbean for the next 10 years, based on humane and humanitarian criteria and with clear and mandatory application, in order to truly achieve the "spirit of Cartagena".

Conclusion

The challenges of protecting refugees and forced migrants in the Cartagena+30 framework stem from the significant increase of displaced persons, who are forced to migrate due to various reasons, as well as the lack of normative instruments that impose legal obligations of protection and reception for States.

The solution to this situation seems to be the broad implementation of the "spirit of Cartagena". In this sense, the review process of the Cartagena Declaration, titled Cartagena+30, which will culminate in the Brazil Declaration and Plan of Action, is strategically poised to move forward in this direction.

---

[106] Available at: <http://www.acnur.org/t3/fileadmin/Documentos/Proteccion/ Cartagena30/ Cartagena30_Boletim_Fev_2014.pdf? View = 1>.

[107] See: < http://www.acnur.org/cartagena30/pt-br/antecedentes-e-desafios> (free translation)

[108] See footnote 56

What needs to be verified is whether there will be political will to face the challenges; especially the ones of a conceptual nature, in order for real forms of protection and, consequently, sovereign flexibility to take place,[109] ensuring both rights for refugees and forced migrants and obligations for States.

One hopes that the true "transformative potential of the refuge"[110], stemming from international solidarity and humanitarianism that mark the "spirit of Cartagena" is in place, so that real and permanent solutions, not only provisional and *ad hoc* ones, assist in the development of International Refugee Law and of other forms of protection of forced migrants, thus avoiding that either is diminished and allowing that the current and upcoming challenges of the next 10 years in our region are adequately faced.

References

ACNUR. *Nota conceitual. Comemoração do 30° Aniversário da Declaração de Cartagena*. Abril de 2013.

ACNUR. *Plan de Acción de México: El impacto de la solidariedad regional*, 2007. Available at: <http://www.acnur.org/t3/fileadmin/scripts/doc. php?file=biblioteca/pdf/5484>.

CARNEIRO, Wellington P. A Declaração de Cartagena de 1984 e os Desafios da Proteção Internacional dos Refugiados, 20 Anos Depois. In SILVA, César Augusto (org.). *Direitos Humanos e Refugiados*. Dourados (MS): Editora UFGD, 2012.

COSTA, Daniel. Introductory note to the Brasilia Declaration on the Protection of Refugees and Stateless Persons in the Americas. *International Legal Materials*, v. 50, n. 3, 2011, p. 357-363.

DEMANT, Eva. 30 años de la Declaración de Cartagena sobre Refugiados. Avances y desafíos de la protección de refugiados en Latinoamérica. *Agenda Internacional*, XX, n. 31, 2013, p. 131-140.

DICKER, Nicole; MANSFIELD, Joanna. *Filling the protection gap: current trends in complementary protection in Canada, Mexico and Australia*. UNHCR, 2012.

EL-HINNAWI, Essam. *Environmental Refugees*. Nairobi: UNEP, 1985.

FISCHEL DE ANDRADE, José Henrique. *Direito Internacional dos Refugiados - Evolução Histórica (1921-1952)*. Rio de Janeiro: Renovar, 1996.

GLOVER, Stephen; GOTT, Ceri et al. *Migration: an Economic and Social Analysis*. The Research, Development and Statistics Directorate. Occasional Paper n. 67, 2001.

HATHAWAY, James. *The Rights of Refugees under International Law*. Cambridge, Cambridge University Press, 2005.

HOBSBAWM, Eric. *Era dos Extremos - o breve século XX: 1914-1991*. 2ª ed. 10ª reimpressão. São Paulo: Companhia das Letras, 1995.

INTERNATIONAL FEDERADTION OF THE RED CROSS AND RED CRESCENT. *World Disasters Report*, 2012. Available at: <http://www.ifrcmedia.org/assets/pages/wdr2012/download/index.html>.

JAROCHINSKI SILVA, João Carlos. Uma análise sobre os fluxos migratórios mistos. In RAMOS, André Carvalho; RODRIGUES, Gilberto; ALMEIDA, Guilherme Assis (orgs.). *60 Anos de ACNUR: perspectivas de futuro*. São Paulo: CLA Cultural, 2011, p. 201-220.

JUBILUT, Liliana Lyra. *O Direito Internacional dos Refugiados e sua aplicação no ordenamento jurídico brasileiro*. São Paulo: Método, 2007.

_____. Fora and Programmes for Refugees in Latin America. In ABASS, Ademola; IPPOLITO, Francesca. *Regional Approaches to the Protection of Asylum Seekers*. Surrey: Ashgate Publishing, 2014, p. 245-266.

JUBILUT, Liliana Lyra; APOLINÁRIO, Silvia Menicucci de O. S. A necessidade de proteção

---

[109] JUBILUT, APOLINÁRIO, JAROCHINSKI SILVA, Op. cit.

[110] Ibid (free translation).

internacional no âmbito da migração. *Revista Direito GV*, v. 6, n. 1, 2010, p. 275- 294.

_____. O Direito Internacional dos Refugiados e seu Contexto Atual na América Latina. In ROSA, Renata de Melo; DOMÍNGUEZ AVILA, Carlos Federico (orgs.). *América Latina no Labirinto Global - Economia, Política e Segurança*. Brasília: CRV, 2012, p. 353-369.

_____. A população refugiada no Brasil: em busca da proteção integral. *Universitas - Relações Internacionais*, v. 6, n. 2, 2008, p. 9-38.

JUBILUT, Liliana Lyra; APOLINÁRIO, Silvia Menicucci de O. S.; JAROCHINSKI SILVA, João Carlos. O Potencial Transformador do Refúgio: aprofundamento da solidariedade e da limitação à soberania como legado da Declaração de Cartagena e de seus processos revisionais. In RAMINA, Larissa; FRIEDRICH, Tatyana Scheila. (coords.). *Coleção Direito Internacional Multifacetado – Direitos Humanos, Guerra e Paz*. Curitiba: Juruá, 2014, p. 173-198.

JUBILUT, Liliana Lyra; CARNEIRO, Wellington. Resettlement in Solidarity: a regional new approach towards a more humane durable solution. *Refugee Survey Quarterly*, v. 30, n. 3, 2011, p. 63-86.

JUBILUT, Liliana Lyra; RAMOS, Érika Pires. Regionalism: a strategy for dealing with crisis migration. *Forced Migration Review*, 45, February 2014, p. 66-67.

LACZKO, Frank; AGHAZARM, Christine (ed.). Migration, *Environment and Climate Change: Assessing the Evidence*. IOM, 2009. Available at: <http://publications. iom.int/bookstore/free/migration_and_environment.pdf >.

MURILLO GONZALEZ, Juan Carlos. El derecho de asilo y la protección de refugiados en el continente americano. In ACNUR. *La protección internacional de refugiados en las Américas*. Quito: ACNUR, 2011, p. 51-74.

PIOVESAN, Flávia; JUBILUT, Liliana Lyra. The 1951 Convention and the Americas: Regional Developments. In ZIMMERMANN, Andreas (org.). *Commentary on the 1951 Convention Relating to the Status of Refugees and its 1967 Protocol*. Oxford: Oxford University Press, 2011, p. 205-224.

RAMOS, Erika Pires. *Refugiados Ambientais: e m busca de reconhecimento pelo Direito Internacional*. Tese de Doutorado apresentada à Faculdade de Direito da USP, 2011.

SPINDLER, William. The Mexico Plan of Action: protecting refugees through international solidarity. *Forced Migration Review*, 24, November 2005.

UNHCR. *Global Trends 2013*. UNHCR, 2014.

UNU - EHS. As Ranks of "Environmental refugees" swell worldwide, calls grow for better definition, recognition, support. *World day for disaster reduction* (press release), 2005.

LATIN-AMERICA AND REFUGEES: A PANORAMIC VIEW (2016)[*]

Liliana Lyra Jubilut[**]

Latin America is a peculiar region in relation to protection through asylum. On the one hand, it has a long-lasting and still operating tradition of political asylum that coexists with an expanded recognition of refugee status based both on the 1951 Convention on Refugees and its 1967 Protocol[1] and the Cartagena Declaration[2] (a regional 1984 document that states that a person can be a refugee if s/he is fleeing gross and generalized violation of human rights, which has become a normative guideline in refugee protection in Latin America).

On the other hand, it is a region that still "produces" asylum seekers but also receives intra and extraregional refugees, having similar numbers of UNHCR's persons of concern (over 7,5 million by the end of 2015[3]) from the region and in the region.

In order to try to paint a panoramic view of refugees and the region, this post presents the current main challenges and developments in refugee issues in Latin America. In relation to challenges, it is important to highlight two on-going refugee-producing situations in Latin America[***]. Colombia[4] has a long-standing conflict situation that may be on the verge of ending, but that during its over 50 years has produced massive forced displacement, both internally (with over 7 million IDPs) and externally (with over 350,000 refugees). This flow of forced migrants placed a challenge to the region, especially to Colombia's neighboring countries in terms of

* Acknowledgement: This post is a contribution to the symposium "Movement of People" which was inspired by the Conference "Movement of People" that was held at the University of Hamburg the 23 and 24 September of 2016.

** Liliana Lyra Jubilut is a Professor at Universidade Católica de Santos (Brazil) and has been working with refugee issues for over 17 years.

1 http://www.unhcr.org/3b66c2aa10.

2 http://www.unhcr.org/about-us/background/45dc19084/cartagena-declaration-refugees-adopted-colloquium-international-protection.html

3 http://www.unhcr.org/statistics/unhcrstats/576408cd7/unhcr-global-trends-2015.html

*** Since this text was written a third massive flow of forced displaced persons has been increasing in Latin America (especially in South America): the one steaming from the situation in Venezuela.

4 http://reporting.unhcr.org/sites/default/files/UNHCR%20Colombia%20Factsheet%20-%20October%202016.pdf

registration, refugee status determination procedures and integration.

A second refugee-producing situation in the region is the displacement in the Northern Triangle of Central America[5]. Encompassing Guatemala, Honduras and El Salvador, this region has seen its refugee numbers increase five-times from 2012 to 2015. Forced displacement there is due to violence, specially related to the actions of organized crime gang activities and gender-based violence. Moreover, it adds to the already challenging scenario of mass displacement, a new factor for the region: the displacement on unaccompanied or separated children.[6]

To deal with both these challenges the region needs to focus on a third one: the actual and proper implementation of refugee-related laws to ascertain integral protection. Meaning the protection of all the rights refugees are entitled too in all phases of their refugeehood, integral protection requires the correct application of International Refugee Law, national legislation dealing with refugee status, and Human Rights standards. Even though most of the countries in the region are part of the international refugee regime[7] and/or have incorporated the regional instruments of refugee protection[8], it is relevant that these norms are applied in practice with a view of actually protecting refugees, and that an increased dialogue is in play between Refugee Law and Human Rights in the region so as to guarantee maximum and effective protection.

In this sense, it is important that refugee legislation and refugee status determination standards remain available and are properly applied in the region. New forms of protection (such as the MERCOSUR residence agreement[9]) are relevant but they should coexist with Refugee Law protection. In this regards the idea of maximum protection brought along by human rights standards is key and the States of Latin America have to take it into consideration in setting up solutions to refugee crisis – existing, emerging and future ones.

Despite these challenges, the region has also engaged in actions regarding refugee protection that can be seen as positive developments in the sense that they enlarge the humanitarian protection space and, therefore, can lead to better refugee protection. Two such actions need to be highlighted, as they strengthen refugee protection by adding new perspectives and approaches to the current international refugee regime with regional "twists". They are: resettlement in solidarity initiative and humanitarian visas.

Resettlement in solidarity was proposed by Brazil during the debates of the Mexico Declaration and Plan of Action[10] in commemoration of the 20 anniversary of the Cartagena Declaration in 2004 and was incorporated in the final document. The States of Latin America decided not only to accept asylum seekers from Colombia into their territories but also to assist the neighboring countries to the conflict by accepting to resettled Colombian refugees. Brazil, Argentina, Paraguay,

---

[5]   http://reporting.unhcr.org/sites/default/files/UNHCR%20Colombia%20Factsheet%20-%20October%202016.pdf

[6] https://www.unicef.org/infobycountry/honduras_86561.html

[7] http://www.acnur.org/t3/fileadmin/Documentos/BDL/2004/2549.pdf

[8] http://www.acnur.org/t3/fileadmin/Documentos/BDL/2004/2542.pdf

[9] http://help.unhcr.org/brazil/en/asylum-claim/mercosur-residence-agreement/

[10] https://www.oas.org/dil/mexico_declaration_plan_of_action_16nov2004.pdf

Uruguay and Chile established resettlement programs[11] – either from scratch or from building on their emerging practices.

Resettlement in solidarity[12] has been in practice since 2004 and has expanded to receiving extraregional refugees such as Palestinians (mainly in Chile and Brazil[13]) and more recently Syrians (in Uruguay).**** It is an effort in both responsibility sharing and regional protection of refugees, and even if it remains an initiative that involves small numbers, it is a positive development in refugee protection in Latin America.

More recently the region has developed a new strategy for enhancing the humanitarian space of protection. This time focused on ascertaining safe ways for forced migrants to access safe territories: the granting of humanitarian visas.[14] This can be seen as a form of complementary protection as it is not only designed for refugees but for people in need of international protection, having already benefitted for instance victims of trafficking or smuggling of people (like in Mexico and Argentina) and also for people fleeing the aftermath of the earthquake of 2010 in Haiti (like in Brazil). Nevertheless, it can also be of assistance to refugees, as has been seen in the case of Syrians who have been granted humanitarian visas by both Brazil and Argentina.[15]

All in all, it can be said that, in a panoramic view of the region, although Latin America still faces challenges in relation to refugee protection, they seem to relate to practical and implementation issues. Therefore, they can be faced with the strengthening of refugee law and human rights standards that are already set in the norms of the countries of the region. It is better and more humane implementation that seem to be key here, much like what has based the region's novel proposals for refugee protection in the resettlement in solidarity and humanitarian visas initiatives.

---

[11] http://www.unhcr.org/57c983557.pdf

[12] http://www.unhcr.org/research/working/4fd5d9c79/pillar-protection-solidarity-resettlement-refugees-latin-america-ana-guglielmelli.html

[13] https://academic.oup.com/rsq/article-abstract/30/3/63/1566119

**** In terms of refugees from the region a recent novelty is the resettlement of persons fleeing the situation of the Northern Triangle of Central America in Uruguay.

[14] http://www.fmreview.org/es/node/3272.html

[15] http://www.coha.org/latin-american-countries-response-to-the-syrian-refugee-crisis-the-brazilian-argentinian-and-the-uruguayan-examples/

CONCLUSION

It is possible to affirm, based on this collection of essays, that there are good practices regarding refugees' protection in both Latin America and in Brazil. From the adoption of international (with the vast majority of the countries of the region being a part of the international regime for refugee protection through the 1951 Convention and/or the 1967 Protocol), regional (with the Cartagena Declaration and the documents deriving from its review process), and national norms on the topics (laws, other regulations and the incorporations by 15 States of the Cartagena Declaration into their national legislation[1] and of 14 States having the right of asylum in their constitutional orders[2]), to the proposals of novel approaches to protection – such as the resettlement in solidarity initiative and humanitarian visas.

Nevertheless, there is reasons for concern in the current scenario. The region has been seeing the adoption by some countries of new restrictive migration laws and policies, which are not in keeping with human rights ideals and norms, and, that could also affect refugees. Closure of bordures – real or disguised in policies that mean in practice that persons in need of international protection cannot access safe territories – are also taking place. As well as the creation of obstacles for adequate access to refugee status determination procedures, and, thus, to adequate international protection. In the case of Brazil, the current challenges relies on how the country will apply International Refugee Law and protection mechanisms to the flow of Venezuelans arriving in it, as well as on the adequate handling of the pending 85,000 asylum requests in the country.

These measures, albeit happening at the national and not on the regional level, may bring into question (at least in part) the perspective of Latin America as a region constantly developing and expanding a humanitarian protection space that benefits refugees and other forced migrants. However, and in spite of the justified concern that they bring, if one looks into the broader context, one will find that the region is still trying to maintain its reputation as well as to cooperate with the improvement of the international refugee regime. Examples of this are the recent adoptions of the San José Action Statement[3] and the *Marco Integral Regional para la Protección y Soluciones* (MIRPS – Regional Integral Framework for Protection and

---

[1] http://www.acnur.org/fileadmin/scripts/doc.php?file=fileadmin/Documentos/BDL/2004/2542
[2] http://www.acnur.org/fileadmin/scripts/doc.php?file=fileadmin/Documentos/BDL/2010/8014
[3] http://www.refworld.org/docid/57a8a4854.html

Solutions[4]) towards the Comprehensive Refugees Response Framework of UNHCR and aiming at the protection of refugees from Central America; as well as the 100 points of Brasília[5], which puts together the region's contributions to the Global Compact of Refugees. Moreover, the review process of the Cartagena Declaration is still on going, with recent meetings taking stock of the three first years of the Brazil Declaration and Plan of Action and its implementation.

In light of this apparently contradictory scenario it is extremely relevant to remind the region, and the countries who compose it, of their history of international protection to forced migrants as well as their humanitarian commitments, so that the "spirit of Cartagena" can be respected and strengthened and refugees' (and other forced migrants) protection can happen adequately. This book aimed to be an instrument in these endeavour. By describing the good practices, the humanitarian protection space and the commitments to refugee protection in recent years in Brazil and in Latin America, it calls for the region to keep the positive policies and innovations in International Refugee Law; so that they can (i) be in place for those who need them, (ii) be the starting ground for new actions and, (iii) maybe even, serve as inspiration for similar practices around the world.

Liliana Lyra Jubilut
March 2018

---

[4]   http://www.acnur.org/que-hace/proteccion/hacia-un-pacto-mundial-sobre-refugiados/marco-de-respuesta-integral-para-los-refugiados-crrf/marco-integral-regional-para-la-proteccion-y-soluciones-mirps/
[5] http://www.acnur.org/fileadmin/scripts/doc.php?file=fileadmin/Documentos/BDL/2018/11590